MOD ART

Copyright © 2018 Omnibus Press
(A Division of Music Sales Limited)

Designed & Art Directed by Michael Bell Design.
Picture Research by Paul Anderson.
Additional Picture Research by Sarah Datblygu.

ISBN 978.1.78305.968.3
Order No. OP56441

Special Edition
ISBN 978.1.78760.139.0
Order No. OP57893

Exclusive Distributors
Music Sales Limited
14/15 Berners Street, London, W1T 3LJ,
United Kingdom.

Music Sales Pty Limited
Level 4, 30-32 Carrington Street, Sydney, NSW 2000,
Australia.

Every effort has been made to trace the copyright holders of
the photographs in this book but one or two were unreachable.
We would be grateful if the photographers concerned would
contact us.

Printed in China.

A catalogue record for this book is available from the British Library.

Visit Omnibus Press on the web at www.omnibuspress.com

'For mum, dad and Carol, who always encouraged me in art when I was a kid.'

MOD ART

**MUSIC AND GRAPHICS
FASHION AND ART
MOD DESIGN
FROM THE 1950s TO 1990s**

PAUL 'SMILER' ANDERSON

OMNIBUS PRESS

LONDON / NEW YORK / PARIS / SYDNEY / COPENHAGEN / BERLIN / MADRID / TOKYO

v

INTRODUCTION

"Art is anything you can get away with." Or so said Canadian philosopher Marshall McLuhan. With that in mind I feel confident enough to present this book. People will often disagree about exactly what art is meant to be. By the same token, the definition of Mod is just as curious, misunderstood and argued over.

For some, Mod is a mere pastime with which to fill their spare hours. Others view it as an all-encompassing ideal; they dive in and completely immerse themselves in the world, forever travelling deeper and deeper, yet never quite plunging the depths. Mod may be a strict lifestyle choice with a clear vision that insulates against fresh ideas.

Yet others would dismiss this notion outright, seeing Mod as a route to enlightenment, to discovering diverse styles in everything from music and clothing to architecture and art. In truth, there is no definitive answer.

From the 1940s' baby boom emerged the generation of young people who would shape the nation two decades later. As jet planes zoomed across the sky and music filled the air, the older generation stood open-mouthed at teenagers pushing against boundaries and challenging established ideas. These fathers and mothers may have fought the war to secure their children's freedom, but the rollercoaster ride of individualism, hedonism, sexual revolution and social protest the youngsters went on was not what their parents had imagined. Real Mods tore up the rule books, as well as everything else expected of them. Instead, they designed, created and moulded a new world, with fresh young eyes.

Mod was always going to be a troubled soul. By its very nature it was destined to live fast and die young: the relentless pursuit of 'the next big thing' sealed Mod's own fate. Desperate to move forward, boundaries became blurred, lines were crossed; eventually the whole culture was swallowed up and disappeared from view.

By the mid-70s, the youthquake that was Punk had become the new teenage revolt. Unforgiving of the direction that the 60s visionaries had taken them, hippy fantasies and self-indulgent Prog Rock desires were terminated. Year Zero was the rallying cry. Destruction may have been in their master plan but, in fact, the whole Punk ethos filtered out all the junk that came after the early Modernist dreams had faded. Long hair, big collars and flares were seen as fashion crimes. The answer was to strip it all back: clean lines, short hair, narrow trousers and three-minute records were the brutal, speed-fuelled visions embraced by the new generation.

When Margaret Thatcher addressed the crowd at Harrogate Conference Centre in March 1982, she covered many subjects in her speech, including defence, industry and youth crime. With the latter she focused on the gradual erosion of morality in this country. Young people of the 1980s were the product of a permissive society, and that is where the blame obviously lay. "We are reaping what was sown in the sixties. The fashionable theories and permissive claptrap set the scene for a society in which the old virtues of discipline and self-restraint were denigrated," bemoaned Thatcher. What she seems not to have noticed is that the decade also gave way to aspiration, entrepreneurialism and individualism. All virtues that she championed.

Good ideas can never die completely. There is always someone to pick up the baton. Often viewed by the originators as charlatans, a parody of the archetypal concept, the truth is that, amongst whatever pale imitations, there will always be a minority filled with a passion to propagate the original idea in its pure form. They, in due course, enhance the original design and the cycle begins again. Just as new shoots grow old and die, Mod is forever reinventing itself and the evolutionary cycle seems never ending.

Mod and Art are great bedfellows. They both have in common the desire to make you pay attention and look.

PAUL 'SMILER' ANDERSON

POP INTO ART
OR ART INTO POP?
COMBINING ART
AND MUSIC
IN 1960s BRITAIN

1 *Just What Is It That Makes Today's Homes So Different, So Appealing?*
Richard Hamilton, 1956.

It's early 1952, and there is an air of excitement surrounding the premises of 17 Dover Street, Piccadilly. For this is the home of the Institute of Contemporary Arts in London. At what is seen to be the first meeting of the newly formed Independent Group, artist and sculptor Eduardo Paolozzi has set up an episcope and is projecting images consisting of comic strips, war magazines, glamour girls, various graphics and advertising he had collated from American magazines collected while living in Paris after the war. The lecture that accompanies the show is entitled 'Bunk.' This is a whole new way forward in the world of art.

The Independent Group consisted of young intellectuals: painters, writers, critics, sculptors and architects that would include fine artist John McHale, art critic Lawrence Alloway and artist Richard Hamilton. Together, they developed an alternative modernism where high culture met mass culture. Now there were conversations about philosophy and science alongside the reality of contemporary culture including the sophisticated advertising, glamour and colourful images coming from the USA.

In August 1955, McHale was awarded a scholarship to study with German-born American artist Josef Albers at the Design Department of Yale University, and he returned to London in June 1956 armed with a trunk full of US magazines containing glamour girls, superheroes and modern domestic appliances. This had an immediate impact on the group, who fell in love with the whole concept of the 'American dream.'

In January that year, London's Tate Gallery had already been host to an exhibition entitled 'Modern Art In The United States,' which displayed the talents of abstract expressionists. Now, seven months later, the Whitechapel Art Gallery threw open its doors to showcase 'This is Tomorrow,' an exhibition that included work from the Independent Group, notably Nigel Henderson and his disturbing collage *Head Of Man* and Richard Hamilton's collage *Just What Is It That Makes Today's Homes So Different, So Appealing?*, the latter of which was influenced by McHale's magazine haul and embodied the fascination with the mass-produced American obsession to sell an ever-growing array of food, gadgets and products, all while pursuing the Moon in the Space Race.

1 *For Men Only – Starring MM And BB*, Peter Phillips, 1961.

2 David Stone Martin's artwork on Lionel Hampton Quartet 12" Clef Records, 1953.

3 *Vertigo* film poster, Saul Bass, 1958.

"...living to a large extent in a myth world..."

RICHARD HOGGART

Of course this fascination wasn't just the exclusive preserve of the intellectual. In Britain, between 1956 and 1963, the number of 15–19-year-olds increased by 20 per cent. On a street-level, young people with limited resources had already asserted their affiliation to the Land of Opportunity through their choice of music – initially revivalist, or modern jazz and later rock'n'roll. They also dressed to establish a presence, partially encouraged by screen idols such as Marlon Brando in *The Wild One* and James Dean in *Rebel Without A Cause.* 1956, though, was the year that Elvis Presley would notch up six chart hits in the UK and American influence would be found much nearer to home, in the cafés and the milk bars of dreary suburban England. Leeds-born writer Richard Hoggart was a staff tutor at the University of Hull when his book *The Uses Of Literacy* was published in 1957. In it he writes of an encounter, presumably around 1956, with some 'Juke Box Boys' in a northern milk bar: "Their clothes, their hairstyles, their facial expressions all indicate [that they] are living to a large extent in a myth world compounded of a few simple elements which they take to be American life."

Hoggart laments the diluting of the British national identity, as he could find no positives in the boys' fascination with a distant land and its creation of mass culture through advertising. He continues: "Like the cafés I described in an earlier chapter, the milk bars indicate at once, in the nastiness of their modernistic knick-knacks, their glaring showiness, an aesthetic breakdown so complete... I have in mind... the kind of milk bar – there is one in almost every northern town with more than, say, fifteen thousand inhabitants – which has become the regular evening rendezvous for some of the young men."

Hoggart was 38 years old in 1956... he belonged to another generation. Pop art was immediate, strikingly colourful, and a release from the established rules. Writers and art critics alike bemoaned that it offered nothing meaningful, while in the USA, consumer goods were increasingly presented as a lifestyle choice, and expression of identity.

Richard Hamilton was teaching design at the Royal College of Art in London. The college boasted some fantastic artists, including Peter Blake, Richard Smith, Derek Boshier, Pauline Boty, Patrick Caulfield, David Hockney and Peter Phillips. These were the people who were excited by an ever-changing world that wanted to distance itself from the constraints of life after the Second World War.

They had a mutual enthusiasm for mass culture and media icons. Peter Blake, for one, would show his love of American culture in his self-portrait of 1961 in which he is seen wearing denim, baseball boots and an array of badges including the largest, a crest-shaped Stars and Stripes, all while clutching a copy of *Elvis Monthly.*

When I'm watching my TV
And that man comes on to tell me
How white my shirts can be
But he can't be a man cause he doesn't smoke
The same cigarettes as me

'(I CAN'T GET NO) SATISFACTION' MICK JAGGER & KEITH RICHARDS

"We weren't all at the Royal College together," states Peter. "I was there from 1953 to 1956 and they all arrived in 1959 and were there through until 1961, so actually there was a six-year gap. When I was there it would have been the end of the kitchen sink school. John Bratby was there because he was doing a fourth year and the next year would have been the young artists picking up on American and abstract expressionism, so I was kind of in a void between the figurative painters and the abstract expressionists. Later there was that fantastic year where it was Hockney, Kitaj, Pete Phillips, Boshier, and Pauline Boty was in the stained glass school. Pat Caulfield was the next year. By then I was beginning to be established so I wasn't actually with them."

These young British artists were also aware that across the Atlantic, people like Jasper Johns, Andy Warhol, Roy Lichtenstein and Robert Rauschenberg were also pushing the limits of what could be accepted as art. Truly fantastic work could also be seen in the graphic design of American film posters by the likes of Saul Bass, or David Stone Martin's artwork on the sleeves of American jazz records.

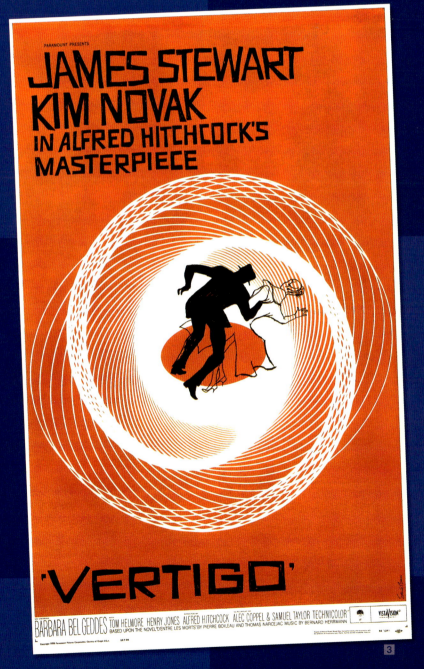

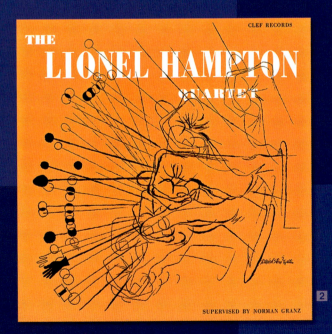

Paris had always been seen to be the centre of gravity in the art world, until, that is, the 1940s, when the focus fell upon New York City. Paris was still very influential – and always will be – but suddenly it wasn't the city around which all artistic expression revolved. The Second World War had put an end to that: the established artists, such as Piet Mondrian, Max Ernst, Jacques Lipchitz and Fernand Léger had taken refuge in New York. This resulted in the next evolution in the art world with the likes of Mark Rothko and Jackson Pollock leading the charge.

1 *Tribute To The American Working People*, Honoré Sharrer, 1951.
2 *With Love To Jean-Paul Belmondo*, Pauline Boty, 1962.

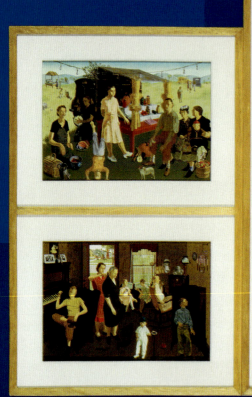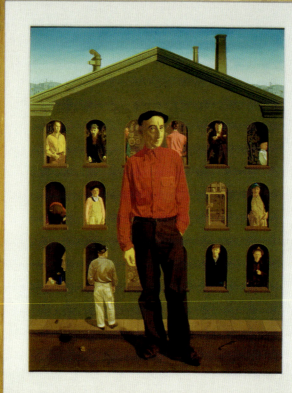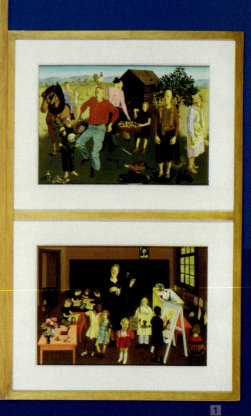

Back in Britain, the most internationally renowned painters were Francis Bacon, Graham Sutherland and Ben Nicholson, whose influences were more set in the traditions of the European painters of the twenties and thirties. The media, though, was soon taking note of the younger generation, who took their influence from the transatlantic cutting-edge styles.

Peter Blake remembers: "The main influences on my work would have been certain parts of art history such as the Flemish Primitives Van Eyck and Vermeer, Diego Velázquez, the Spanish painter, and then from more recent times, a group of artists working in America called The Magic Realists with the main one being a woman called Honoré Sharrer. She was the main, single influence. I think it wasn't particularly a love for America as such, but in most cases 'the best of' came from America. I was generally interested in rock'n'roll, people like The Everly Brothers just happened to be American.

It wasn't an interest in the fact that they were American people. It was just what they did was the best and they happened to come from America."

On February 4, 1962, *The Sunday Times Magazine* included a feature on Peter Blake, 'Pioneer of Pop Art.' Later the same month, the BBC arts television programme *Monitor* aired an episode called 'Pop Goes The Easel.'

Peter Blake: "It was interesting to do. It was Ken Russell's first feature-length film for television so he was inventing, and he was a brilliant filmmaker. Making it with David Boshier, Peter Phillips and Pauline Boty… we were all friends. It was a new kind of experience to be acting with such a good filmmaker. It was meant to portray life in a day and that included going to the fair, wrestling and all those different wonderful things, so it was fascinating to do.

The Twisting scene at the end was filmed at the artist Richard Smith's studio. It was a party kind of set-up, which degenerated into total drunkenness. They filmed the scene with someone up in the beams, I think it was one of London's first loft spaces and it was very cool. Hockney was there too, and we were all twisting like mad and pretty drunk by then. I think Ken [Russell] just set up a party, let us get on with it and then he filmed us."

Although a fantastic piece of television, the only let down is that Pauline Boty doesn't get to speak as much as the others about her work. Instead she is featured in a surreal piece of film, being chased down the curving corridors of BBCTV Centre by a blind old lady in a wheelchair.

Boty was a fantastic representative for female artists and makes an illuminating case study. Nicknamed 'The Wimbledon Bardot,' on account of her resemblance to the French film star Brigitte, Boty proved that beauty and brains could go hand in hand. She was a sophisticated, strong-minded, well-educated artist, who enjoyed the visual and performance elements of her pop culture identity. She was hip enough to meet Bob Dylan off the plane on his first visit to England in December 1962, and later to dance on *Ready Steady Go!*. After the documentary, Boty embarked upon a brief acting career, but it was art that remained her priority. Her paintings often included idols such as Marilyn Monroe or Jean-Paul Belmondo, and she was not afraid to tackle female sexuality through the presentation of her erotic images of women.

In 1959, art critic Raymond Cogniat and the French Minister of Cultural Affairs, André Malraux, launched and set up the 'Biennale de Paris,' a presentation of youthful creativity worldwide. The Biennale of 1963 would see England's own pop art breakthrough. The British Council presented a collection of paintings and sculptures that originated in the nucleus of the English pop art movement: Alan Jones, Blake, Boshier, Hockney and Phillips were all picked as representatives. The French section of painters always vote for the Prix des Jeunes Artistes, their judgement usually biased towards anybody influenced by the École de Paris (School of Paris). On this occasion, however, having been so impressed with the British section, a group of forward-looking young artists formed a pressure group in their favour. Blake, Phillips and Boshier's work was considered but was deemed too radical for the more conservative of the judges. However, Alan Jones was eventually awarded the grand prize, and 'le pop art Anglais' was the talk of the town.

In London, various new art galleries opened, which would engage with the emerging new wave of artists. In 1963, art dealer John Kasmin opened up a gallery in New Bond Street that would show the work of David Hockney as well as American artists such as Kenneth Noland. Around the same period, an art dealer who would become synonymous with the sixties, Robert Fraser, opened up an eponymously named gallery in Duke Street that represented British pop art and American artists such as Jim Dine and Claes Oldenburg. It became a crucial nexus of the movement, where film stars, wealthy collectors, celebrities, and pop groups such as The Beatles and the Stones could mingle with avant-garde artists.

One of the movement's true pioneers was Victor Musgrave, who had opened Gallery One in 1953. He had shown works by French artist Yves Klein and, in 1962, was the first to show the work of Bridget Riley, whose early op art paintings represent the free spirit of the era (later, in 1966, Riley would have an exhibition of her work at New York's Museum of Modern Art). The vitality of British art was demonstrated in the 'New Generation' series of exhibitions held from 1964 at the Whitechapel Gallery and directed by Bryan Robertson.

However, London's gallery kingpin was the Marlborough, owned by Vienna-born entrepreneur Frank Lloyd. He had offered contracts to the top artists in the country that gave them more money and security; among others, he signed Francis Bacon, Henry Moore, Graham Sutherland and Barbara Hepworth. At the time he also set up galleries in Rome and New York. By now London could boast around 160 galleries of all shapes and sizes.

1

❝ ...degenerated into total drunkenness. ❞

PETER BLAKE

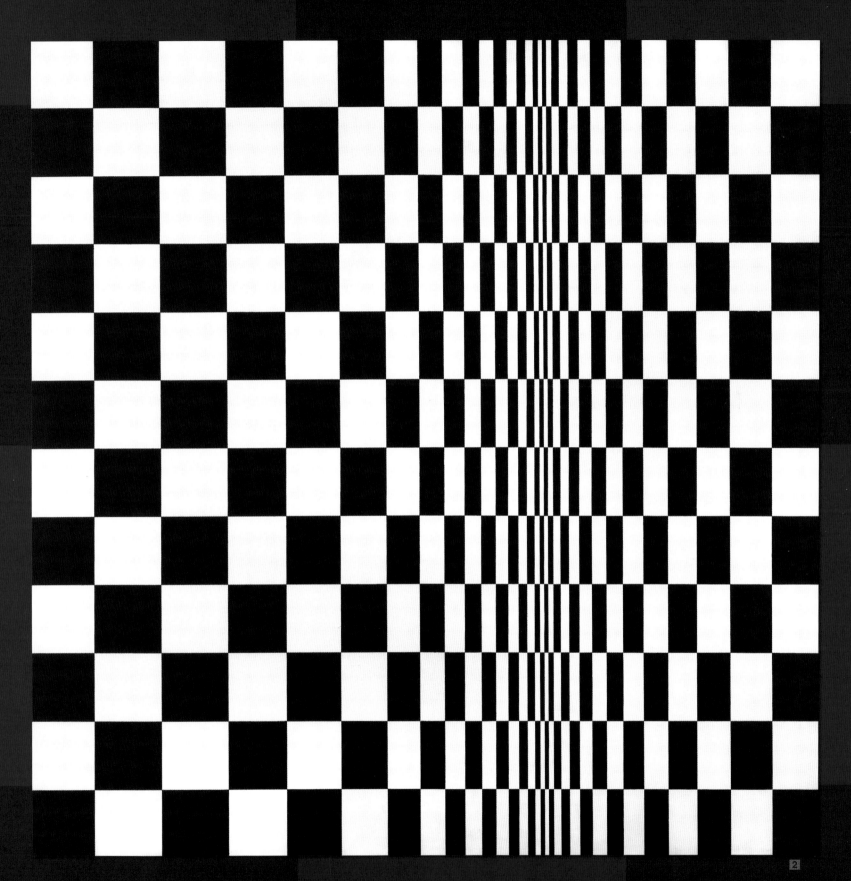

1 *Gift*, Kenneth Noland, 1961–2.

2 *Movement In Squares*, Bridget Riley, 1961.

The underground counterculture had been thriving since the start of the 1960s. The Beatniks had always mixed jazz, drugs, art and reading. The words of William Burroughs, Allen Ginsberg, Gregory Corso and Jack Kerouac were of utmost importance to them.

On June 11, 1965, around 7,000 people attended the Royal Albert Hall for the four-hour-long International Poetry Incarnation, an event that featured, among others, Lawrence Ferlinghetti, Ginsberg and Corso. For an event that had only been set up 10 days earlier and was sparsely advertised, the turnout alone showed that there was a huge interest in change. The International Poetry Incarnation was worlds away from the basic type of protest seen on the Campaign for Nuclear Disarmament (CND) Aldermaston marches; poetry was no longer confined to the written word on the printed page – the whole essence of performance was equally vital. The poetry itself was no longer bound by the limitations of right-wing or left-wing politics but embraced the use of psychedelic drugs while examining the frontiers of madness and LSD-induced internal liberation. It was through this event that one of London's most famous galleries came to be.

Barry Miles, one of the event's organisers, had been running the alternative bookshop Better Books in London's Charing Cross Road, which promoted American avant-garde literature. With new, more traditional owners arriving in the form of Collins, Better Books' original concept seemed doomed. So Miles set about establishing his own bookstore, although he had no money to put his ideas into practice. Through Paolo Lionni, a writer and art director of several national magazines, Miles met John Dunbar who was planning on opening an art gallery and with John's friend, pop star Peter Asher, as a silent partner, the three young men combined their ideas into a company called Miles, Asher and Dunbar Limited (MAD). In September 1965, the Indica Books and Gallery at Mason's Yard – an outlet for art and literature – was born.

"The thing that got it going was seeing the Albert Hall totally full for this loony reading thing. We thought: 'Fuck, thousands of people paid a quid or whatever. We could do a shop!' We didn't want to do just old pictures. We wanted to show what was going on and I just went from one artist to another really. Robert Fraser was doing the same around that time. We got to know each other in Venice in '66 and bonded over drugs and so on. We were never rivals and we were both very helpful to each other and encouraged each other a lot."

1 *Love Wall*, Peter Blake, 1961.
2 *Sand, Wind And Tide Series*, Boyle Family, 1969.

John Dunbar recalls: "Marc Feld, who later changed his name to Bolan, was at art school just around the corner. He helped us put the shelves up. He was really nice and helpful. [Paul] McCartney was an enthusiastic helper. He didn't put the money up for it, that was Peter Asher, but he helped set it up and made the wrapping paper."

The 1960s proved to be a real merging point between music and art. If you were to ask somebody "What do Pete Townshend, Eric Clapton, Ray Davies, John Lennon and Keith Richards all have in common?" you could answer that they'd all been in highly successful music groups of the period. You could also say that they all, among many others of their kind, attended art college long before making it in music. At art college, social barriers tumbled and working-class students mixed with middle-class intellectuals to forge a real pop art movement.

John Dunbar: "I got involved with people like Andrew Loog Oldham when I was very young. He was a friend of Peter Meaden [first manager of The Who]. They used to hang out together. Meaden's girlfriend, Gina, was my girlfriend's friend so we used to hang out together at these parties around Hampstead and such places. Andrew was such a good hustler. He was hustling from the word go and then he found the Stones. Peter Meaden, meanwhile, had The Who but they were called The High Numbers and made that record 'Zoot Suit.' But Peter was so kind of manic that he talked himself out of it somehow. He was very into purple hearts and he fell by the wayside somehow. He talked himself out of shit and put people off by that overwhelming jabbering. I wasn't really shocked that Peter never made it because I hung out with him and could just see him fucking up. He was so full on. Andrew just happened to have a more forceful personality because I think Peter could have made it through The Who. I mean, it could have been mega."

Peter Blake has his own take on what happened: "I think what happened was that immediately after the Second World War there was a Labour government giving grants to people, and some who wouldn't have gone to either art school or into the theatre had the opportunity to. So people started going to art school in the late 1940s and 1950s, and people like me were coming to fruition by the 1960s and that culminated in new photographers, actors and painters. Almost every band had at least one member who had been to art school."

John Dunbar was there among the influx of pop music artists meeting the pop art artists. He was more than willing to introduce these musicians to the work of exciting creative characters such as Mark Boyle.

Glaswegian Mark Boyle, alongside his partner Joan Mills, was famous for creating *Earth Studies*, which were randomly chosen, highly accurate, painted three-dimensional casts of areas of the Earth's surface using resin and fibreglass as well as natural materials from the scene, such as twigs, pebbles and leaves.

“...at least one member who had been to art school.”

PETER BLAKE

John Dunbar: "The analogy of what was happening at the time is that it was like a fucking big wave that went through London, spread right throughout the world, and I was in it. So you are not aware of it as a wave, if you see what I mean. But in retrospect that is kind of how it was. Y'know, tumbling around in this wave with all sorts of other people who you would bash into and meet. We just knew it was a very small town in those days. You just kind of knew everybody. We obviously turned people like Paul [McCartney] and John [Lennon] on to various things, because we had been to university so we turned them on to various ideas of chemistry vis-à-vis drugs and so on, as well as general art things.

"John was always drawing. Paul wanted to be middle class basically. I introduced them to all the loony stuff, such as conceptual art, from Yoko Ono to Takis. Then there were all the people I put on, such as Mark Boyle. Mark was a good talker and did all the light shows for the UFO [club] and stuff but at the same time he was very strict about his randomness. He liked the whole idea of being random. Stick a pin in a map, go there, chuck a stick behind his shoulder and make a square of wherever the stick landed and lift that up, absolutely. Mark Boyle in a way is pop. He takes any bit of ground and puts it up. People, you know, arty types, would say 'You can't be random! You have to choose it!' No definitely not. That was his kind of thing. With people like Paul [McCartney] and John [Lennon], they wanted to know things from us and we were interested in their scene as well. It was an interaction. It wasn't just one-sided guru shit you know."

Art wasn't just about creativity: destruction was just as important. Gustav Metzger had come to Britain in 1939 as a refugee, having been born to Polish-Jewish parents in Germany. In 1943, his parents were arrested by the Nazis and never seen again. This was a major factor for the pure hatred that Gustav held towards war. He was as much a political activist as he was an artist, and he became involved with CND in the 1950s. In 1959, he began his work, which he would eventually term 'auto-destructive art.'

On July 3, 1961, Metzger attracted a crowd of people at the South Bank in London. He was dressed in a combat jacket, helmet, pilot's goggles, oxygen mask and gauntlets, not only for protective use but also to emphasise his image as a revolutionary. Metzger then proceeded to spray hydrochloric acid onto three stretched nylon canvases on metal frames. The nylon began disintegrating into sections – just as the art was being created, it was also being destroyed. As the last sheet dissolved it revealed a view of St Paul's Cathedral in the background. Metzger's destructive art was a clear comment upon the destructive power of the Nuclear Age.

By 1965, Metzger's experiments led to the *Liquid Crystal Environment*, made using heat-sensitive liquid crystals placed between glass slides and inserted into projectors. The slides were rotated to create movement within the liquid, and as the crystals were heated they changed colour. The way-out patterns produced within the various slides were then simultaneously projected onto screens around the exhibition space. These were later used as a backdrop for a gig featuring Cream, The Who and The Herd at London's Roundhouse.

1

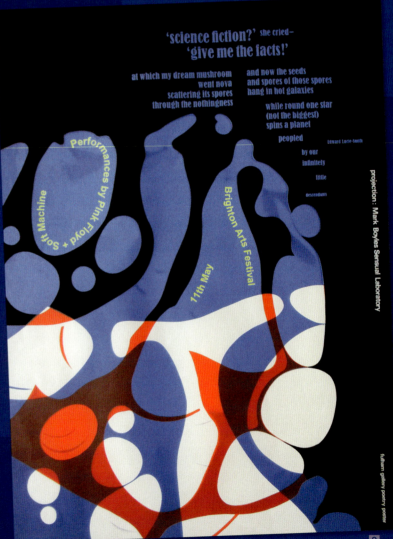

'science fiction?' she cried–
'give me the facts!'

at which my dream mushroom
went nova
scattering its spores
through the nothingness

and now the seeds
and spores of those spores
hang in hot galaxies

while round one star
(not the biggest)
spins a planet

peopled
Edward Lucie-Smith
by our
infinitely
little
descendants

Performances by Pink Floyd + Soft Machine

Brighton Arts Festival

11th May

projection: Mark Boyles Sensual Laboratory

fulham gallery poetry poster

2

> **"I don't think I am especially interested in destruction..."**
>
> MARK BOYLE

The Sensual Laboratory London
published by fulham gallery London

[3]

His light shows would go on to become backdrops in the underground music venue the UFO club, including those for the group Soft Machine, their US tour with Jimi Hendrix and several of their shows at Middle Earth in Covent Garden. Later, in 1970, Boyle was quoted as saying, "I don't think I'm especially interested in destruction as an aspect of everything... Things are created and survive only by destruction of other things."

The Sensual Laboratory London
published by fulham gallery London

[3]

In September 1966, some 15 months after the Poetry Incarnation, a Destruction in Art Symposium took place at the Africa Centre and various locations around London. It gathered 50 different artists from 10 different countries. Included as representatives were Metzger and Boyle, who although sharing similar ideals, were also very different. In Metzger's case, he believed that the final product – his creative piece ending in ultimate destruction – eliminated the artist's ego. Boyle could claim a similar stance with his random approach. Boyle had also been experimenting with light projection since 1962. He used Aldiss projectors, a mixture of chemicals, 35mm slides, insects and other living specimens to create a series of images that were in constant movement and mutation.

[1] Gustav Metzger, South Bank, 1961.

[2] One of the posters sold at the Brighton Arts Festival, 1968, for Pink Floyd's performance. Designed by the renowned artist Tom Adams with inspiration from his friend and collaborator, Mark Boyle, who created *The Sensual Laboratory*, a lightshow used by both Jimi Hendrix and Pink Floyd.

[3] Two colour variants of *The Sensual Laboratory* poster, 1968. Also designed by Tom Adams, inspired by Mark Boyle's lightshow. The poster could be purchased at Tom's gallery in Fulham and at concerts where the lightshow was used.

By now, pop had certainly entered the world of art and the only thing the artists were bound by was the limitations of their own imaginations. As the use of drugs escalated during the period, so did the boundaries of vision among those using them. In the early part of the decade, amphetamines such as benzedrine, dexedrine, methadrine, durophet, purple hearts and French blues were the drugs of choice. These would increase energy and confidence and give an overall feeling of well-being. By 1965, drugs had moved on, just like the kids and the art world, and the New Kid on the Block was lysergic acid diethylamide (LSD), or 'acid,' as it was commonly known. LSD is a derivative of ergot, a rye fungus, and is a colourless and odourless substance. Swiss chemist Albert Hoffman discovered it by accident when taking it led to heightened awareness and a distortion of colour and sound. In other words, it was a powerful hallucinogen, the ingestion of which many non-conformists (artists, writers, musicians) believed to expand their talents. The downside, of course, was that it could also produce severe psychotic reactions and mental disorder. However, many were prepared to take that risk, and the latter half of the sixties would indeed prove to be the start of a ground-breaking period in both music and art.

For some, drugs were certainly not a new experience, as John Dunbar recalls: "I was going to Paris quite a lot but I really discovered drugs while hitchhiking, and I wound up in Greece around '61 or '62. At the time I was 16 or 17. There were lots of drugs around Athens... opium, puff and stuff. I'd got turned on to smoking dope before that though, from a Scottish guy who came back from abroad with drawing boards packed with nice Lebanese hash. I was still at school then pretty much."

Dunbar would witness the effects of drugs on a band from start to finish, first hand. He'd got to know The Beatles in their early, clean-living days and watched them transform both creatively and musically into an unstoppable force while under the influence of various narcotics. "Bob Dylan turned The Beatles on to drugs in America. A few months before they went, I was in this club, smoking a little hash pipe. John Lennon goes past and says 'Is that drugs?' in a shocked voice. I said 'Yeah, it's a bit of hash,' and we had a chat about it but he was just a drinker.

They came back from America all interested in drugs, smoking puff and everything. Acid came in around 1965, the same time as the poetry reading [the International Poetry Incarnation] at the Albert Hall. The poet John Esam brought back some liquid acid from Switzerland, from Sandoz I think. That was my first trip. Acid was very confusing memory-wise, it just separates you off in a funny sort of way. Drugs definitely have an effect. I think it can be used in a positive way but it can be very dangerous as well. In '67, Peter Whitehead took some shots of me and Lennon arriving at the 14 Hour Technicolour Dream [a 1967 concert held at Alexandra Palace, with Pink Floyd headlining]. We'd been in John's house in Weybridge and we suddenly remembered the event. So we got his driver, Terry Dorran, got in the Roller or whatever it was. I remember looking out of the back window at the sky and it was totally clear... then suddenly there were these fucking fireworks going off! We arrived at the Ally Pally basically ok, but tripping. There's footage of us there."

John Dunbar had in fact been very influential in Lennon's meeting with Yoko Ono. The couple had met at the Indica Gallery in November 1966 at Yoko's 'Unfinished Paintings And Objects,' which Robert Fraser had sponsored. Lennon was impressed by the exhibition's humour, which included an apple on sale for £200 and a step ladder that led up to the ceiling and a hanging magnifying glass on a chain that when peered through would pick out tiny letters on the ceiling spelling the word 'yes.' Lennon was fascinated by its positivity.

Peter Blake recalls: "Robert [Fraser] was essential to it all. He was a close friend of the Stones and The Beatles and he probably supplied their drugs at the time, as he himself took various drugs. He was incredibly important. As for the Indica Gallery, I remember when Yoko Ono came to London, she came to a symposium of conceptual art. She stayed with a friend of mine called John Latham and they came to the pub we used in Notting Hill called the Princedale one Saturday morning. She was just a young Japanese kid really, very well known in the States but not really known here. Then when she got the show in Indica she asked me whether I could find get some of my students, because I taught at the Royal College, who could actually make the pieces.

When you see photographs of that Indica show it's usually Yoko, John Dunbar and Barry Miles. Sometimes Robert Fraser is in them and lurking in the background are two young men with big full beards. They are my students, who actually made all the pieces and constructed the whole show."

"...discovered drugs while hitchhiking... ...drugs around Athens... opium, puff and stuff."

JOHN DUNBAR

Colin Self

Exhibition at the Robert Fraser Gallery, 1966, featuring works by the leading pop artists of the time, including Peter Blake. Robert Fraser himself was keen to ingratiate himself into the 'pop' scene of the period, befriending both The Beatles and the Stones.

Dunbar, meanwhile, has fond memories: "I'm very proud of Indica, it was great. It did a lot of good and brought people together in all kinds of ways. Everybody that came through London arrived there. It helped kick off a whole bunch of stuff. The whole point of Indica was to be non-high-falutin.' People could just come there, and did, from junkies to megastars and princes. I did it because I was married [to Marianne Faithfull] and had a kid basically. Once that broke up I lost interest basically. There was no money. It was very difficult to make it pay because there were fuck all paying punters. People like McCartney bought things, which helped you keep going for a few months. It was never going to be a money-making venture. I just thought we might get a bit of support, you know, be able to survive. I had no fantasies about making a fortune. I'm not Andrew [Loog Oldham]! He was a businessman and hustler. I totally never have been." He continues: "There were things happening all the time; recordings, shows, happenings, parties and lots of drugs. There was a lot of acid but it became too overwhelming I guess. Some people did fantastically well and got riches beyond their wildest dreams pretty quickly as well as lots of attention. That changes people, always does. Then there were other people dropping out."

" ...I saw her and instantly fell in love..." "

PETER BLAKE

The year 1967 could be seen as the culmination of the art world mixing with pop. On June 1, the eighth Beatles studio album was released. The initial, most striking thing about *Sgt. Pepper's Lonely Hearts Club Band* was the cover. Art-directed by Robert Fraser, designed by Peter Blake and his then wife, Jann Haworth, and photographed by Michael Cooper, it featured a collage of life-size cardboard cut-outs of celebrities and waxwork dummies. The Beatles themselves had been asked to choose famous people they admired and these became the cut-outs that surrounded the band: actors, comedians, sportsmen, writers and religious gurus, which included Diana Dors, Aleister Crowley, Marilyn Monroe, Oscar Wilde, Sonny Liston, Bob Dylan, Fred Astaire and Tony Curtis.

Even though Blake and Haworth only made £200 for their work on the design, Peter Blake's career will forever be linked with that album cover.

However, it nearly never came about. In fact, a hippie collective, known as The Fool, had designed the initial artwork for the album cover. Robert Fraser saw it and insisted The Beatles commission Peter Blake instead. Blake recalls: "The reason that happened was that Robert Fraser had seen the design they had done and it was a very psychedelic design by Simon Posthuma and Marijke Koger. They were a Dutch design group and [Fraser] proposed that they had [the cover] done by an artist rather than a designer, so that's how it came about."

The album would go on to win four Grammy awards that year, including for Best Album Cover, Graphic Arts.

Sadly, Pauline Boty would not be around to witness her great friend Blake's escalation in the music world. Having married the literary agent Clive Goodwin, Boty became pregnant. During a prenatal examination it was discovered that she had leukaemia. She refused to have an abortion or receive treatment in case it harmed the foetus. Her daughter, Boty Goodwin, was born in February 1966. Boty died at the Royal Marsden Hospital on July 1 that year, aged just 28.

Peter Blake recalls with much sadness: "I think I saw her and instantly fell in love with her and it was a kind of unrequited love. We were great friends and she said that classic line 'I love you but I don't love you in that way.' So we were terrific friends and always stayed that way. She had various boyfriends all the time and we went out a few times to private viewings and such. Then she married Clive Goodwin, sadly she had leukaemia while she was pregnant. She had the choice of having treatment and losing the baby or just having the baby. Anyway the baby was born and the leukaemia got worse and worse. I hadn't seen her for a while and I was having lunch at the Royal College and her closest friend, Natalie, said 'Pauline is very ill. She said she'd really like to see you.' We literally drove from the Royal College round to the Royal Marsden Hospital. She had died minutes earlier and I'd just missed her."

Smoke cigars? He practically paints with them

Creative people take to Wills

And wisely too. Pop artists swear blind they paint better on a Wills cigar. And if an artist should happen to dip his Toledo in the paint by mistake . . . well, who knows . . . it may be the start to a completely new trend in pop art.

The point is, Wills have put an end to all those age old prejudices about cigars – like, cigars are the privilege only of millionaires or Americans. In fact, Wills say cigars aren't a privilege at all. They're a fact of life to anyone who enjoys smoking them – anyone from Royal Academicians down to pavement artists. You see, anyone with years of experience knows how to make good cigars. But Wills know the people they're making them for as well. That's why their cigars are available everywhere at the right prices for hundreds of thousands who, a few years ago, wouldn't have even dreamed of a puff.

PICADOR · TOLEDO · WILLS WHIFFS
VAN DYCK · CASTELLA · EMBASSY

W.D.&H.O.WILLS

CIGARMAKERS-PACEMAKERS

P 80C

Robert Fraser Gallery
69 Duke street London W1
October 20 to November 27 1965

Peter Blake

DOKTOR K. TORTUR

1

2

It would be Robert Fraser who would push the art-meets-pop-meets-drugs world beyond the limit. On June 29, 1967, Fraser was sentenced to six months' imprisonment and fined £200 costs. Alongside him, also facing sentencing, were two of Britain's pop stars.

The scenario had started earlier that year, on February 12, to be precise, when police officers raided Keith Richards' home, known as 'Redlands,' in West Wittering, Sussex. Having been tipped off by the press that a drug party was taking place, officers turned up and arrested several revellers.

The eventual outcome was that Robert Fraser – an old Etonian, son of a rich banker, art dealer, dandy and drug addict – was found guilty to the charge of the possession of illegal substances, along with two members of the pop elite.

Judge Leslie Kenneth Allen Block, chairman of the bench at Chichester Court, was known to be unforgiving and stern, and proved this in his severe sentences for the first-time offenders. Jagger was found guilty of being in possession of four tablets containing amphetamine sulphate and methamphetamine hydrochloride. He was sentenced to three months in Brixton Prison and ordered to pay £100 costs.

Keith Richards felt the full force of the law, as he was handed a year's imprisonment and £500 court costs for allowing his home to be used for the purpose of smoking cannabis. While Fraser was found in possession of heroin and eight capsules of methamphetamine hydrochloride and so got his hefty prison sentence. Both were to be detained in Wormwood Scrubs.

The artist Richard Hamilton, who had produced the 1956 collage *Just What Is It That Makes Today's Homes So Different, So Appealing?*, was appalled. It seemed apt that he would be the artist to produce a series of works capturing this piece of social history. He began an array of paintings that would be known as the *Swingeing London 67* series. (A year earlier, *Time* magazine (April 1966) had reported on the London-based social revolution leading to permissiveness, the article including the phrase 'Swinging London.' Judge Block had clearly duly noted this apt phrase, because during his harsh sentencing of the pair, he mentioned that they should receive a "swingeing sentence.")

The paintings would centre on a photograph taken by *Daily Mail* photographer John Twine, of Jagger and Fraser handcuffed together in the back of a police van. Working with pencil, watercolour, pastel and a metalised acetate, in order to highlight the handcuffs, the paintings were both extremely striking and a wry comment on the draconian sentences handed down during the supposedly hedonistic Swinging Sixties.

The Who recorded covers of 'The Last Time' and 'Under My Thumb' as a single at De Lane Lea Studios, London. The intention was to help Jagger and Richards make bail. The songs were rush recorded and the record appeared in shops within just a week, but by the time the single was made available, the two fall guys had already been released. Fraser was collected from jail in a shiny black limousine, which delivered him back to his flat in Mount Street, Mayfair.

In 1968, Fraser exhibited Hamilton's *Swingeing London* works at his gallery at 69 Duke Street, London where he'd also displayed John Lennon's 'You Are Here' exhibition, both of which would prove to be his biggest shows.

In complete contrast to Blake's vivid and colourful *Sgt. Pepper* cover, The Beatles' 'White album' cover was totally white, with the words 'The Beatles' embossed in the bottom right-hand corner. Richard Hamilton designed the cover, on Fraser's recommendation. Fraser could also claim another influence on The Beatles' career, as it was he who sold Paul McCartney a painting of an apple, *Le Jeu De Mourre*, by the Belgian surrealist artist René Magritte. This is believed to have been the inspiration for Apple Corps Limited, The Beatles' creative outlet that would include music, film, electronics and the ill-fated Apple Boutique clothing shop.

John Dunbar also played a part in it. "Apple ended up being diabolical. I backed right off that whole scene. The idea of Apple Corps was started in my flat in Bentinck Street. We were taking trips and drawing on the walls and stuff. We started talking about doing something with the money that was coming in. Then the idea of a company called Apple came up. It was all about doing wonderful things. I mean, they tried but it all kind of fucked up. It could have been great but it all just got out of hand. Too many cooks, basically. I was certainly naive... we all were to some extent, apart from a few like Andrew Loog Oldham and so on."

As the 1960s came to an end it would prove to be the decade most associated with the combined force of drugs, music and art. No period since has ever come close.

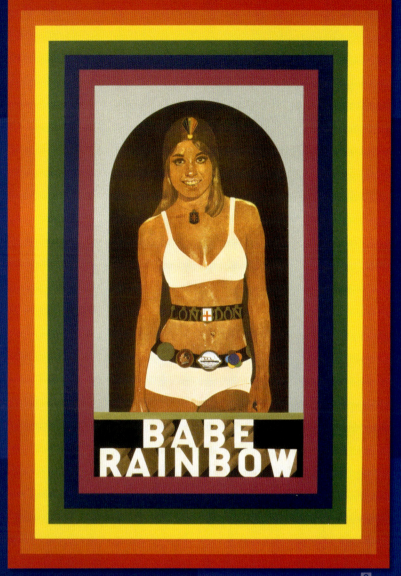

3

1 Peter Blake exhibition at the Robert Fraser Gallery, 1966.
Doktor K. Tortur was a mythological wrestler.
Wrestling is a subject matter that has fascinated Peter Blake for most of his life.
2 *Swingeing London 67*, Richard Hamilton, 1968-69.
3 *Babe Rainbow*, Peter Blake, 1968.
4 *Ice Cream*, Evelyne Axell, 1964.

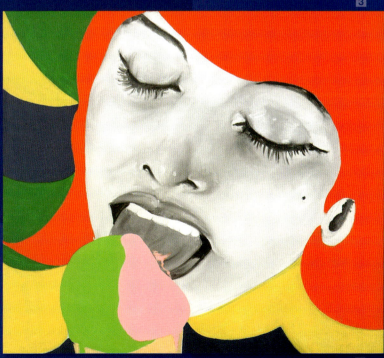

4

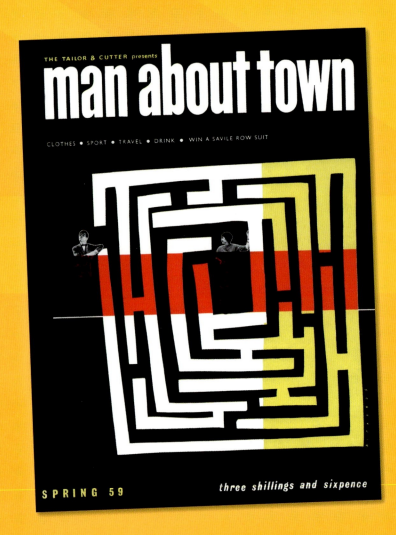

THE TAILOR & CUTTER presents

man about town

CLOTHES • SPORT • TRAVEL • DRINK • WIN A SAVILE ROW SUIT

SPRING 59   three shillings and sixpence

HERE COME THE TONY BOYS

❝ ...we shall henceforth refer to them as Macaronis... ❞

JOHN TAYLOR

October 1957. Paul Anka's 'Diana' is number one in the UK charts. Elvis Presley has four records in the Top 20, and Buddy Holly and Jerry Lee Lewis are keeping him company there. Britain's pretender to the Elvis crown, Tommy Steele, is among them, too, and celebrating his first year as a star. Take a look in a *Melody Maker* magazine from that time, though, and all the talk is of jazz: Count Basie, Lionel Hampton, Duke Ellington and Louis Armstrong were the big names. British names that get a mention include Johnny Dankworth, Lonnie Donegan and the aforementioned Steele. It's like rock'n'roll never happened.

Man About Town quarterly magazine was directed at exactly the kind of person in the title, middle-to-upper-class men who knew to buy their suits from the likes of Hawes & Curtis in Dover Street, W.1, spade-toe brogues from Russell & Bromley in New Bond Street, and to entertain that young filly from the typing pool with dinner at Murray's Cabaret Club in Beak Street. The magazine's editor, 36-year-old John Taylor, came up with the concept and launched the magazine in 1950. Taylor, who was also the editor of *Tailor And Cutter* magazine, aimed the *Man About Town* at an audience that had been starved, through war-time austerity, of the finer things in life: good wine, smart clothes – preferably from Savile Row – and beautiful women.

When the autumn 1957 edition hit the shelves its bright red cover featured the usual cover character, a middle-aged, mutton-chopped man, pouring champagne into a woman's slipper. Among the contents advertised are the words 'Tony Boy – The new horror.' Turning to page nine we are treated to a full page under the banner 'Teddytorial,' where John Taylor rather astutely make notes of the emerging youth fashion, which is moving away from the American-influenced 'Teddy Boy' look towards a newer, Italian/continental style. The mood of the piece is extremely derisory. While admitting that it is a heralding in a significant moment in the history of fashion, with a style that has emerged from the bottom of the social-class scale, it is quick to denounce the look as nothing more than a "layabout level fad." A cartoon by Taylor accompanies the piece. The 'Tony' label is never explained but could have been directed towards Tony Curtis haircuts, or maybe even 'Anthony' and Cleopatra. As negative as the article is, it really might be the very first of its kind on the emerging fashion trend that would go on to be called 'Mod.'

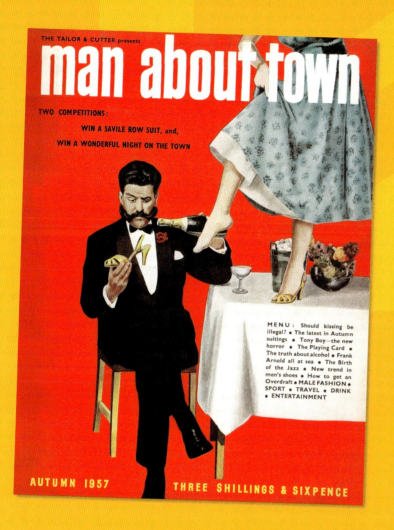

out goes the
TEDDY BOY
in comes the
TONY BOY

Our street corners are looking different. Whereas they were once supported by retrospective looking lads, they are now being kept in perpendicular rigidity by a strange pseudo Mediterranean race. The Teddy Boy is giving way to the Tony Boy.

Basis for the fashion trend among the lads at the end of the street is the Italianate influences of extremely short, top-heavy jackets, wide widely draped shoulders, very rounded jacket fronts, at least three buttons probably fastened on the top one, and a narrow turn-upless trouser which uses an interior stiffening inside the lower part of the trouser and gives the effect of a plain deep cuff. The effect is of a peg top jacket—heavy across the shoulders and gathered in fittingly around the hips.

With this ensemble a tie is often dispensed with and the other end of the Tony Boy is dolled up in those sharply pointed, apparently weltless slippers which the retail shoe shops assure us are "Made in Italy", and which it seems like you'd have to have a toe amputated to get into. The causes and effects of the style are interesting.

For one thing this seems to be about the first time in the history of masculine clothes that a fashion has originated at anywhere other than the top of the social scale. Fashion has always been snobbish—and it remains snobbish. For our money the social scale won't allow this style to climb any higher than the level at which it has started.

(The trend for the British short jacket continues, of course—but its silhouette is neater in shoulder width, slightly squarer in shoulder shape; and more fitting at the waist, more flaring at the hem.)

It has always been the Kiss of Death to any fashion for it to be adopted by the lads on the corner, so it is very doubtful if this style will get any wider recognition than it will inevitably receive at layabout level.

What is interesting to note, however, is the shift in emphasis by the adolescent class to Italian styled clothes rather than American styled clothes as has been the habit at the lower end of fashion hitherto. Some journals have howled that the Italian fashion movement has endangered the British tailoring lead—but this new circumstance seems to suggest that it is not the British clothing trade which will be affected so much as the American fashion trade.

The Teddy Boy was, in effect, not an Edwardian figure but a kind of Mississippi Gambler shape (remember his string tie, his wide wide shoulders, his diving-boot shoes). The replacement to the Teddy Boy is the Tony Boy; and you have been warned not to do as the Romans do.

MAN ABOUT TOWN, AUTUMN, 1957

TEDDYTORIAL

John Taylor went on to largely ignore the latest youth style in subsequent editions of the magazine, but it ate away at him enough to give the 'Tony Boys' full pages in two issues over the next year and a half. In spring 1958, he penned 'Macaroni – and not the first time,' in which he likened the new breed to that of a group of 18th-century men influenced by Italian style and calling themselves 'The Macaronis.' He even quoted from an article in a 1772 edition of *Town And Country*, which ridiculed the group. Taylor states: "The contemporary Macaroni – for we shall henceforth refer to them as Macaronis – seems to share at least his shoe fashion with that of his 18th-century predecessor – but the coat styles are reversed in that the first M.'s was so long that the coat pockets were out of reach and the inside breast pocket was first introduced. Nowadays the Macaroni wears a funny little curved bum-freezer jacket and trousers that certainly are cut loose enough to be neo-breeches. Thus we have Number Three in the post-war list of exaggerations: First – the Spiv; Second – the Teddy-Boy; Third – the Macaroni."

The last mention Taylor gives to the new breed comes by way of a mocking poem entitled 'Friends Romans Countrymen,' which was published in the spring 1959 edition.

Macaroni – and not the first time

The weirder youths nowadays seem to be taking their extreme fashions from Italy instead of America as was once their wont—or their will.

But it isn't the first time that a reprehensible sartorial cult has filtered through to Britain from the Italian area. In the Eighteenth Century a set of peculiar young men in the London area, who had travelled in Italy, began to inject Italian influence into their clothes.

Their cult was supposed to be a protest against the foolish fashions of the day, but actually their clothes soon outstripped in ridiculousness even the fanciful styles they were supposed to be improving upon.

Their extremes became the laughing stock of the time; and as a cult always has to have an identification, the public dubbed these layabouts The Macaronis.

In 1772, *Town and Country Magazine* reported of them: "They make a ridiculous figure with hats an inch in the brim that do not cover but lie upon the head, with about two pounds of fictitious hair formed into what is called a 'club' hanging down on their shoulders. The end of the skirt of their coat reaches the first button of their breeches which are either brown striped or white, their sleeves are so tight that they can only with difficulty get their hands through the cuffs . . . their legs are covered with all the colours of the rainbow. Their shoes are merely slippers and their buckles within an inch of the toe. Such a figure, essenced and perfumed, with a bunch of lace sticking out under its chin, puzzles the common passenger to determine the thing's sex."

The contemporary Macaroni—for we shall henceforth refer to them as Macaronis—seems to share at least his shoe fashion with that of his Eighteenth Century predecessor—but the coat styles are reversed in that the First M.'s was so long that the coat pockets were out of reach and the inside breast pocket was first introduced. Nowadays the Macaroni wears a funny little curved bum-freezer jacket and trousers which certainly are cut close enough to be neo-breeches.

Thus we have Number Three in the Post-War list of exaggerations: First—the Spiv; Second—the Teddy-Boy; Third—the Macaroni.

MAN ABOUT TOWN, SPRING, 1958

Spaghetti – the very first time

According to legend, the art of making macaroni products was discovered through the carelessness of a Chinese maiden many hundreds of years ago.

While busy preparing her daily batch of bread dough, the girl was courted so ardently by an Italian sailor that she forgot all about the dough on the stove.

The dough overflowed from the pan and dripped in strings that quickly dried in the sun.

The sailor, whose name was Spaghetti, gathered up the strings of dried dough and took them back to his ship where they were boiled in broth.

Before the war there were only two firms in Britain making macaroni products. The remainder of Britain's consumption of this type of food had to be imported from abroad. Now there are a dozen macaroni firms in this country making altogether 300 tons a week, and production is constantly increasing to cater for a demand stimulated by foreign travel. And not only are we making more macaroni and spaghetti, but the British product is claimed to be superior in quality to that imported.

Remember: 1: Spaghetti and macaroni are at their best when slightly cheesy. Do not overcook.

2: A little butter added to hot drained macaroni, spaghetti or noodles before the sauce is poured on will keep it from sticking together.

3: Macaroni and spaghetti double in bulk in cooking. Noodles swell only about one-fourth.

4: If you have some left over from a meal, store in a cool place. To use for another meal, freshen by running hot or cold water through it.

MACARONI-SALMON SALAD

Combine and toss together until well blended:
● 2 cups cooked and cooled elbow or shell MACARONI ● 1 cup diced cucumber ● 1 tin salmon flaked ● 1 dessert spoon grated onion ● 1 teaspoon finely chopped Parsley ● ½ cup Mayonnaise ● ¼ teaspoon pepper.

Fiends Romans Countrymen

I really was insulted when they come to 'ear my case,
For just becos I'd bashed some white 'aired geezer in the face,
They called me "Teddy Boy";
I said "Now—steady, boy,
"Even tho' I'm on probation, still a lad 'as got 'is pride
"An' that 'Teddy' connotation is unjust, Milord," I cried,
For Edwardian is passe and the current rulin' passion
Is the short coat, Jeans and pointed shoes of the Italian fashion.

We're the Toni Boys—
Me an' me crony boys—
We're dead to rights, awfentick, Macaroni Boys:
We've got them littul jackits woot stops just above the 'ips,
We got Julius Caesar 'aircuts an' them shoes wiv pointed tips
An' see wears 'em night and day; Gor Blimey 'ow me bunion nips!
We're the phoney Macaroni Toni Boys.

Lancaster Gate Italianate are quite a sight to see
The coats we've bort are proper short, but all the boys agree
Another inch 'll
Look most Provincial.
We've never bin to ole Turin, or Rome; but short inspection
Shows from our 'air and cloes we wear we're Ities by inflexion;
And when we're standin' on the corner, said one witty geezer,
We seem 'ell bent to represent the Leanin' Shower of Pisa.

We're the Toni Boys,
Not moan and groaney boys,
But payin' for this gear has left us stoney boys.
We've suffered ter be smart; it just ain't easy to be slickers;
My bottom's ruddy cold from this short coat and narrer nickers;
An' I'd ne to amputate two toes to wear these winkle pickers;
We're the phoney Macaroni Toni Boys.

Our tastes are very simple, Cappucino will support us,
We realise the white faced girls in black tights who escort us
Prefer us soulless
To Rock and Roll-less;
We never 'eard of 'Orace; except 'Orace Brown the grocer,
And Gallic Wars, and Latin clause, and Nero, we don't know Sir.
We think that schoolin' 's foolin'; but, though given more to spivvin'
We, in our way, spread, day by day, the Latin Way of Livin'.

We're the Toni Boys,
We stand aloney boys,
A wicked lot of sinners—no Baloney, boys,
In Regents Park we carve up filthy words on all the trees
We take our Cappucino straight—no lumps of sugar please—
And sometimes we deface the walls in public lavatories;
We're the phoney Macaroni Toni Boys.

A visitor to London, should 'e suddenly intrude
An' watch the stars of coffee bars, might suddenly conclude
The British Yeoman
'As gorn all Roman:
'E'd dig the rounded jackits, and the suits striped like a blazer
And the shirts like littul skirts, an' all the 'aircuts wiv a razor,
The taut-stretched pants, the slouching stance (the fashion's really catchin'),
The shoe points like stilettos, and the flick-knife smartly matchin'.

We're the Toni Boys,
The Cannelloni Boys,
All sorts; we're thins and shorts and fat and boney boys.
We don't fear unemployment, Mate, in fact we grab at it,
And though Life's full of problems, why, we never crab at it;
We've got the answer to all problems—'ave a stab at it
Like the phoney Macaroni Toni Boys.

J.T.

MAN ABOUT TOWN, SPRING, 1959

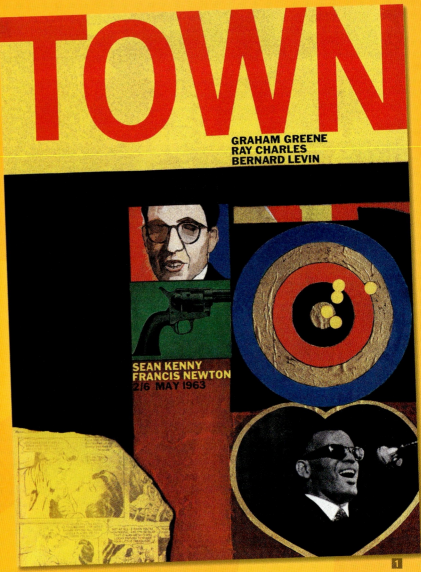

TOWN

GRAHAM GREENE
RAY CHARLES
BERNARD LEVIN

SEAN KENNY
FRANCIS NEWTON
2/6 MAY 1963

[1]

IN FACT IT'S THE MAN IN THE BLADES SUIT

It had to happen. Savile Row standards and the new crisp International look have met. At Blades. Blades craftsmen cut for Today, with the expertise of many Yesterdays. They are using the best materials, the traditional, and the new light and middle weights . . . The man in the Blades suit is tailored for today, elegant everywhere. A Blades suit is a Blades suit is a Blades suit. Who said that? We do. Blades are at 25, Dover Street, W1 Telephone GRO 5601

THE 1960s CLOTHING REVOLUTION: BOUTIQUES AND ADS

"...the beginning of the end of the old Savile Row. "

STANLEY KILGOUR

1 Blades Suits, July 1963.
2 The most desirable driving shoes, June 1965.

Most people know that quality healthcare in London can be found on Harley Street, and those that go there are often adorned in the best suits the city has to offer – from the sartorial institution that is Savile Row. What most people don't realise, however, is that it wasn't always this way.

Back in the early 1800s, the practice of making clothes was seen as a contemptible trade to be undertaken by the lower classes in under-lit basements. That is, until Henry Poole became the man responsible for changing everything. His father, also Henry, began as a private volunteer in the army making good clothes for the officers during the Napoleonic wars. In 1828, he purchased 4 and 5 Burlington Street as premises in which he could make uniforms for the military. He'd also managed to send young Henry to some very good schools, where he managed to break down social barriers and meet an array of wealthy and fashionable young men. Young Poole assembled a group of cutters, and with the help of the newly established railways, he could visit the country seats of these men and fit them for hunting clothes.

In 1846, when his father passed away, young Poole had the great idea of making the back entrance to his father's shop (then a stable block in Savile Row) the main entrance. At the time, Savile Row was teeming with wealthy doctors and fashionable surgeons, who at the impertinence of a mere tailor invading their sanctuary, were driven to seek refuge in their droves and move to Harley Street. Other tailors settled in their abandoned premises, making Henry Poole the founding father of Savile Row.

By the mid-1950s, while Savile Row could still lay claim to being the home of the best quality and most exclusive tailoring services in England, it was out of touch with the desires and demands of the fashionable youth. The fact that these hip, young people couldn't afford such prices didn't matter: they were the new 'fling society' – buy it, wear it, fling it and buy another. Why invest a lot of money in a quality suit when it would be unfashionable before the year was out? Why not buy four or five cheap ones that may only last a year but would be on trend? Stanley Kilgour – co-founder of the historic Savile Row tailors now known as Kilgour, claimed: "You can now see the beginning of the end of the old Savile Row."

When Kilgour, French and Stanbury opened their number 10 shop in Dover Street, they discarded their 80-guinea suits in favour of those for 54 guineas. Rupert Lycett Green then offered off-the-peg suits at 42 guineas in his Blades boutique in Burlington Gardens. It soon became hard to justify paying between £75 and £100 for a single suit when you could buy a few at £15 each. The old institution was caught off guard.

There is a great moment during the film *Doctor In Clover* (1966), during which an aging doctor, played by suave cad actor Leslie Phillips, is going through a mid-life crisis. He strolls down Carnaby Street, passing Raoul's shoe shop, and Domino Male and Paul's Male boutiques, and enters a shop where a young male assistant, played by Nicky Henson, confronts him. When Phillips explains that he wants something "with it," he is asked by the boutique assistant if the item is for his son. Phillips then explains that he wishes to appear younger looking. "We can sort you out with clothes but... physically... your hair is a bit old world." "Where do you think I should get it cut?" enquires the doctor. The assistant laughs and says "I don't think you should lose anymore. Try getting it styled."

A moment in a film, of course, but a grim reality. In fact, by the time the old brigade and the establishment had finally realised that there was a male fashion revolution taking place, it was practically over. By 1967, at the ripe old age of 31, John Stephen had watched his empire of boutiques – including the aforementioned Domino Male and Paul's Male – grow and grow, while the blinkered, established clothes stores poured scorn on any idea of there being a demand for male fashion, dismissing the whole thing as a flash in the pan. In fact the revolution was seen as some kind of feminine joke for many years; that is, until they saw visionaries such as Stephen driving around in Rolls Royces. Stephen's thirst for success was still unquenched, though, and even in 1967, a decade after his initial steps into the business, he was still putting in a 72-hour week. He owned most of the boutiques in Carnaby Street and now was steadily building an empire that would see his stores open in the USA and across Europe.

1 John Stephen's His Clothes boutique, June 1961.

2 American cool via Sweden from Cecil Gee, March 1964.

He's got a three-litre Bentley and a four-figure income. He has to dress at Smart Weston

He buys a luxurious wool-and-mohair MAGNI Topcoat, exclusive to Smart Weston. He likes its Swedish excellence of style tailored knee-length, with flap pockets, side vents, arm stitching, half belt and leather buttons. In Navy, Camel or Grey. 24 gns.

Smart Weston store for men

Coventry Street by Piccadilly Circus W1. Late night Thursday until 8 pm — open all day Saturday. Also Brompton Road, Knightsbridge/Shaftesbury Avenue (Smart Bros)/Kings Road, Chelsea/Golders Green Road, NW11/ and branches throughout London, Birmingham and at Manchester.

3

4

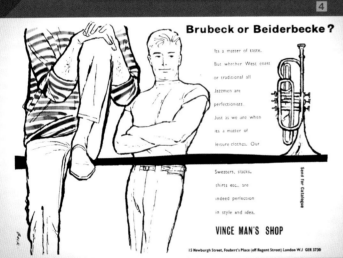

Brubeck or Beiderbecke?

Its a matter of taste.

But whether West coast or traditional all Jazzmen are perfectionists.

Just as we are when its a matter of leisure clothes. Our

Sweaters, slacks, shirts etc., are indeed perfection in style and idea.

Send for Catalogue

VINCE MAN'S SHOP

15 Newburgh Street, Foubert's Place (off Regent Street) London W.1 GER 3730

Stephen had not been alone or indeed the first in his quest to serve young people's fashion demands. At the end of the Second World War, Cecil Gee had opened up in Charing Cross Road and became known as the 'Spiv King.' He had tried pioneering an American look that was all tight trousers, kipper ties and floral shirts before moving to Shaftesbury Avenue, from where he imported the Italian Brioni fashions. Smart Weston was also aimed at the fashion-conscious young and imported Scandinavian, Yugoslav and Italian goods, while Bill Green, who owned and ran Vince's in Newburgh Street, Soho, had imported continental fashions since 1954.

Clothes boutique owner Lloyd Johnson: "When I first came to London my first job was at Cecil Gee's in Charing Cross Road, and that was great because it was right on the route to Denmark Street and all the guitar shops. In the basement were a coffee bar and all the band uniforms. You know, stuff like Bo Diddley used to wear – tartan coloured jackets with a cumberband and a bow tie. So the likes of Kenny Ball and his Jazzmen, Acker Bilk and all those types, were the customers downstairs. But upstairs it was all the kids who were going off to buy guitars. So they'd get The Beatles, The Rolling Stones, the Small Faces, St Louis Union and those types of people. All the bouncers from the Soho clubs and all the hoods went there because they had some special shirts that had no neck band and came down very low, so anybody that had a huge neck, it didn't strangle them. We sold knitwear to the Small Faces and I remember Mike McVay sold John Lennon the Levi jacket that he wore on the front cover of the *Rubber Soul* album.'

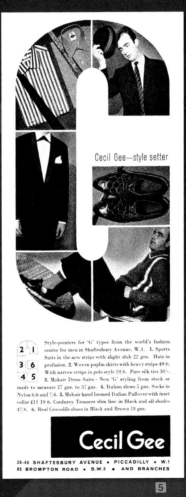

Cecil Gee—style setter

Style-pointers for 'G' types from the world's fashion centre for men in Shaftesbury Avenue, W.1. 1. Sports Suits in the new stripe with slight slub 22 gns. Hats in profusion. 2. Woven poplin shirts with heavy stripe 49/6. With narrow stripe in polo style 59/6. Pure silk ties 30/-. 3. Mohair Dress Suits – New 'G' styling from stock or made to measure 27 gns. to 37 gns. 4. Italian shoes 5 gns. Socks in Nylon 6/6 and 7/6. 5. Mohair hand loomed Italian Pullover with inset collar £11 19 6. Corduroy Trousers slim line in Black and all shades 47/6. 6. Real Crocodile shoes in Black and Brown 18 gns.

Cecil Gee

39-45 SHAFTESBURY AVENUE • PICCADILLY • W.1
85 BROMPTON ROAD • S.W.3 • AND BRANCHES

5

Grandees

Slacks keep that impeccable just-pressed look with stretch

If you're a man who gets around, these slacks are for you. Relax in them, and feel immaculate wearing them. How about those button-on stirrups for out of town and any Sports, you'll play better Golf in them—they never lose their shape.

Thank Cecil Gee and Bri-Nylon for this fabulous four-season trouser. Slimly styled in charcoal, navy and small diced check they cost 99/6 available at

BRI NYLON

Cecil Gee

Main Store: 39/45 Shaftesbury Avenue, Piccadilly, London W1. Open all day Saturdays. 85 Brompton Rd, SW3, 313 Oxford St., W1, and branches.

6

3 Smart Weston targets the top end of the market, December 1964.

4 Vince Man ad in the Beaulieu Jazz Festival Programme, August 1959.

5 Style setting from Cecil Gee, April 1962.

6 Strides by Cecil, April 1964.

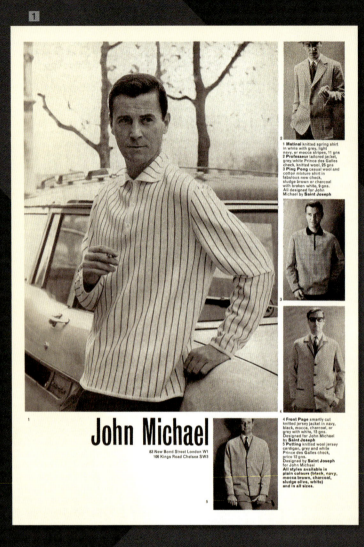

The two were rivals in the same game, but with different philosophies: "Carnaby Street is my creation. In a way I feel about it like Michelangelo felt about the beautiful statues he created," John Stephen once said, while John Ingram was far less generous when he stated that "Carnaby Street takes the fashion ideas from the very few and then bastardises them and over-does them so that you're not getting just a nasty thing but an over-exaggerated, cheap nasty thing."

It seems almost ironic that Carnaby Street runs parallel to Savile Row, divided only by Kingly Street and Regent Street – both with a common purpose and yet thoroughly divided by taste and class.

If John Stephen was ever to have any real competition in being at the forefront of advancing British male fashion, then that would come in the form of John Michael Ingram. Never wanting his clothes to be way-out or gimmicky, John Michael catered for men who wanted to be well dressed in quality merchandise, all at a reasonable price. He opened his first shop in the King's Road, Chelsea, in 1957 and a year later, he owned another store on Old Compton Street. By 1967, Ingram had 17 shops under various names, such as Guy, which specialised in ties and cufflinks, Sportique (casual and leisurewear) and The Westerner (you guessed it – Western/cowboy-style garments).

> **" Carnaby Street takes the fashion ideas from the few and then bastardises them... "**
>
> JOHN INGRAM

In 1966, the Ken Ashton-directed film *A Tale Of Two Streets* (shown on ATV in April 1967) compared the two streets. Sadly, the film gained favour for neither, as Savile Row was portrayed as a snob-ridden dinosaur and Carnaby Street was seen as too inarticulate.

Strangely enough it would be Regent Street, running in between the two sartorial streets, that would find the common ground. Up to that point, it was tailoring houses with branches nationwide that dominated high street fashion. Burtons, Hepworths, John Collier, John Temple, Hector Powe and Neville Reed – these retailers long had an unwritten understanding that they would offer similar styles, that their garments would pretty much look the same. Nobody wanted to rock the boat in the quest to remain King of the High Street. Then the sixties came along, demands changed and a veritable fashion war broke out.

At the beginning of the decade, Burtons decided to expand its business and John Collier attempted to keep its products low in price, while Hepworths made the bold decision to take on English fashion designer Hardy Amies to design a range for them. It was Hepworths who gained here, by championing a name linked with Savile Row and style. They got rid of mass production and employed cutters in every store. It was a huge success and was the first time a mass-consumer public had bought into a designer's name alone, and not just a high street brand. Burtons always remained steadfastly popular, however, as while it refused to go down the route of gimmicks, it was prepared to offer the individual customer exactly what he wanted.

On the other hand, many of the smaller clothes boutiques away from the high street flourished by offering exactly that: something gimmicky, something different. In 1965, Esquire, based in Kensington Church Street, had co-owner Willie Bowman making biannual trips to Europe in order to buy clobber, as well as importing goods from the continent. Michael's Man Boutique – mainly aimed at the 17–25-year-old market – also specialised in imports, and its director, Leslie Frankel, had been going on buying trips abroad since the start of the sixties. Meanwhile, having only opened in June 1965, the Ivy Shop in Richmond, quickly gained success by looking to America for its inspiration. John Simons and Jeffrey Kaye pushed the Ivy League look in shirts, trousers and jackets. Other shops cashed in on fads, and boutiques such as Paul's Menswear in Carnaby Street (run by Paul and Susi Spiegal) boasted that they could recreate any new idea within 24 hours of it being seen.

Granny Takes A Trip boutique in World's End was at 488 King's Road, Chelsea. Specialising in second-hand men and women's clothes and Victoriana, it was run by founders Nigel Waymouth, John Pearse and Sheila Troy. It soon began to stock new clothing, including floral shirts and white Venetian cloth trousers with flared bottoms. In January 1967, Waymouth and designer Michael Mayhew painted a giant mural of a woman's face on the outside wall of the store. It reflected their departure from selling second-hand Victoriana to stocking new and original designs. By June 1968, the picture had been replaced by the front half of a genuine 1948 Dodge saloon, its nose 'sticking out' of the building as though it had crashed through the wall.

1 Country look for urban life, April 1964.

2 Three shirts in one, March 1965.

3 The American Dream available in... Surrey, July 1966.

4 Smart American businessman look for the discerning Modernist, March 1966.

Soft tweed Stroller jacket in fawn Houndstooth check with Ghillie collar and side flap pockets. Also available in dark brown and navy blue – 79s 6d

michael's **MAN** boutique

15 The Broadway, Ealing, W5
74 High Road, Wood Green, N22
76 High Street, Putney, SW15
42 The Broadway, Southall
161 High Street, Acton, W3
30b Fife Road, Kingston

Please quote measurements when ordering.
Postage and packing 2s 6d extra.
Postal enquiries to the Ealing branch

1

The King's Road area had certainly become The Place To Be Seen by the mid-sixties. Just Men at 9 Tryon Street, just off the King's Road, was run by four of designer John Michael Ingram's graduates. The manager, Michael Dacie, offered a one-week, made-to-measure service on trousers and jackets. But probably the best new boutique in that area was Hung On You, at 22 Cale Street. Its proprietor, Michael Rainey, had named the shop after a Righteous Brothers song. Hung On You specialised in brightly coloured clothes and could count The Beatles, the Stones, The Action and The Who among its customers. It sold ready-to-wear suits for 33 guineas, but also offered a made-to-measure service in which Rainey or fellow designer Christopher Lynch could offer a suit in maybe an olive-velveteen or forties-style stripes, all in just 10 days. "We're not tailors but we will make things up for people if we think they're good," stated Rainey.

Most of the old established order, though, was too afraid to experiment. Scared of alienating their elder clientele but being mocked by the young for being stuck in the past, they had to find a compromise. This would eventually come in the shape of a store within a store, or 'shops in shops.'

Simpsons of Piccadilly was the first to achieve this. Sometime around late 1963, one-time *Town* magazine's fashion editor Gordon Deighton set up 'Trend' in the department store. Trend created a vogue for herringbone in shirts, suits and jackets. Austin Reed in Regent Street followed shortly, with another ex-*Town* magazine fashion editor, Colin Woodhead, designing and buying for the shop's new department known as 'Cue,' overlooked by Australian Graeme Tonge. In fact, the Kingsway branch of Austin Reed was making a steady loss until the entire store was converted to 'Cue,' after which it made good profits.

❝ We're not tailors... ❞

MICHAEL RAINEY

Austin Reed's new boutique department aimed at the young.

1 October 1965.

2 December 1966.

3 Simpson Piccadilly fab holiday gear, July 1965.

Cue men have a lean and lively look.
Cue is Austin Reed's dazzling new shop within a shop... an Aladdin's cave, a cornucopia of brilliant new clothes for men. Take this suit, for instance. You'll identify at once with the 3-button jacket, its two vents, soft shoulders, raised seams and of course, its clover leaf lapels. And you'll warm to the handsome, straight-cut trousers with their plain fronts and bottoms. Yours for about 28 gns. Better take your Cue . . . come along to Austin Reed in Regent Street and see for yourself.

CUE AT AUSTIN REED

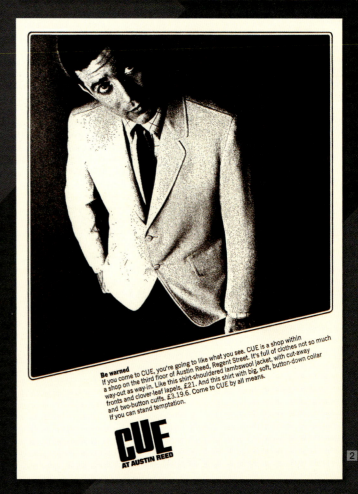

Be warned
If you come to CUE, you're going to like what you see. CUE is a shop within a shop on the third floor of Austin Reed, Regent Street. It's full of clothes not so much way-out as way-in. Like this shirt-shouldered lambswool jacket, with cut-away fronts and clover-leaf lapels, £21. And this shirt with big, soft, button-down collar and two-button cuffs, £3.19.6. Come to CUE by all means.
If you can stand temptation.

CUE AT AUSTIN REED

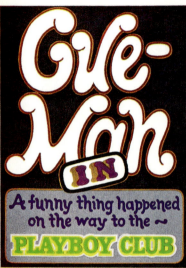

"...eventually got the sack from Cecil Gee's..."

LLOYD JOHNSON

Back to Lloyd Johnson: "I eventually got the sack from Cecil Gee's for insulting the manager because he was bullying another worker. I looked in the *Standard* for a job and saw one being advertised at Austin Reed's Cue department. This was around August 1966, I know that's correct because we used to play 'Autumn '66' by The Spencer Davis Group at Cecil Gee's and by September I was working at Cue. I was interviewed by Colin Woodhead and I told him I'd been sacked for insulting the manager but he liked my honesty and I pretty much started straight away.

"I'd gone to Austin Reed's because I thought it was better than Carnaby Street. They had these fabulous high-collar button-downs; in the collar they had a metal strip that you could bend and achieve a perfect roll collar. They were made in bleeding Madras from fantastic fabrics. They were also importing John White's American jackets. It was a two-button jacket with a square-top collar and a rounded narrow lapel. It was a black blazer that had three lines of contrasting white stitching around the lapels and the pocket flaps and white buttons. They were really top-end American clothing. They had Irish tweeds where you get a herringbone with a coloured stripe running through it. All hook-vent Ivy League stuff, and three-piece corduroy suits. Some of the stuff was edging towards the French thing, such as the Shetland sweaters. Colin Woodhead was so far ahead of anything else. Even the advertising was great, the Cue Man drawings were done by Alan Aldridge."

All the big stores would follow in the footsteps of Austin Reed and Simpsons – Aquascutum, Moss Bros., Jaeger. Indeed, luxury department store Harrods had pioneered the idea of young people wanting to wear different clothes from their parents, and had set up a youth department within the store, called 'Young Men's.' But it wasn't until the summer of 1967, after realising that in Carnaby Street the rents had gone up 1,000 per cent and pulling in an annual turnover of £5 million, that Harrods finally gave over a part of its store to teenagers, calling it 'Way In.' But from the Mod perspective, by then it was all too late.

Some people, though, still appreciated the shop's efforts to get with it. As top Mod Willie Deasy fondly remembers, "Way In made lovely clothes. Velvet jackets for men, it went quite upmarket. I went in there one day and nicked five left shoes. I went back about two weeks later and they'd put the right shoes out, so I took them too! They had no idea of security. Later on they started bringing in security tags, but you could put your hand over them and once you were out of Way In you were in Harrods. Different people, they didn't give a fuck. The alarms sometimes went off but they didn't care. I'd never go to somewhere like Irvine Sellars. I never had anything cheap made, I always wanted something different. It was like the thing with the bowling shoes, you know, different colours. That Way In stuff was really different and classy." While Mod was a male-dominated scene and there may have been a revolution in men's clothing, women's boutiques were on the up too.

"I found the Way In"

Our friend here has just found some of the best men's clothes he's ever seen. No wonder he's smiling.

"I found a cotton seersucker shirt with deep cutaway collar for 75/-. With white and 8 colours to choose from, I couldn't go wrong."

"I found a double breasted French raincoat, cut slightly longer with a half belt. £15."

"I found a double breasted, flared high-buttoning suit with deep side vents and cigarette shape trousers for £32. They call the colour faint navy."

"I found a short, slim-cut dressing gown in a wild Senegal print for £7.15.0. If that doesn't surprise the milkman, nothing will."

"I found a cotton batiste shirt with a deep polo collar for 69/6. And a slightly wider silk tie with square ends for 30/-."

Way In, Hans Crescent, S.W.1. Tuesday-Friday open 9.30 a.m. till 7 p.m. Saturday open 9.30 a.m. till 5 p.m. Closed Monday.

3

" They had no idea about security. "

'TOP MOD' WILLIE DEASY

At number one Marlborough Court, just off Carnaby Street, was Foale and Tuffin, which drew in clientele between the ages of 16 and 35. Sally Tuffin and Marion Foale, both of whom had left the Royal College of Art in 1961, designed the clothes. Although quite expensive, the quality was much higher than that of Carnaby Street boutiques. *Ready Steady Go!* presenter Cathy McGowan would shop there.

Trecamp was at 46 Carnaby Street and was the first girl's boutique that opened there, in autumn 1965. Owned by John Stephen, nothing was particularly expensive and it had dressing rooms papered with six-foot-tall pictures of men in bathing trunks. Prices started with leather belts at 10s, 6d, up to leather brush jackets at guineas.

Top Gear and Countdown were at 135a–137 King's Road. Both were owned by model Pat Booth and hat designer James Wedge. Top Gear had a great canopy over the door with a Mod target emblazoned across it, an image that their carrier bags also featured.

"We had a grand opening with Mick Jagger..."

THERESA KERR

The shop quickly gained a reputation for selling 'Mod' gear to the Chelsea dollies and the rich and famous, including Marianne Faithfull and The Beatles. It sold hats designed by James Wedge, way-out clothing designed by Royal College of Art students, and shoes, bags, suits and dresses. Foale and Tuffin was its main supplier. Countdown was next door, to the right of Top Gear, and featured a quite basic black-on-white stencilled shop sign and a fantastic polished-silver metal interior, and was the more expensive of the two. The white tunic-dress that Mick Jagger wore at the 1969 Hyde Park concert? It came from Countdown.

Also in the King's Road was Bazaar, opened by Welsh fashion designer and British fashion icon Mary Quant in 1955, with the help of her husband Alexander Plunkett-Greene and former solicitor Archie McNair. Bazaar was famous for pioneering the 'Chelsea look.' Quant had been unhappy with the clothes on offer so decided to design her own, and became known as the woman 'who started it all.' Quant was also happy to champion bright young designers, including among others Jean Muir, Jan Stevens, Gerald McCann and Harvey Gould. Prices were reasonable for the quality on offer.

Biba was at 87 Abingdon Road and owned by Barbara Hulanicki and her husband, Stephen Fitz-Simon. All designs were exclusive and considered inexpensive for the time. Customers included Cathy McGowan and singer Cilla Black. Biba had started as a mail order business in 1964 and believing that Quant and other boutiques' prices were too high for the young, Hulanicki was the first to promote the 'knock down, throw away and buy another' philosophy.

The boutique Hem and Fringe was opened by ex-*Ready Steady Go!* dance demonstrator Patrick Kerr and his wife, Theresa, at 35 Moreton Street, London S.W.1. The stock here would change every three weeks and was priced very cheaply, from about £2 to £8. Theresa Kerr: "We started Hem and Fringe in '65. We had a grand opening with Mick Jagger and lots of celebrities of the day. I remember Marianne Faithfull was pregnant at the time. We had all these people working for us who were art school people. A lot of them were at Ealing Art School or the Royal College of Art. These people were all involved in the design, so that if anybody wanted anything special we could make it up because the cutters and machinists were on site."

Denis Confrey was a Mod at the time, and Theresa's brother. He said, "The great thing about Hem and Fringe was that when you walked down the stairs, there was all this space. You weren't inundated. There were a couple of things here and a couple of things there. If they had something you really liked they could make it in a different colour if you wanted. The place had a feel about it. It was a bit like a club, because you walked down the stairs and you knew you were somewhere where the people you were with knew what they were doing."

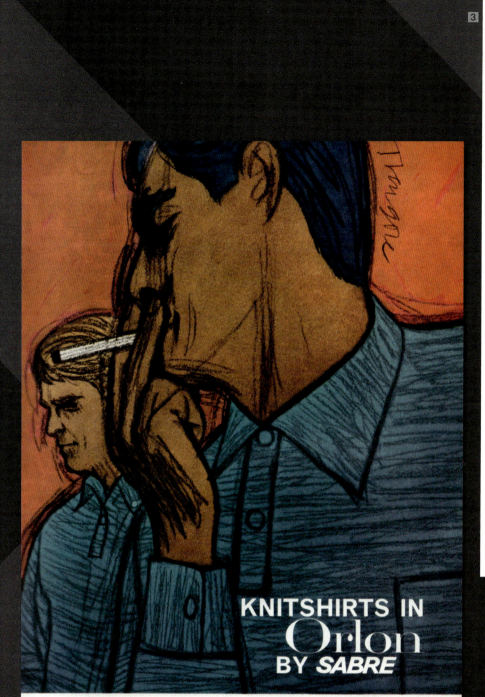

KNITSHIRTS IN Orlon BY *SABRE*

The Braemar Leisureman lives twice as fast. Takes life in his stride: distinctive, rugged, individual. For play time, he plays it cool. He takes his pleasure in Braemar.

BRAEMAR
BRAEMAR KNITWEAR LTD., HAWICK, SCOTLAND

AMBASSADOR: About 13 gns. One from a range of pure Scottish Cashmere leisurewear, priced from 5 gns. at your favourite shop.

1

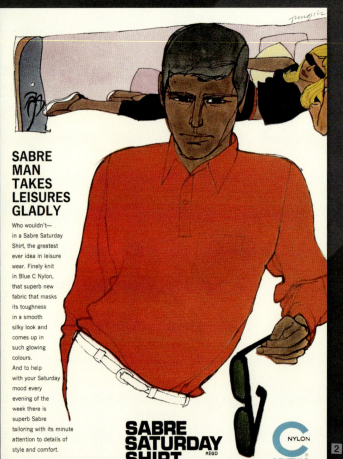

SABRE MAN TAKES LEISURES GLADLY

Who wouldn't—in a Sabre Saturday Shirt, the greatest ever idea in leisure wear. Finely knit in Blue C Nylon, that superb new fabric that masks its toughness in a smooth silky look and comes up in such glowing colours. And to help with your Saturday mood every evening of the week there is superb Sabre tailoring with its minute attention to details of style and comfort.

SABRE SATURDAY SHIRT REGD

C NYLON CHEMSTRAND

2

MEN WITH DRIVE

Accelerate into Smart Weston

Change up into the car coats that will be lapping the field for seasons to come

Left **SVEN**. Specification: Proofed whipcord, heavy knitted collar. Lining—half quilted, half tartan. Removable back half-belt. Black; Brown and Navy. 15 gns. Another continental entry **HOLGER**. Specification: Iridescent poplin, knitted collar. Padded belt, easy-action shoulder line. Spice Brown. 18 gns.

CONTINENTAL *Valmeline* at *The* **Smart Weston** *Store for Men*

COVENTRY STREET by Piccadilly Circus W1 □ & 84 BROMPTON ROAD □ KNIGHTSBRIDGE SW3 □ BRANCHES THROUGHOUT LONDON & AT MANCHESTER

3

1 Cardigans never looked so cool, December 1964.

2 Sabre leisure shirts, April 1965.

3 E-Type flashness, October 1962.

4 Drawing on the popularity of scooters and the young, May 1962.

BRI-LON
for the **look** of it

BRI-LON
for the **feel** of it

BRI-LON
for the **sense** of it

No fuss to this fibre. It's BRI·LON. Easy-clean, easy-dry, machine-washable and still handsome Stay-bright colours. Man's sweater shirt in Navajo blue by Sabre, about 59/6; girl's jumper in pale blue by Playfair, about 63/-.

**SHOES FOR
YOUNG WOMEN
OF TOMORROW**

SANDIE 39/11 Red, string, honey or hazel softee
D fitting • Creflex wedge soles • Sizes 2-8.

Clarks

NEAREST SHOP 7 WRITE CLARKS, DEPT. HW 27, STREET, SOMERSET.—AND ASK FOR ILLUSTRATED LEAFLET.

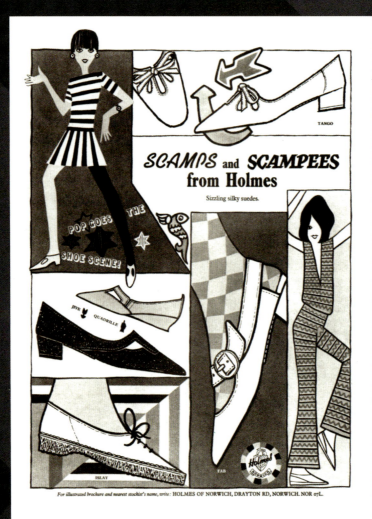

**SCAMPS and SCAMPEES
from Holmes**

Sizzling silky suedes.

For illustrated brochure and nearest stockist's name, write : HOLMES OF NORWICH, DRAYTON RD, NORWICH, NOR 07L.

**THE KINK
AND THE NON-KINK
'TERYLENE' SKIRT** A Kink, by the name
of Dave, had a yen
for this 'Terylene' skirt. Neat, he said. The model was mad about it as well. It was
the crush-proof part that sold her (besides, it washed without shrinking or losing
its charm). 'Terylene' is always such great news value.

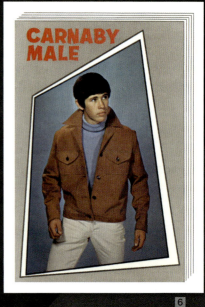

1 Targets and bowling, April 1966.

2 Shoes for Modybody girls, May 1966.

3 Mod parkas and desert boots, May 1966.

4 Kinky fun with Dave, May 1966.

5 Twiggy double take, May 1967.

6 Carnaby Male flyer, summer 1967.

7 Pages from Modern Man catalogue, 1967.

8 Pages from Modern Man catalogue, 1968.

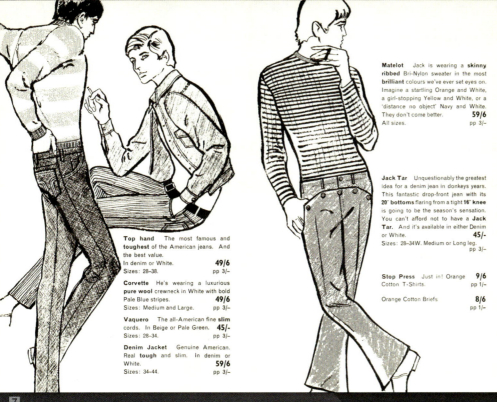

Matelot Jack is wearing a **skinny ribbed** Bri-Nylon sweater in the most **brilliant** colours we've ever set eyes on. Imagine a startling Orange and White, a girl-stopping Yellow and White, or a 'distance no object' Navy and White. They don't come better. **59/6**
All sizes. pp 3/–

Jack Tar Unquestionably the greatest idea for a denim jean in donkeys years. This fantastic drop-front jean with its **20″ bottoms** flaring from a tight **16″ knee** is going to be the season's sensation. You can't afford not to have a **Jack Tar.** And it's available in either Denim or White. **45/–**
Sizes: 28–34W. Medium or Long leg. pp 3/–

Stop Press Just in! Orange Cotton T-Shirts. **9/6** pp 1/–

Orange Cotton Briefs **8/6** pp 1/–

Top hand The most famous and **toughest** of the American jeans. And the best value.
In denim or White. **49/6**
Sizes: 28–38. pp 3/–

Corvette He's wearing a luxurious **pure wool** crewneck in White with bold Pale Blue stripes. **49/6**
Sizes: Medium and Large. pp 3/–

Vaquero The all-American fine **slim** cords. In Beige or Pale Green. **45/–**
Sizes: 28–34. pp 3/–

Denim Jacket Genuine American. Real **tough** and slim. In denim or White. **59/6**
Sizes: 34–44. pp 3/–

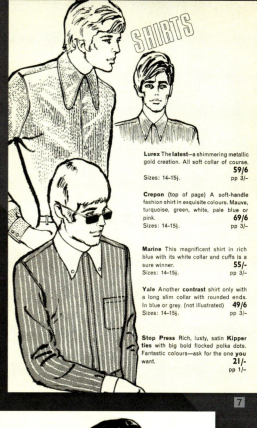

SHIRTS

Lurex The **latest**—a shimmering metallic gold creation. All soft collar of course. **59/6**
Sizes: 14–15½. pp 3/–

Crepon (top of page) A soft-handle fashion shirt in exquisite colours. Mauve, turquoise, green, white, pale blue or pink. **69/6**
Sizes: 14–15½. pp 3/–

Marine This magnificent shirt in rich blue with its white collar and cuffs is a sure winner. **55/–**
Sizes: 14–15½. pp 3/–

Yale Another **contrast** shirt only with a long slim collar with rounded ends. In blue or grey. (not illustrated) **49/6**
Sizes: 14–15½. pp 3/–

Stop Press Rich, lusty, satin **Kipper ties** with big bold flocked polka dots. Fantastic colours—ask for the one **you** want. **21/–**
pp 1/–

Far Left
Battle Blouse The **latest** jean jacket but now in a great **washable** cotton. Available separately or pair it up as a new **lightweight suit!** Jacket in Red, Sand or Navy—complete with matching belt. **6.19.6**
Sizes: 34–40 pp 3/–

Lightweight hipsters in Navy or Sand. **3.5.0**
Sizes: 28–34W. S.M.L. Leg pp 3/–

Polo Sweater He's wearing a pure all-wool fashioned one. In White, Sky, Tan, Brown, Green or Black. **55/–**
Sizes: M.L. pp 3/–

Roma A brilliant **Italian designed** sweater in Green (as shown), Orange, Lemon or Brown. **Fabulous for the Beach.** **45/–**
Sizes: M.L. pp 3/–

Vaquero Cords The **latest** from the USA. Tough, Slimcut. In either Beige, Green or Navy. **59/6**
Sizes: 28–34W. S.M.L. Leg pp 3/–

◀

Outrider A superb **lightweight** all-lined, all-nylon zip-up. Warm woven neck and cuffs. In Royal Tan or Navy.
Sizes: 34–40 **4.19.6**
pp 3/–

Pompey Mk. II A swinging bold naval flare—genuine 22 in. **plus** old-time adjusters at back. In a fabulous face-cloth. In Navy Only.

Same high '**V**' style as on page **14.**

Sizes: 28–34W S.M.L. Leg **79/6**
pp 3/–

RAVER'S MAP OF LONDON

BOUTIQUES SHOWN
Adam
Adam W.1.
Anello & Davide
Bernard Hones
Biba's Postal Boutique
Chelsea Cobblers
Countdown
Cue, Austin Reed
Donis
Domino Male
Foale & Tuffin
Granny Takes a Trip
Guy
Hem & Fringe
His Clothes
Irvine Sellars
John Michael
John Stephen
Lord John
Paul's Boutique
Poco
Quorum
Ravel
Simon Shop
Sportique
Susan Locke
The Shop
The Village Shop
Top Gear
Topper Shoes
Trecamp
Victoria & Albert
Vince
Wild West Won
You and I
Chelsea Antique Market

DISCOTHEQUES SHOWN
Big L Discotheque
Birdland
Blaise's Club
Carna B Hive
Cromwellian
Dolly's
Deep Hole Bistro
Elbow Room
Flamingo
'In' Place
Last Chance
Le Kilt
La Discotheque Club
One Hundred Club
Marquee
The Scotch
Tiffany's
Tiles
Whiskey A-Go-Go

EATERS
Crank's Health Restaurant
Chelsea Kitchen
Guys And Dolls

1 *Rave* magazine's guide to all that's happening
and swinging in the West End, April 1966.
2 Memories from original Portsmouth Mod, Ian Hebditch,
for his thesis 'A Personal Recollection Of The Mods', 1971.

EXAMPLES OF DRESS.
1965 - 1966.
WORN BY PEOPLE I KNEW
PERSONALLY.

1. QUARTERED SUEDE COAT, HERRINGBONE TROUSERS, MOTORORING SHOES FROM RAVEL'S.

2. MOHAIR JACKET WITH DEEP (3") POCKET FLAPS AND NARROW TROUSER TURNUPS.

3. BOTTLE GREEN SUIT, NARROW BRIMMED HAT.

4. OP ART SWEATER, JEANS, BASEBALL BOOTS. TYPICAL CASUAL WEAR.

5. GOLD. SILK MOHAIR SUIT.

It's not all GO

READY STEADY GO!
HOW POP ART LANDED
IN OUR LIVING ROOMS

**"...way ahead of its time.
...it was really
kind of an elite club..."**

THERESA KERR

1 Cathy McGowan on set with Arnold Schwartzman.
2 Arnold's design of the *Ready Steady Go!* logo.
3 The Beatles.
4 James Brown.
5 Cathy with Dusty Springfield.
All photos taken on set by Arnold during rehearsals.

"*Ready Steady Go!* was way ahead of its time. *Juke Box Jury*, *Six-Five Special* and *Thank Your Lucky Stars* had already been around for a while, but they were so old fashioned. To get on *Ready Steady Go!*, it was really kind of an elite club," Theresa Kerr remembers fondly. Theresa at the time, along with her partner Patrick, was the dance demonstrator on the programme.

Ready Steady Go! was the most bang-up-to-the-minute television programme of the sixties. From the opening sequence to the final credits everything about the programme screamed NOW! The title sequences changed constantly and usually featured a small film accompanied by a current chart hit. The person responsible for the credits was Arnold Schwartzman.

Arnold was born in Wapping, East London, and later he and his family moved to Margate. He studied for two years at the Thanet School of Arts and Crafts before progressing to the Canterbury College of Art where he obtained the National Diploma in Design. As soon as he graduated he was conscripted to the army for two years, serving in Germany and South Korea.

In July 1957, having been demobbed, Arnold found himself on a train going home. It was on this journey that he noticed two teenagers in strange attire and guitars playing a form of music alien to him. Rock'n'roll had passed him by while he'd been away.

"My first job was as a graphic designer for Southern TV Southampton in 1959. Later I was engaged by Associated-Rediffusion Television, London. There I worked on a number of shows including drama, news and public affairs, children's programmes and of course *Ready, Steady Go!*. I can't recall the year that I took over designing the opening title sequences, the design of the logo, record sleeves invitations, etc. There were several other of my colleagues in the graphics department working on the titles prior to me."

The logo Arnold produced for *Ready, Steady Go!* was outstanding and modern, with a slight similarity to the 1962 Dexter Gordon Blue Note album *GO*. "Although the Dexter Gordon cover pre-dates my logo, I had in fact never seen it. The similarity is the fact that they both spell out the word GO with an arrow. My idea was to take the word 'go' and to emulate the groove of a record and integrate it into the letter 'O'. Television in those days was black and white so the only time you saw them in colour were on the invitation cards, which were blue."

Every Friday, Arnold would go down to the small Studio 9 in the basement of Television House to photograph the show's rehearsals with his 35mm camera, which led to him capturing some great artists, including James Brown, The Beatles, Dusty Springfield, The Kinks and the Stones.

3

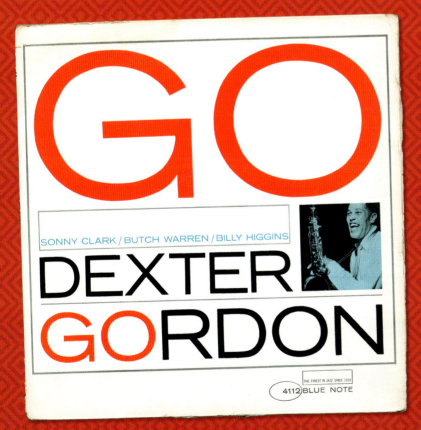

4

5

Around every six weeks, Arnold was brought in to recreate the opening titles for the show. The array of titles included a pop art-influenced version, which involved cut-out photos of people, a pinball machine and targets flashing on the screen to the tune of Manfred Mann's '5-4-3-2-1'; surfers, American footballers, a baseball game, lions, dancers and a rocket taking off to the sound of The Animals' 'I'm Crying'; a Rocker couple on a motorbike and a Mod couple on a Series 1 Lambretta riding off from traffic lights to 'Wipe Out' by The Surfaris; various photos of a girl in sunglasses with fleeting drawings flashing over her eyes accompanied by Manfred Mann's 'Hubble Bubble (Toil and Trouble)'; shots of a girl playing a medley of instruments alongside 'Land Of 1,000 Dances' by Wilson Pickett; and flashing shots of one girl in a stripy top sat on a zebra and another in a top with 'USA' emblazoned across it, both toting guns to Manfred Mann's 'I've Got My Mojo Working.'

Alfred: "Two storyboards of stills from my opening title sequences were a skateboarding sequence that was cut to The Who's track 'My Generation.' We shot the skateboarding sequences on the sloop at Wembley football stadium. I managed to recruit students from the Royal College of Art, who were one of the first groups in the UK to adopt the skateboarding craze. The other sequence was The Rolling Stones' 'Satisfaction.' Mick Jagger and Andrew Loog Oldham came to see me with their demo disc, and I told them the piece was too long for my purpose. They responded that they were producing a single, and left me with what I assume was a one-off demo; scratched into the shellac was the title 'Satisfaction.' I gave the record to my younger sister as she was a great Stones fan; to this day, she won't tell me what happened to it!"

Arnold had wholeheartedly embraced the new art forms. "Most of my influences came from the United States – designers such as Milton Glaser and Seymour Chwast. Peter Blake was my main one in the UK."

The other striking feature on *Ready Steady Go!* was the stage backdrops, in front of which the bands performed. Nicholas Ferguson, the set designer, was in his early twenties when he was asked to join the programme.

" ...my influences came from the United States... "

ARNOLD SCHWARTZMAN

1 Dusty Springfield and Long John Baldry.
2 Ray Davies of The Kinks. Photo by Arnold Schwartzman.
3 Opening title sequence to *Ready Steady Go!* featuring 'My Generation' music.

 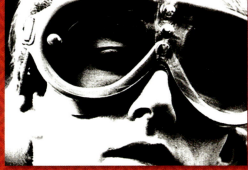 

  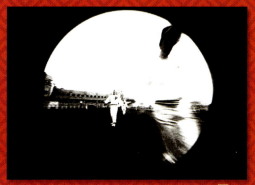

1 Opening title sequence to *Ready Steady Go!* featuring 'Satisfaction' music. 2 *RSG*, Nicholas Ferguson, 1965.

"...he loved the idea of me being an artist starving in the garret...

NICHOLAS FERGUSON

Ferguson was brought up in Scotland and through his mother he got to see lots of French, Russian and German films at an art cinema called the Cosmo in Glasgow. When the family came to London, his mother took him to the Everyman cinema in Hampstead. Nicholas believes that it was his father's left-wing views that influenced his mother's viewing habits, as she avoided American cinema at all costs. The films Ferguson saw during that period had a profound effect on him in later life and a huge influence on his work. "My mother, who was self-educated, was brought up in a convent so she wasn't that educated, but she was a bright woman. My father was a Communist, so what is interesting there is the links. Because in the 1930s, a lot of the Communists were in France – Picasso and Matisse and all those people were Communists, too. What happened was that in England, there were left-wing groups educating the working classes. They had a magazine called the *Worker's Weekly* in the 1920s and 1930s. What was great about these [magazines] was that you could buy books cheaply, so my father would order these books, but my mother would read them. She read all of Bernard Shaw's works and all the things she'd never learned at school."

Nicholas studied at the Chelsea College of Art where he was tutored by Elisabeth Frink and Robert Clatworthy. He then went on to University College London's Slade School of Art, which boasted Sir William Coldstream, the sculptor Henry Moore and Lucien Freud as teaching staff, all of whom would help model the young Ferguson. In his postgraduate year, Ferguson studied film as well as stage design.

"I failed my 11-plus so I wouldn't have gone to a grammar school but a secondary modern," Nicholas laughs. "My step-mother said 'He can't do that!,' so the little money my father had went towards my education. I went to a private school in Hampstead where I did art, acted and painted scenery. I mean, my spelling is poor. I can't add up very well but I do love reading. I got to do drawing, painting and made films at school. My father encouraged it, he loved the idea of me being an artist starving in the garret."

1 Martha Reeves and The Vandellas on set.
2 Arnold captures The Beatles rehearsing.

While at art school, Ferguson attended parties and got to know David Hockney who was studying at the Royal College. At the time, Ferguson was impressed by American artists such as Robert Rauschenberg, but he was also looking further afield. In these early years he travelled all over, taking in the art and culture of France, Russia and Japan. But it was in the USA that he came across another artist with whom he didn't see eye to eye.

"In 1960, I got to know an American concert pianist, James Mathis, and he asked me to go to New York with him. I stayed with his friend Ivan Davies and his wife, because James was always on concert tours. They seemed to know everyone in New York, because – as it is in London – if you are involved in music you would get to meet people. I had some wonderful introductions. New York seemed quite small then. I went to a party and was introduced to Andy Warhol. I don't think I liked him and he didn't like me. We were talking but not getting on at all well. I thought he was pretentious because they'd got one of his coffee table books, which was of drawings of feet and all those bloody Campbell soup tins. What a load of nonsense, I thought. Later I changed my view on it, and I realised it was actually very interesting. At the time, though, I was so young and opinionated on what I liked and didn't like it was just very extreme and stupid at times. Still, when you are 20, you say things that you really mean, but it's not a very educated view. Although, I had been to the 'This Is Tomorrow' exhibition at Whitechapel, and I thought it was fascinating and that was sort of the beginning of pop art, so it must have influenced me unconsciously. I related that more to what had gone on in Europe from the twenties and the thirties – Picasso, Matisse and French artists like Sonia Delaunay. I think the roots of what we were doing came more from her and her husband. Everybody went to Paris in the thirties from England and all over the world. Paris was the centre of art and so all these influences were there. So the pop art thing and my extreme use of colour all stems from that period. Prior to 1965, I wouldn't have used as bright a red in my paintings. When I left Slade I went into design, and I didn't do as much painting, and if I did it was rather sombre abstracts, like Rothko. What happened was that what I had learned from the pop scene made me bolder. Another influence was the German artist called Kurt Schwitters, who made collages. I'd seen them at the Marlborough Gallery around 1960, which was Francis Bacon's gallery, so I was very plugged into what was going on."

"...went to a party and was introduced to Andy Warhol.

NICHOLAS FERGUSON

Nicholas was 24 years old when he joined the television network Rediffusion in 1962. His father wasn't happy though; he thought it was dreadful, his son working for a commercial company and not the BBC.

"I think I was almost the oldest of the team except for Elkan Allan, who was the executive producer, and the presenter Keith Fordyce. I was a year older than [*Ready Steady Go!* producer] Vicki Wickham I knew nothing of real pop music at all; I mean, we'd had dances at school, at which was played some pop music, but I only really knew classical music. My boss, Michael Yates, told me that he thought I'd enjoy doing [*Ready Steady Go!*]. So I went and looked at the set, and the sets were dreadful. The guy before had spent all the budget money for the entire series. I was left with a budget of something like £13.50 per week to do the scenery. I suddenly thought about what they call 'below line costs', so I had to ask the boss if we could have photographs done for nothing. He said 'yes, any size'. So I went to the photographic department and asked how big they could make them and they basically said any size you want them. They were really skilled people, so I could do a piece of artwork about 10in x 8in and then take it up to the photographers' bench camera and they could make very, very good copies, so when the 10in x 8in was blown up big it looked fantastic, because they'd got the tones right. I could also have free paint, so everything I ever painted in the studio was either black, off-white or red. Even though the show was filmed in black and white, the atmosphere had to be right."

For somebody who had never shown an interest in pop music, Ferguson was about to witness the biggest pop phenomenon of the period.

"I was on the fourth floor [of Television House] and I thought I'd go down and see what these people [The Beatles] looked like. So I went down to the studio and looked over the balcony to where they were rehearsing, and I thought, God they are really good. They were miming of course – everybody did – but they came across fantastic. Anyway, as I walked off I heard all this noise, so I went out on the same level as the balcony to a window that overlooked the front entrance of the Kingsway building. It was packed with teenagers, thousands of them – mostly girls – and the traffic didn't move at all. It was just people. They had to put wire over the front of the building because they were going to push the glass front doors in."

" ...knew nothing of real pop music at all... "

NICHOLAS FERGUSON

READY STEADY GO

MOD ART 58

Ready Steady Go! was all about the visuals, and the scenery was paramount to its success. The show was very much known for being bang-up-to-date, so the artwork had to be created at the very last minute.

"The night before the show, I didn't really know what I was going to do but I'd have some pictures saved from things like American magazines. I'd use maybe a picture of Marlene Dietrich, a picture of Rembrandt's son Titus, various *Ready Steady Go!* designs, bits of medals, a picture of a Mod, Dusty Springfield and ballet people. Then I'd go over to WHSmith across the road from the studio to buy magazines to cut up; get some lettering, then take it upstairs. Each collage took about three hours, although it could be all afternoon or all evening if I couldn't get it right. As I'd been to art school I knew what I was doing in the sense of abstract shapes. I could make it work, but you had to know how to work in black and white.

The key thing was, being a painter, you had to see things tonally. You have to know how the greys work otherwise it will look dull. So I knew how to make things jump out, some recede a bit and other bits look mysterious."

Through various art and music circles, Ferguson became friendly with Brian Epstein and undertook some work for his artists, including Cilla Black and, of course, The Beatles, for whom he created the backdrops to their appearances on *Thank Your Lucky Stars* and the US show *Hullabaloo*.

1 *Callas And Jagger*, Nicholas Ferguson, 1965.

Eventually, Ferguson was to move away from his career in art and became involved in film making and direction. He would go on to direct two classic TV music shows: *So It Goes* with presenter Tony Wilson, which would champion the burgeoning punk rock movement, and *Marc!* with Marc Bolan, just before his death in September 1977. He would make music videos for various artists including Wings, Elton John, Paul McCartney and David Bowie. He then moved on to directing mainstream television, including a stint at *Coronation Street*. There are few who can boast such an extensive and varied CV. Thankfully, Nicholas Ferguson can.

Arnold Schwartzman didn't fair too badly, either. He went on to become the concept planning executive for Erwin, Wasey & Co. advertising, where he won awards for his television commercials for Coca-Cola and Philips electrical, and in 1968, he joined the board of the Conran Design Group as graphics director. He also became a TV commercial director, as well as directing with Mick Jagger a radio commercial to promote 'Brown Sugar.' And while he conceived and art-directed the poster for the Stones' *Sticky Fingers* album [the album cover was conceived by Andy Warhol and designed by Craig Braun], he was also an illustrator and art consultant for the *Sunday Times* and Warner Bros. Records.

"Later, after my days in broadcasting, I became an advertising art director where one of my major accounts was Coca-Cola. For two of my film commercials for Coke I hired The Who to compose and perform the soundtrack," he recalls.

In 1978, the legendary designer and filmmaker Saul Bass invited Schwartzman to join him as his design director in Hollywood. In 1981, Schwartzman went on to make *Genocide*, a film about the Holocaust, narrated by Orson Welles and Elizabeth Taylor. It went on to win the Academy Award for Best Documentary Feature that year. The following year, he was appointed Director of Design for the 1984 Los Angeles Olympic Games.

In 2002, Schwartzman was awarded an OBE for services to the British film industry in the USA. He is also a governor of the British Academy of Film and Television Arts Los Angeles (BAFTA/LA), and serves on the Board of Hollywood Heritage, Inc.

"My fondest memory from those early days was of a rather boisterous *RSG!* team Xmas party at the Cheshire Cheese in Fleet Street! I still keep in touch with *RSG!*'s director Michael Lindsay-Hogg, who lives near me in Los Angeles, plus producer Vicki Wickham and Nicholas Ferguson."

Schwartzman has gone full circle and finds himself at many of the leading art institutions throughout the world, the difference being that he is the one lecturing on graphic design and film.

1 Nicholas Ferguson at home, 2013.

2 LP featuring Patrick & Theresa Kerr dancing on the cover.

3 *Dusty And Marlene*, Nicholas Ferguson, 1965.

"...hired The Who to compose and perform the soundtrack..."

ARNOLD SCHWARTZMAN

EDDY GRIMSTEAD: THE UNCONSCIOUS PROPHET OF THE NEW POP ART AND ANTI-ART MOVEMENT

On a cold and rainy day in early May 1964, photographer Cyril Maitland and reporter Nick Davies found themselves outside Peckham Employment Exchange chatting to a group of nine Mods on six scooters, many of the machines adorned with chrome extras, including petrol pump attendant John Roger's display of 43. While the scooters are the main feature of the two-page article that would adorn the *Daily Mirror*'s centre pages, clothes are also given a mention: "This is what the Mods will be wearing this summer; white shirts with long, pointed collars; slim single-colour ties; very lightweight jackets in tartan or bright-coloured stripes in an Italian style; trousers, slim, without turn-ups, in lilac, tangerine or orange."

❝This is what the Mods will be wearing...❞

NICK DAVIS: *DAILY MIRROR*

" Not a piece of chrome will be in sight... **"**

NICK DAVIS: *DAILY MIRROR*

The article states that in the world of Mods, you are finished at the ripe old age of 20. It also says that stripped-down scooters – a "back to the basic look" – will be the new style. "Not a piece of chrome will be in sight," the article ends. Though looking at the images of the chrome-laden chariots, its hard to think of them as anything but an art form unto their own.

While Eddy Grimstead rightfully wins plaudits for being the best-known scooter customiser, the initial idea came from further afield.

Andre Baldet was a French scooter dealer based in Northampton and in August 1957, he offered the first dedicated dealer special, although it happened by accident. It came about as he took collection of four new Minerva grey Vespa 150 Continentals from the Bristol-based Douglas factory. Two were damaged in transport and this gave Baldet the problem of how to sell them while avoiding additional cost. At the time, he was selling and repairing pushbikes at his Moto Vespa Shop in Newland. He suggested to his painter that they could cover up the damage with the same black paint they used on the bicycles. Baldet then painted the other damaged scooter, with blue as a secondary colour. Both scooters sold almost immediately, and he was so impressed, he painted the other two undamaged scooters with red and green as secondary colours, adding to each a star-shaped badge on the leg shield declaring 'By Baldet of Northampton.' He then named the new, special range Arc-En-Ciel (French for 'rainbow').

Andre also realised the potential of chrome extras and accessories, and he can claim to be the first to sell scooters with special paint and accessories included. He would carry this idea forward when in March 1960, he opened up a Moto Baldet dealership in Hendon, North London and his special two-tone Vespas could be seen zooming around all over the city.

In March 1961, Scoot-A-Long, based on the Old Kent Road, London, offered special edition Lambrettas with chrome and copper side panels and varying paint schemes on the Series 2 TV and LI models. Scoot-A-Long's George Wells described himself as "London's original chromium plating and individual two-toning artist."

ter.. Status symbols of the riding Mods

...tooned ...horns,

...Britain's ...d above

...Like the ...l filling ... lamps,

But the chrome is on the way out

four Alpine horns, six chrome mascots, four mirrors and two badges.

John's 43 "extras" have cost him £75. There are others who have as many as 50, 60 and even 70 glittering status symbols on their scooters.

They are the trend-setting Mods. The Mod elite of the "scooter schools."

The Mods first hit the headlines with their sense of dress.

The girls in long skirts, boys' shirts and no make-up. The boys in collarless suits, high-necked shirts and Texan boots.

They are opposite to the Rockers, the leather-clad young ones with their tonup motor-bikes.

The fashion houses and stores caught on, and the clothes the trend-setter...

Pictures by CYRIL MAITLAND
Story by NICK DAVIES

Mods wore TWO YEARS AGO are now in the shops.

Now the Mod girls design their own skirts, and dresses and coats.

Or they go with the boys to the Mecca of Mods . . . Carnaby Street, W.1, where Mr. John Stephen (he's 27) creates clothes for the wavy-haired people who like to keep one jump ahead of everyone else

Tartan

This is the gear the Mods will be wearing this summer:

White shirts with long-pointed collars; slim single colour ties; very light-weight jackets in tartan or bright-coloured stripes in an Italian style; trousers, slim, without turn-ups, in lilac, tangerene or orange.

The days when Purple Heart drug tablets were the trend have gone. It's IN to drink vodka.

It's a world where the youngsters live only for the future.

Where you are considered to be finished . . . old fashioned . . . at the ripe age of 20.

For the Mod believes in the creed of the conveyor belt. A perpetual motion in which to stop is to cease.

Already these scooter status symbols are out of date.

Tomorrow, they say, the scooters will be stripped bare.

Not a piece of chrome will be in sight.

S OF ...BBY

...others and children. ...ow the time has come ... focus on middle-aged ...n.

...y can benefit in terms ... longer life. Too many ...ave forgotten the value ... keeping fit and stay-... fit.

...hard-hitting report to ...rliament from twelve ...ecialists — headed by ...rd Cohen of Birken-...ead, one of Britain's ...p physicians — spot-...ghts what is wrong ...th the present Govern-...ent approach to health ...ucation.

Spending

...ays that in the present ...proach to the nation's ...alth education prob-...m there is:

...T ENOUGH emphasis ... finding out why ...eople are unhealthy ...d in trying to persuade ...em to get fit.

...O MUCH EMPHASIS is ...t on getting them well ...ain after sickness.

...report says that the ...vernment now spends ...200,000 a year on health ...ucation.

...at is needed, Parlia-...ent is told, is an extra ...00,000 spent every ...ar for five years—in ...der to show what bene-...s can be obtained.

THE BARE LOOK
Micky White's scooter has no status symbols. It's tomorrow's "bare" look for Mod machines.

Forty-three gleaming bits and pieces on John Rogers's scooter.   But they're going out of fashion

Throughout the fifties, various scooter clubs sprang up all over the country, with owners customising their own scooters, but it would be the Mods in the early sixties that made the personalising of the vehicles commonplace. And so we return to the dealer who became synonymous with the scooter: Eddy Grimstead.

1 Eddy Grimstead outside Newbury Park shop.
2 Vespa GS and Lambretta LI, Burdett Road.
3 Lambretta TV200.
4 Inside the Eddy Grimstead shop on Barking Road, East Ham, 1962/63.
5 Eddy Grimstead, Barking Road, Lambretta GTs.

Grimstead was born on September 23, 1933 and came from a working-class, East End family. Eddy's grandfather had launched his own business selling cycles in 1908 at Beckton Road, Canning Town. Eddy's father then took on the business and learned how to make more money by hiring out pushbikes at 3d per half hour. Eddy himself entered the business in 1951 and he soon took over running a small cycle and moped shop in Brentwood Road, Romford.

However, National Service, between the years of 1953 and 1955, soon cut short any dreams of building up an empire. But as soon as Grimstead was demobbed, he set about investing the £100 he had managed to save by renting a one-room derelict shop in Burdette Road, E.14, and started his own business selling cycles and mopeds. Two years later, he took his first scooter, a Vespa, and it sold immediately. He leapt on the chance to change his stock and began selling motorcycles and scooters.

Eddy worked hard – he was his own salesman and mechanic. By 1959, he was doing so well that he opened up another branch in Radcliff Road, East Ham.

In late 1961, Grimstead started his practice of painting scooters with different colours and selling them with added extras, mainly on Lambretta Series 2 and Vespa GS150 models, but also on any model that he needed to sell. The following year saw him open another branch, this time in Barking Road, East Ham. It was the biggest of the Grimstead showrooms and it was here that he acquired his first agency for Honda. They would specialise in scooters, motorcycles and three-wheeled cars, and also started a postal service for spares that resulted in orders from as far away as Malaya. Eddy wanted each branch to function as its own entity, and so he installed mechanics, workshops and spare parts to ensure an efficient service for the customer.

3

4

It was during that year that Grimstead first started using the advertisement "specialist customised used scooters," and this is where the inaugural reference to the 'Hurricane' and 'Imperial' specials can be found. Initially, these special names referred to the paint scheme only and not to any standard upgrade in engine capacity. The paint schemes were also available on the humble Vespa 150 Sportique and Lambretta LI models.

5

"...reminiscent of the finish of the classic fairground rides..."

ROGER: EDDY GRIMSTEAD'S COUSIN

From May 1962, Grimstead found the newly introduced Vespa GS160 much easier to work on, as its detailing lent itself to the easy application of two-toning and chroming, particularly as both side panels could easily be removed. While he had previously tried to increase the engine capacity of the GS150, without a great deal of success, a new oversize piston kit was also available for the GS160 to take the engine to nearer 180cc, and this proved to be a big selling point. Eddy's cousin, Roger, who worked at the Barking Road branch, remembers it well: "My spraying method and masking was quite involved and time-consuming. Firstly, the area to be painted would be 'flatted down' inside the masked-off spray area in order to provide a 'key' for the new paint. Then a layer of silver would be sprayed, to give a metallic look to the finished product. Then, we'd apply a coloured lacquer on top of this silver base coat. The lacquer was the clever part, as it gave a very unusual look, somewhat reminiscent of the finish of the classic fairground rides – it was unique in the world of road vehicles." Available colours included British Racing Green, Magenta, Flam Orange, Flam Yellow, Flam Blue and, his own favourite, Vauxhall Cavern Green.

Contrary to the popular myth, it was March 1963 before Eddy started much more widely advertising his own special edition scooters as Vespa Hurricane and Lambretta Imperial. Adverts from 1964 show Vespa GS160 Hurricanes and SX200 Imperials. Many believed his first special edition scooters (SS180 Hurricane Vespa (SS200 at additional cost) and SX200 Imperial Lambretta) to have been produced from 1965, but this is mainly due to the large amount of additional advertising for these models that flooded the market at this time.

The famous '100mph speedometer' was introduced on the 1965 SS model, and was actually a 100kmh speedometer that had not been recalibrated and therefore gave speed readings much higher than the actual road speed. In the spring of 1964, Issue 35 of *Ark* (the magazine of the Royal College of Art) included an article entitled 'Fine Artz View Of Teenage Cults' that proclaimed, "The cult of today is the culture of tomorrow." The issue also included a feature on Eddy, declaring that: "Mr Grimstead is an unconscious prophet of the new pop and anti-art movement among the young."

1 Grimstead SS Hurricane, Beehive Lane.

Motor Cycling

THURSDAY, MAY 25, 1961

9ᵈ

MOTOR CYCLING

with **SCOOTER WEEKLY**

★ *In this issue...*

WHITSUN SPORT REPORTS

UNSURPASSABLE

By Appointment
To H.R.H. The Duke of Edinburgh
Manufacturers of Vespa Scooters
Douglas (Sales & Service) Ltd.
Bristol.

The man that **gets ahead** gets there on a **Vespa** Gran sport

Make your **vespa** more attractive

handlebar mirror

fly screen

rear luggage rack

horn cover

rear crashbar and footrest

luggage rack

front crashbar

front bumper

with **GENUINE VESPA ACCESSORIES**

These words of praise didn't go unnoticed and on August 30, 1964, the *Sunday Times* ran an article by Nicholas Tomalin, entitled 'Cult,' on Grimstead's customising revolution, in which are mentioned the teenagers drawn to his shop in order to purchase flashing wheel spokes, crash bars and the desire to "cover their seats, spare tyres and panniers in leopard, zebra or the latest ocelot-type plastic skin, or maybe go for the latest whip aerial from Japan complete with sculptured plastic naked lady on top."

It also stated there were true fans who could recognise any one of the dozen different types of note made by one of Grimstead's exclusive exhausts from a single revving of the engine. As if to entice the reader to the latest teenage craze, the article went on, "You then buy an anorak from a local seaman's store. A beret, which you shove forward into an artificial frown over your forehead. And you drive off, with your elastic-sided feet pointed outwards at an angle of 45 degrees. Very important, that 45 degrees." The article sums up Eddy's work with the description: "A Grimstead scooter isn't just a means of transport. It's a fantasy object, glowing with rainbow colours, festooned with cult symbols."

PERSONALISE
with genuine
accessories

RIETI
ROMA

by Lambretta

Acton Mod Dave Dry remembers the SX Imperial with fondness and shares his story in his own inimitable way: "This story starts in late 1966... A cold and windy street in East London and two young 'faces' staring intently into the window of a shop which, although closed at this time, displayed a truly exotic array of the most mind-boggling paintwork the likes of which could only previously be seen by visiting a fairground. This shop was Eddy Grimstead's scooter shop and it had fame indeed to drag two West London boys from Shepherd's Bush to this outpost close to the edge of known civilisation – there was life beyond the West End!

"Despite the shop not being open, a deal was done on the spot. At least it was in the mind of one of the pair. On this matter there was only one doubt – what does he do about the GT...? Stood parked in the gutter was the most glorious road burner of the sixties: the Lambretta TV200, or GT, as it was universally called, and this one was more than a bit special. This one made even the grey street people take a second look! Wow!... Black and maroon paint with plain chrome side panels and front mudguard.

Not to mention it was the ultimate 'traffic light Grand Prix' drag bike. Open the throttle wide – Let the clutch in nice'n'slow. 40 in first... no sweat! This was the scooter that beat Lotus Cortina's away from road junctions. The last word in street cool! Sorry, baby you've gotta go...

TOP OF THE IT PARADE!

See me at the National Lambretta Rally, Beaulieu, Hampshire, July 18/19.

on your new

Lambretta *150* SPECIAL 'PACEMAKER'

You're certainly 'IT'—you're the star of a streamlined, dream-lined hit—when you ride the new LAMBRETTA 'PACEMAKER'. Hop on the top of the scooter pops—pull out the stops and W-H-O-O-M! You're really swingin'—on a *real* scooter with real performance.
For you—the light-hearted, easy-to-handle 'PACEMAKER' with thrilling extra power—right on the beat, right up your street—right on any road to anywhere. Yet the tax and insurance are exactly the same as for an ordinary 150cc. machine. Gear but NOT dear—it's HERE!... the NEW 150 'PACEMAKER'—go see it at your dealers now!

To: Lambretta Concessionaires Ltd
Trojan Works · Purley Way · Croydon · Surrey
*Please send me full details of Lambretta,
the world's finest scooter*

Name ....

Address ....

....

LP 21

Smee's

THE WORLD'S FINEST SCOOTER

July, 1964

"...Grimstead's product could not be ignored."

DAVE DRY: ACTON MOD

1 Scooters at Clacton, March 1964.
2 Phil Luderman's customised TV175 in Battersea Park, 1962.

"The deal was done – this time in reality – and a beautiful, white SX200 with green pearl lacquered panel work was all mine!... What a babe to die for?

"So, you've finally 'cottoned on'? This is my story and, more importantly, my SX!

"Wherever you lived in and around London, the Grimstead's product could not be ignored. Even the teenager living in West London could be seduced by the lure of Eddy Grimstead's finest customs being sold at the same price as the boring, non-customised offerings as seen at the local scooter dealer. The end result, in this case, was the purchase of SX200 UOY42F in white and green – beautiful! On picking up this gleaming Lambretta at a very busy Burdette Road shop on a Saturday morning, the salesman mentioned that there was a petrol garage down the road and that there was only a small amount of fuel in the tank. How right he was? The tank was topped up at this garage, but for the next couple of miles or so of the journey home, quite a number of new scooters were witnessed being pushed back towards the garage by proud new owners that had ignored the salesman's sage advice.

"Selective and heavy polishing later rubbed away the yellow pinstripes between the white and the green paint of the Lambretta and someone, slightly later, relieved the scooter of the green and white side panels in the car park at Isleworth Poly. These were replaced with white fibreglass offerings from Pride and Clarke's in Stockwell and the SX was finally sold for the grand sum of £65."

Grimstead was the Scooter King, but there were also many 'bit players' in the world of scooters, such as Speedways of Acton and Woodford Scooters, with their 'Z Type' SS 180s also getting in on the act. The most prominent challenger, however, was Arthur Francis of Watford and his legendary S Type Lambrettas. Francis' product was much fancied at the time as it covered a sporting market that had an enormous attraction to many of the younger scooterists of the day.

Lambretta Concessionaires and Vespa Douglas also dabbled in the 'custom scene.' The UK was the biggest foreign market for both Innocenti (Lambretta) and Piaggio (Vespa) and, to this end, the importers could and did demand that the manufacturers in Italy produced models for perceived demands in the UK market. The classic example of this 'arm twisting' must be the Lambretta TV 200, known almost universally as the GT. This was an export-only machine and a machine that Innocenti arguably did not want to manufacture; the vast majority of the production-run of this model were exported to the UK (a smattering did end up in the USA). The model, in fact, could not be sold in Italy, as it lacked the homologation stamps on the frame required by the Italian authorities at that time. Lambretta concessionaires would import white GTs and add colour flashes in alternating paint to customise the vehicles before delivering them to the dealers. Eddy Grimstead would always claim it was due to his influence that they did this... and he was probably right.

Then, just as the *Daily Mirror* article had predicted back in May 1964, scooter enthusiasts started removing all their scooters' accessories.

In an article that appeared in a scooter magazine later that year, entitled 'Mod Strippers Get A Rocket From The Law,' the reporter Belinda Chapman wrote:

"Motor-scooter Mods are having a busy time. After the fad of dressing up the scooters with badges and lamps, came the stripping down process. Any Mod worth his high-heeled boots took his scooter to pieces. Off came the windscreen, mudguards, engine cover, badges and lamps. And in stepped the law...

"For a motor scooter is considered unfit for the road if it has no mudguard, engine cover, hooter or lamp.

"The Mods are unhappy. But 30-year-old Eddy Grimstead is quietly rejoicing."

> **"...Eddy Grimstead is quietly rejoicing."**
>
> **BELINDA CHAPMAN**

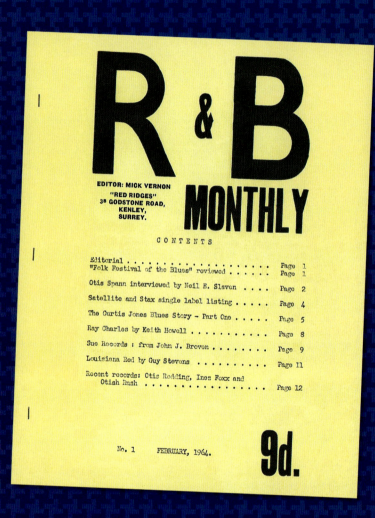

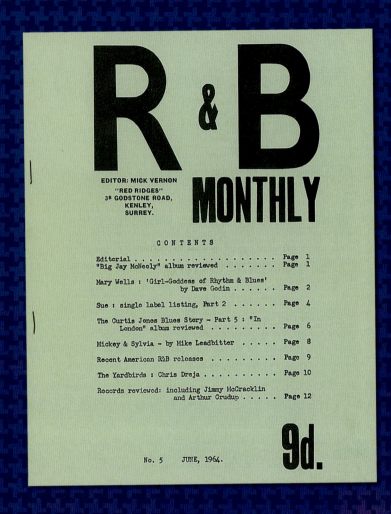

TOPPING UP: 1960s MUSIC FANZINES AND MAGAZINES

" ...not happy about his antics and poses... "

NEIL SLAVEN

One thing Mods loved was 'topping up,' or gaining knowledge about important issues, such as music. James Asman may have revealed the R&B Top 20 in *Record Mirror* but there was no insight into or background provided for the artists involved. Luckily, there were a few music fans who were generous enough to spread the word, ushering in the era of homemade music fanzines.

R&B MONTHLY

One of the best fanzines of its day was *R&B Monthly*. Hailing from Kenley in Surrey, *R&B Monthly* started life in February 1964 and lasted 24 issues, until February 1966. It had slightly erratic release dates: monthly, bi-monthly, no one really seemed to mind. Editor Mick Vernon, alongside assistant editor Neil Slaven, provided a fantastic commentary on the growing music scene, which was at its best in their music reviews and blues artist feature articles. Some of the great live reviews included Sugar Pie DeSanto live at the Marquee, John Lee Hooker live

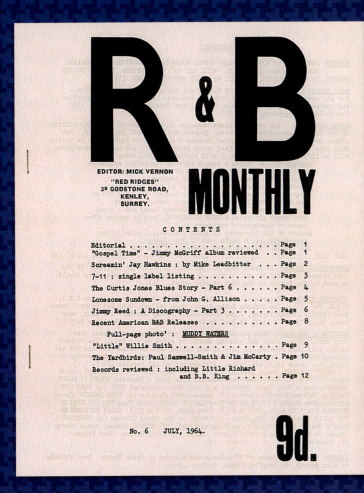

R & B MONTHLY

EDITOR: MICK VERNON
"RED RIDGES"
3B GODSTONE ROAD,
KENLEY,
SURREY.

C O N T E N T S

Editorial . . . . Page 1
"Gospel Time" - Jimmy McGriff album reviewed . . Page 1
Screamin' Jay Hawkins : by Mike Leadbitter . . . Page 2
7-11 : single label listing . . . . Page 3
The Curtis Jones Blues Story - Part 6 . . . . . . Page 4
Lonesome Sundown - from John G. Allison . . . . . Page 5
Jimmy Reed : A Discography - Part 3 . . . . Page 6
Recent American R&B Releases . . . . Page 8
Full-page photo' : MUDDY WATERS
"Little" Willie Smith . . . . Page 9
The Yardbirds: Paul Samwell-Smith & Jim McCarty . Page 10
Records reviewed : including Little Richard and B.B. King . . . . . . Page 12

No. 6 JULY, 1964. 9d.

R & B MONTHLY

EDITOR: MICK VERNON
"RED RIDGES"
3B GODSTONE ROAD,
KENLEY,
SURREY.

C O N T E N T S

Editorial . . . . Page 1
"The Blues of Otis Spann" - album reviewed . . . Page 1
Howlin' Wolf : by Neil E. Slaven . . . . Page 2
Dial : single label listing . . . . Page 3
Tommy Tucker - Bio. and Disco. . . . . Page 4
Carl Perkins talks about Sun/Phillips Records . . Page 6
Full-page photo' : YOUNG JESSIE
John Lee Hooker at the Flamingo Club . . . . . . Page 7
Inez and Charlie Foxx at the Flamingo Club . . . Page 8
Recent American R&B Releases . . . . Page 9
Records reviewed : including Don & Dewey, Tim Whitsett, Homesick James and Frank Frost . . . Page 10

No. 7 AUGUST, 1964. 9d.

at the Flamingo, the 1964 American Folk Blues Festival at Croydon's Fairfield Hall and Screamin' Jay Hawkins at the Flamingo. My personal favourite, though, is a review of Little Walter live at the Marquee in September 1964, in which Neil Slaven mentions the support band, The Hoochie Coochie Men, and states that he is impressed by Rod Stewart, ending the piece "...although, I am still not happy about his antics and poses, which he strikes whilst singing. But we'll be hearing more from him soon, of that I'm sure."

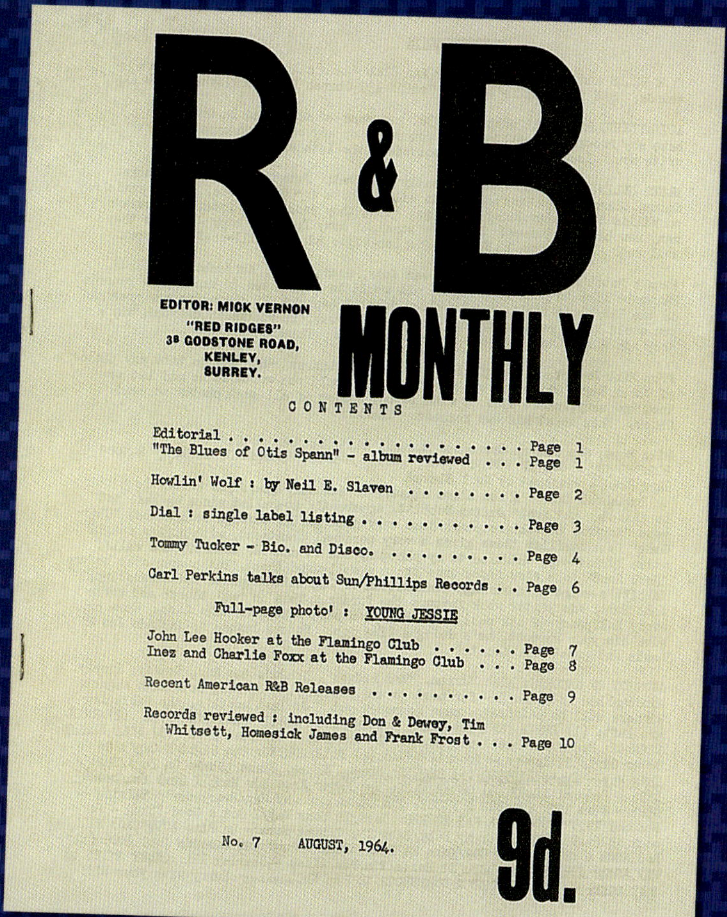

By Issue 9, which came out in October 1964, the cover featured a photo and the overall effect was much more professional. At the time, Mick Vernon was working at Decca, where he went from teaboy to being one of their youngest record producers, with credits including early David Bowie singles, John Mayall & The Bluesbreakers' 1966 album *Bluesbreakers*, in which they teamed up with Eric Clapton (the album is otherwise known as the 'Beano' album due to Clapton reading the comic *The Beano* in the album's cover image) and The Artwoods' 1966 album *Art Gallery*. He then went on to become the founder of the Blue Horizon label.

R & B MONTHLY

EDITOR: MICK VERNON
"RED RIDGES"
3B GODSTONE ROAD,
KENLEY,
SURREY.

C O N T E N T S

Editorial . . . . Page 1
"Portraits In Blues" Sonny Boy Williamson - album reviewed . . . . Page 1
Slim Harpo : by John G. Allinson . . . . Page 2
Crackerjack : single label listing . . . . Page 3
Short Bios: Gladys Knight/Pips - Billy Bland . . Page 4
Discography Part One : Little Walter Jacobs . . . Page 5
Full-page photo' : JERRY BUTLER & IMPRESSIONS
Recent American R&B Releases . . . . Page 9
Records Reviewed: including Shorty Long and Elmore James . . . . . . Page 11
Duke & Peacock Records Matrix/Pressing Details . . Page 12

No. 8 SEPTEMBER, 1964. 9d.

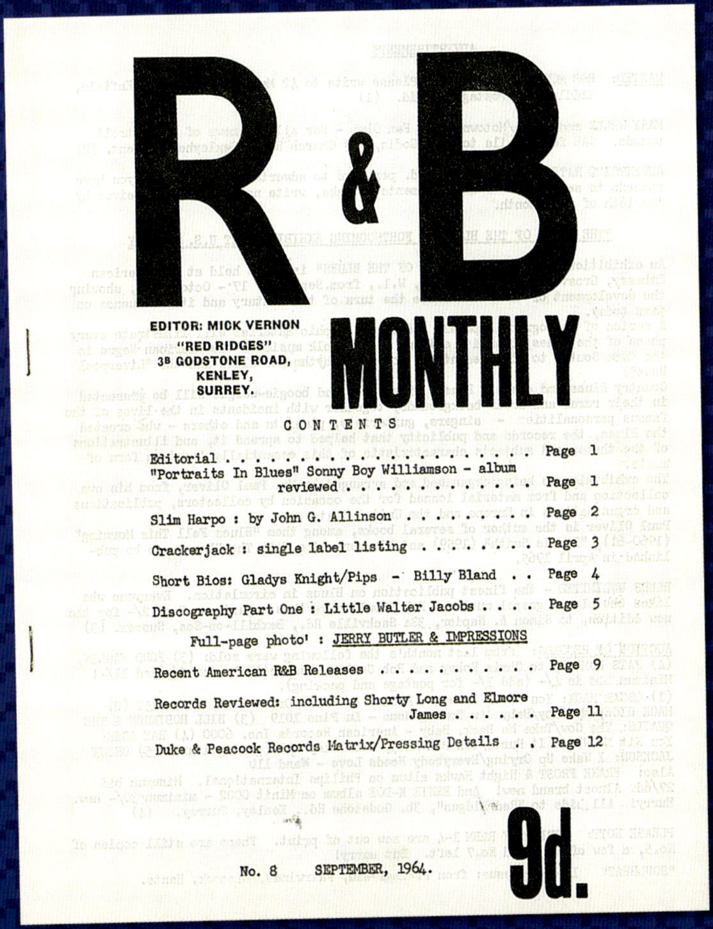

R&B MONTHLY
Editor: MICK VERNON
Assistant Editor: NEIL E. SLAVEN
1/-
No. 15. APRIL, 1965.
3ª GODSTONE ROAD, KENLEY, SURREY

Photo: **BUDDY GUY**   Mick Vernon.
at Klooks Kleek

R&B MONTHLY
Editor: MICK VERNON
Assistant Editor: NEIL E. SLAVEN
1/-
No. 19 AUGUST, 1965.
3ª GODSTONE ROAD, KENLEY, SURREY

ANTOINE FATS DOMINO
1949 - 1958

R&B MONTHLY
Editor: MICK VERNON
Assistant Editor: NEIL E. SLAVEN
1'6
No. 23 DECEMBER, 1965
3ª GODSTONE ROAD, KENLEY, SURREY

THE FOLK BLUES FESTIVAL 1965
From left top to right: Eddie Boyd, Fred McDowell,
Freddie Below, Buddy Guy, James Moore (Willie Mae's
Manager), J.B.Lenore, Jimmy Lee Robinson, Roosevelt
Sykes, Mama Thornton, Doctor Ross and Shakey Horton.

R&B MONTHLY
Editor: MICK VERNON
Assistant Editor: NEIL E. SLAVEN
1/-
No. 16 MAY, 1965.
3ª GODSTONE ROAD, KENLEY, SURREY

JOHNNY WATSON, LARRY WILLIAMS and his wife HELEN.
Decca Studios, Monday 5th. April.

R&B MONTHLY
Editor: MICK VERNON
Assistant Editor: NEIL E. SLAVEN
1'6
No. 21 OCTOBER, 1965
3ª GODSTONE ROAD, KENLEY, SURREY

LIGHTNIN' HOPKINS
Photo' courtesy of Arhoolie Records

R&B MONTHLY
Editor: MICK VERNON
Assistant Editor: NEIL E. SLAVEN
3/-
No. 24 JANUARY/FEBRUARY 1966
3ª GODSTONE ROAD, KENLEY, SURREY

Top left: EDDIE BOYD   Top right: DOCTOR ROSS
Bottom left: JOHNNY 'GUITAR' WATSON
Bottom right: BO DIDDLEY with The Duchess

R&B MONTHLY
Editor: MICK VERNON
Assistant Editor: NEIL E. SLAVEN
1/-
No. 17. JUNE, 1965.
3ª GODSTONE ROAD, KENLEY, SURREY

AARON "T-BONE" WALKER
- A DISCOGRAPHY IN THIS ISSUE -

R&B MONTHLY
Editor: MICK VERNON
Assistant Editor: NEIL E. SLAVEN
1'6
No. 22 NOVEMBER, 1965
3ª GODSTONE ROAD, KENLEY, SURREY

CLIFTON JAMES   BO DIDDLEY   THE DUCHESS
Pictured at The Flamingo
Photo : Mick Vernon

R&B SCENE

This was the music fanzine of Roger Eagle, the DJ at the Twisted Wheel in Manchester. Produced from Roger's flat in Chorlton-cum-Hardy, it featured some great artist bios from Mike Leadbitter, plus discographies and reviews. Although it contained many record-label supplied promotional photos, the fanzine was lucky enough to have the talents of local photographer Brian Smith, who captured some great images of the visiting American stars.

R·n·B SCENE

1/-

VOL. 1. No. 4.

LITTLE RICHARD

In this Issue ▶

THE LITTLE WALTER STORY . LaVern Baker FREDDY KING . LITTLE RICHARD DISCOGRAPHY SLIM HARPO . RUFUS THOMAS THE BLUES FESTIVAL 1964

BLUES UNLIMITED

Coming out of Bexhill-on-Sea, on the East Sussex coast, Simon Napier was this fanzine's driving force. Starting life as a typed, mimeographed booklet; later it went on to become a full-fledged magazine. By 1987, the year it ended on Issue 149, it was edited by Mike Rowe.

There were other blues magazines such as Bob Groom's *Blues World*, which lasted until 1970, but by 1966, soul music had taken centre stage and this reflected in the publications. From Plymouth, there was Tony Cummings' fanzine, simply named *Soul*, and that same year would also see Dave Godin, who had formed the Tamla Motown Appreciation Society, bring out his own *Rhythm & Soul USA*, which was highly informative and great quality.

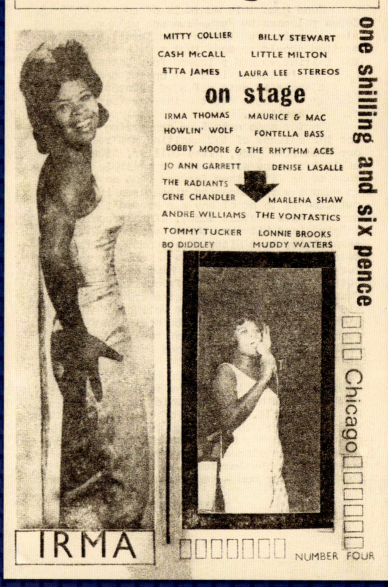

By 1967, *A Chess Full of Goodies* was published by the Chess Checker Appreciation Society in South Woodford. Although it contained biographies, discographies and record reviews, the quality was very poor until a year later, by Issue 6, when the fanzine was bigger and of much better quality.

Far more interesting in 1967 was *Soul Messenger*, otherwise known as 'Uptightan'Outasight,' which was the official magazine for the Atlantic and Stax Appreciation Society. The people behind the 'zine were Janet Martin and Judy Webb, who both worked at the Polydor Offices in Stratford Place, London. Polydor had the UK licence to issue Atlantic releases, so

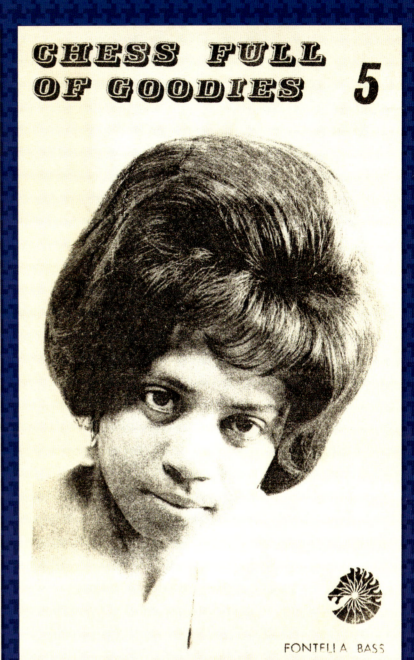

CHESS FULL OF GOODIES NO. 2

LAURA LEE

CHESS FULL OF GOODIES 5

FONTELLA BASS

Janet and Judy were in the ideal position to promote anything new on the label. The club's honorary president was the DJ Johnnie Walker and he would often provide articles for the fanzine.

The first *Soul Messenger* appeared in July 1967, and although it had a good-quality coloured cover, it only featured typed articles free of images. Some photos did appear by the second issue. Sadly, in December 1967, Atlantic's biggest recording artist, Otis Redding, was killed in a plane crash. When Issue 4 appeared in January 1968, the magazine was solely devoted to Otis, and featured written tributes from owner of the Soul City record shop Dave Godin, singer Sharon Tandy, DJ Mike Raven and music writer Tony Hall, among others.

By 1969, Atlantic's musical policy was changing and the magazine would also feature more white artists such as Led Zeppelin, The Rascals, The Allman Brothers Band and Crosby, Stills, Nash & Young.

FEBRUARY, 1964   1/6

JAZZ BEAT

THE LIVELY JAZZ MAGAZINE

BLUES on TV –
Special feature
●
Articles on
RONNIE SCOTT'S
CHARLIE MINGUS
MATT MURPHY
CYRIL DAVIES
and
THEM !
●
CLUB GUIDE
RADIO JAZZ

EXCLUSIVE ELLINGTON – THE MAN

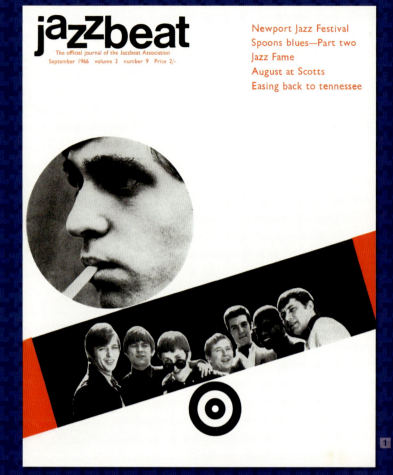

jazzbeat
The official journal of the Jazzbeat Association
September 1966   volume 3   number 9   Price 2/-

Newport Jazz Festival
Spoons blues—Part two
Jazz Fame
August at Scotts
Easing back to tennessee

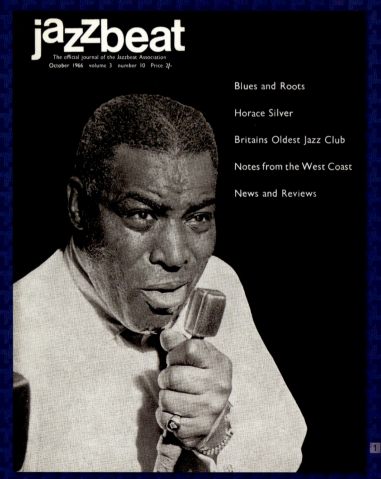

jazzbeat
The official journal of the Jazzbeat Association
October 1966   volume 3   number 10   Price 2/-

Blues and Roots

Horace Silver

Britains Oldest Jazz Club

Notes from the West Coast

News and Reviews

1 *Jazzbeat* magazine, like many other jazz-related publications at the time, would heavily feature blues and R&B articles as the music gained in popularity. Guy Stevens started writing a regular column for it in February 1964.

2 'Call it R&B' advert from UK magazine *Jazz Journal*, February 1963.

Call it MUSIC IN-BETWEEN:

PART 1

R & B

All LPs have 12 titles and all EPs have 4 titles unless otherwise stated

RAY CHARLES

THE RAY CHARLES STORY—Vol. I
Ⓛ HAK 8023 London Atlantic LP (18 titles)
THE RAY CHARLES STORY—Vol. II
Ⓛ HAK 8024 London Atlantic LP (14 titles)
THE ORIGINAL
Ⓛ HAB 8022 London LP
THE GENIUS SINGS THE BLUES
Ⓛ LTZK 15238 London Atlantic LP
RAY CHARLES AT NEWPORT
Ⓛ SAHK 6008 Ⓛ LTZK 15149
London Atlantic LP (8 titles)
Ⓔ REK 1317 London Atlantic EP (2 titles from LP)
THE GREAT RAY CHARLES
Ⓛ LTZK 15134 London Atlantic LP (8 titles)
RAY CHARLES IN PERSON
Ⓛ HAK 2284 London Atlantic LP (7 titles)
WHAT'D I SAY
Ⓛ HAK 2226 London Atlantic LP (10 titles)
Ⓔ REK 1306 London Atlantic EP (3 titles from LP)
YES INDEED
Ⓛ HAK 2168 London Atlantic LP (14 titles)

**RAY CHARLES &
MILT JACKSON**

SOUL BROTHERS
Ⓛ SAHK 6008 Ⓛ LTZK 15146
London Atlantic LP (8 titles)

Many titles from the above records are also available as 45 rpm singles

**ALEXIS KORNER'S
BLUES INCORPORATED**

R & B FROM THE MARQUEE
Ⓛ ACL 1130 Ace of Clubs LP — 19/4

JOE TURNER

BIG JOE RIDES AGAIN
Ⓛ SAHK 6123 Ⓛ LTZK 15205 London Atlantic LP (10 titles)
BOSS OF THE BLUES
Ⓛ SAHK 6019 Ⓛ LTZK 15053 London Atlantic LP (10 titles)
BIG JOE IS HERE
Ⓛ HAK 2931 London Atlantic LP
ROCKIN' THE BLUES
Ⓛ HAK 2173 London Atlantic LP (14 titles)
PRESENTING JOE TURNER
Ⓔ REK 1111 London Atlantic EP (4 titles; 3 from above LP)

H. B. BARNUM

THE BIG VOICE OF BARNUM—H.B. THAT IS!
Ⓛ SF 7500 Ⓛ RD 7500 RCA Victor LP

FATS DOMINO

TWISTIN' THE STOMP
Ⓛ HAP 2447 London LP
WHAT A PARTY!
Ⓛ HAP 2426 London LP
Ⓔ REP 1340 London EP (from LP)

LET THE FOUR WINDS BLOW
Ⓛ HAP 2420 London LP
I MISS YOU SO
Ⓛ HAP 2364 London LP
A LOT OF DOMINOES
Ⓛ HAP 2312 London LP
LET'S PLAY FATS DOMINO
Ⓛ HAP 2223 London LP
THE FABULOUS 'MR D.'
Ⓛ HAP 2135 London LP
THIS IS FATS
Ⓛ HAP 2087 London LP
THIS IS FATS DOMINO
Ⓛ HAP 2073 London LP
HERE STANDS FATS DOMINO
Ⓛ HAP 2052 London LP (12 titles; 1 from HAP 2041)
CARRY ON ROCKIN'
Ⓛ HAP 2041 London LP
FATS ROCK AND ROLLIN'
Ⓛ HAU 2028 London LP
BE MY GUEST
Ⓔ REP 1261 London EP (4 titles; 2 from
THE ROCKIN' 'MR. D.'—Vol. I
Ⓔ REP 1206 London EP (4 titles; 3 f
THE ROCKIN' 'MR. D.'—Vol. II
Ⓔ REP 1207 London EP (4 titles; 3 f
THE ROCKIN' 'MR. D.'—Vol. III
Ⓔ REP 1265 London EP (1 title from
HERE COMES FATS—Part 1
Ⓔ REP 1079 London EP (2 titles fro

HERE COMES FATS—Part 2
Ⓔ REP 1080 London EP (from HAP 2087)
HERE COMES FATS—Part 3
Ⓔ REP 1138 London EP (4 titles; 2 from HAP 2135)
CARRY ON ROCKIN'—Part 1
Ⓔ REP 1115 London EP (from HAP 2041)
CARRY ON ROCKIN'—Part 2
Ⓔ REP 1116 London EP (3 titles from HAP 2041;
1 title from HAU 2028)
BLUES FOR LOVE—Vol. II
Ⓔ REU 1062 London EP (3 titles from HAU 2028;
1 title from HAP 2073)
BLUES FOR LOVE—Vol. III
Ⓔ REP 1117 London EP (from HAP 2087)
BLUES FOR LOVE—Vol. IV
Ⓔ REP 1121 London EP (4 titles; 1 from HAP 2135;
3 from HAP 2073)
(no two EPs contain the same title)

LITTLE RICHARD

THE FABULOUS LITTLE RICHARD

THE DECCA RECORD COMPANY LIMIT

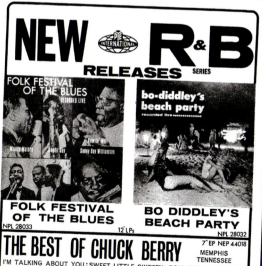

NEW PYE INTERNATIONAL **R&B** SERIES **RELEASES**

FOLK FESTIVAL OF THE BLUES
Recorded Live
Muddy Waters Howlin' Wolf Sonny Boy Williamson
NPL 28033 12" LPs

BO DIDDLEY'S BEACH PARTY
recorded live
NPL 28032

THE BEST OF CHUCK BERRY 7" EP NEP 44018
MEMPHIS TENNESSEE
I'M TALKING ABOUT YOU : SWEET LITTLE SIXTEEN : ROLL OVER BEETHOVEN

CHUCK AND BO vol. 3 7" EP NEP 44017
Deed And Deed I Do   It Don't Take But A Few Minutes   Too Pooped To Pop   Diana

THE STORY OF BO DIDDLEY 7" EP NEP 44019
The Story Of Bo Diddley   Put The Shoes On Willie   Little Girl   Run Diddley Daddy

PYE RECORDS (SALES) LTD., A.T.V. HOUSE, GT. CUMBERLAND PLACE, LONDON, W.I.

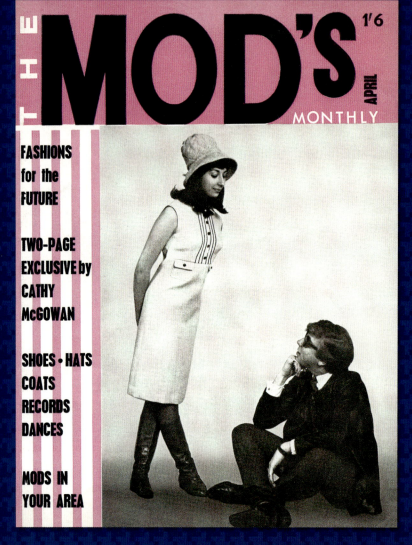

THE MOD'S MONTHLY
1'6
APRIL
MONTHLY

FASHIONS for the FUTURE

TWO-PAGE EXCLUSIVE by CATHY McGOWAN

SHOES • HATS
COATS
RECORDS
DANCES

MODS IN YOUR AREA

THE MOD'S MONTHLY

The first issue of *The Mod's Monthly* appeared in March 1964. I'm not sure how much demand there would have been for such a publication at the time, but the figures editor Mark Burns mentions in the introduction in Issue 1 seem a little far-fetched: "Mods have been waiting a long time for a book of their own and after early advertising, advance orders had reached 50,000 on the first issue." When Issue 2 appeared a month later, Burns says in the intro that the first issue "had completely sold out, but they managed to do a quick reprint and so you could order your copy." He went on to add "...on the third day 5,000 letters swamped the office asking if it could be a weekly."

At just 10 double pages and only 245mm x 85mm, the editors still appeared to struggle to fill such a small and flimsy magazine. 'Cathy McGowan's Look at the Mod Scene Today,' 'Mods of Tomorrow' (future styles) and readers suggested dance steps were just some of the fairly uninspiring features, while much of the rest of the fanzine is given over to photographs of various fashion shoots and the contact details of various clothes suppliers.

Sadly, for 1/6d there isn't much detail of anything and I presume that by the time the actual fanzine had hit the shelves, most items featured would probably have been seen as passé. Whatever the reason, Cathy McGowan didn't stay long as fashion consultant – she was replaced by Vicki Wickham, who then gave way to Jill De Jey.

One of the most interesting features in the fanzine was the letters page, 'Mod Mailbag,' in which readers discussed what the latest groups, clubs, dances and trends were in their region. One of the most interesting examples is from a girl in Leeds, dated July 1964 and entitled 'Real Mods.'

> " Mods have been waiting a long time for a book of their own... "

MARK BURNS: *THE MOD'S MONTHLY*

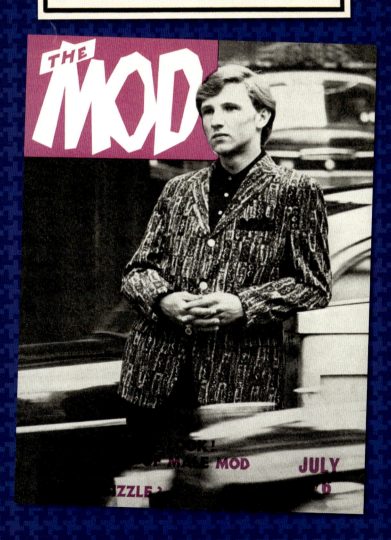

> **❝ ...some of your readers are no longer Mods. ❞**

STEPHANIE BROWN

"I think that your mag is fab and both my boyfriend and myself look forward to reading it, but we also think some of your readers are no longer Mods. My boy wears his hair very long, reaching eight inches below his collar and finished with a fringe just above the eyes. His face is lightly made up and finished with a nice shade of lipstick. Nail lacquer of the same colour completes the effect. He wears bell-bottom trousers, with Cuban heel boots. He wears a bright shiny red P.V.C. jacket, which he purchased from my dress shop. I like bell-bottom jeans with block heeled shoes and a light blue shiny P.V.C. jacket. Let us keep getting your very nice articles."
– Stephanie Brown (Leeds, 16)

Interestingly enough the penultimate issue, dated September 1965, carried a cover story entitled 'Where Have All The Mods Gone?' and bemoaned the fact that the rest of the country had finally cottoned on to new ideas and implanted them into all aspects of pop music, film, theatre, art and literature. It states that the people who despised this outcome the most were the teenagers, who resented old people's (anyone over 25) interest in the Mod scene:

"This upsurge caught hold of almost everybody young in mind and the whole world has gone Mod. Now, everyone between six and sixty is trying to think young. We see women in their fifties wearing the latest 'Mod' gear. City stockbrokers in suits that would not be out of place in Carnaby Street. Young executives in big corporations with hairstyles that would have got them shown the door but a year or two ago. Company directors growing beards and sideboards and asking their Savile Row tailors to make them their next suit just like The Beatles wore."

The magazine ran from March 1964 until October 1965, initially as *The Mod's Monthly* covering seven issues before becoming simply *The Mod* in October 1964, whereupon it ran for a total of 13 issues.

RAVE MAGAZINE

Rave magazine is often wrongly seen as a teenybopper girls' publication, but what some people fail to get is that the magazine's team had its finger on the music scene's pulse. Just as *Ready Steady Go!* was the visual messenger, showing Britain what was happening in the capital, so *Rave* magazine provided a written manifesto to those living in rural areas. Often overlooked are the exclusive photo shoots with various artists and bands. *Rave* also featured some great in-depth interviews and articles.

At 2s 6d, the magazine seemed outrageously expensive but each issue usually contained around 60 pages and measured 10.75in x 8.5in. From its first issue, in February 1964, and throughout the ever-changing decade and beyond, *Rave* kept its audience informed on all the latest from 'the scene.' While early issues concentrated on artists such as Cliff Richard, The Searchers, The Beatles and The Rolling Stones, as *Rave* evolved it made bolder moves, covering lesser-known bands, such as The Action.

Fashion guides appeared, and very cleverly they catered for both male and female. The 'Just Dennis' feature (a boy's slant on fashion) would often see *Rave*'s assistant art director, Dennis Barker, kitted out in the latest clobber with details on price and where to buy the items.

As the sixties wore on, the Swinging London aspect of *Rave* was lost to plastic flowers and free psychedelic posters before becoming very much a magazine aimed at teenage girls.

rave

Where it's all happening!

MARCH
2s 6d

moody blues?
STONES
IN IRELAND
understand
your
animals
Fashion St. W.1.
Cathy McGowan's
New Hairstyle

Annie Hutchison was a young Mod girl who had found work drawing heating implements in the design department of a factory in Slough, when she made the phone call that would change her life and lead to her working on the magazine that she bought religiously every month.

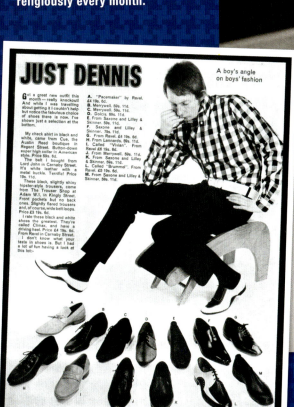

1 Annie Hutchison drawing at *Rave*, 1968. They'd just moved from the original offices, which were across the road, to Tower House, Southampton Street, next to the original Covent Garden and the same building that housed *Nova* and *19* magazines.

"I was seriously into Mod while I was at art school in '63 and '64," remembers Annie. "I was living in Gerrard's Cross with my parents. I would hitch over to Windsor to the Ricky-Tick nights at the Star and Garter and later to the old house [Clewer Mead] by the river, where the Ricky-Tick was relocated. It was terrifying, as I always had to walk past the Hell's Angels at the Cellar Bar by the river on the Eton Windsor borders in my Mod gear. Great times though, as I also went to places like Eel Pie Island and the various Crawdaddy clubs. The Stones, The Yardbirds, The Pretty Things and so many of those old blues greats like Sonny Boy Williamson, Howlin' Wolf and John Lee Hooker. The Spencer Davis Group often played in a club above Burtons, a men's clothing store in Uxbridge.

"Music and dancing went hand in hand with the clothes. There was even a walk that I used to practise down the corridors at art school. You kind of swung your shoulders with a total swaggering confidence. My mum had bought me a full-length brown leather coat for £25 and I worked as a model for evening class art students – at the huge amount of 7 shillings and 6 pence an hour – and I paid her back every week. I judged all my boyfriends by how they were dressed; they had to look good and my first question was always 'What type of scooter have you got, how many lights, what model?' It sounds awful now but to me it was important."

Annie had studied a year of Basic Art at High Wycombe Art School before deciding on the graphic design course, although she sometimes seems to find it unbelievable that she made it on to better things. "During the 'History of Art' lectures on a Friday evening I was always disappearing. It was a big room with this dapper little bearded man with his pointer. The room would be full when he started, then the lights would go down and then you would see a little crack of light in the door as somebody sneaked out. At the end, there was nobody left as we had all crept out to get home in time for *Ready Steady Go!*. Amazingly I passed the History of Art with honours. How did I do that?

"Everybody was doing advertising in the sixties, so I went to what must have been a hundred job interviews and I didn't get anywhere except for people telling me I was wasting their time. Luckily, I met somebody whose daughter was going to the same school that I used to go to. He told me I should go into publishing instead of advertising. So I went to various interviews and eventually met Roger Pinney [art director of *Rave* magazine]. He was impressed but said he didn't have a vacancy at the time. I had no faith in myself but my mum got me to ring him again quite a long time after the first meeting and I landed a job on *Rave* that included being a Model Girl.

1 Annie Hutchison's drawing of the Ricky-Tick, Windsor. It was created whilst she was still at art school and was based on watching the dance moves and the clothes in the club.

❝...seriously into Mod while I was at art school... Music and dance went hand in hand...❞
ANNIE HUTCHISON

"I started on £14.6d a week and I was employed as assistant layout artist to Dennis Barker. Terry Hornett was the editor. Roger Pinney was the art editor, Dennis Barker was the assistant art editor. There were some good features writers such as Jeremy Pascal and Maureen O'Grady. She was fantastic, and knew all there was to know about music. Obviously, search engines like Google didn't exist back then so we'd ask her 'who sang this?' or 'what were the words?' and she always seemed to know. She would also get you a free copy of any album you wanted. Dennis Barker had been at *Rave* since it started, I think, but he was definitely the creative man there. He was incredibly tall and skinny with sandy coloured hair. He was a brilliant artist. He was quite quiet but all the stuff that was going on in his brain was amazing. He was always coming to work saying he'd just seen some new incredible band. A lot of the photography sessions, such as Bowie with the curly hair and smoke behind him, and Hendrix with the pink lights, were directed by him.

Johnny Rave

Talks about your boyfriend problems here!

Hi ravers! Springtime is when everyone is supposed to fall in love, but there are still an awful lot of lonely young people around. A story reached me of two girls who committed suicide because they were convinced they weren't attractive enough to get boyfriends!

If you're depressed about your appearance, don't be. There's always *something* you can do about it if you really try. Dress in a different style, get your hair re-done or go on a diet. I'm not an expert on these matters, but beauty girl Samantha assures me that no girl is a hopeless case!

Jane, who's eighteen and lives in Reading, said in her letter to me that some of her friends have started taking drugs. Because she has quite a lot of money to spend, she finds herself being offered them quite frequently. Other than this she likes her friends very much, but said her mother would be furious if she knew. Should she drop the friends altogether?

Jane, I don't think you can ever hope to build lasting friendships from those you now have. Look around for a crowd who have different ideas of enjoying themselves.

Hilary, who's nineteen and lives in Brighton, wrote to me and said that her boyfriend temporarily has nowhere to live, and has asked her if he can stay for a while in her flat, which she shares with other girls. He's impressed on her that she can trust him, but she's not at all sure. How can she say no without hurting his pride and risking losing him?

Tell him the girls in the flat will make things awkward for you, Hilary, or that you don't want to make things awkward for them. If either of those don't work, just mention that your mother drops in at unexpected times, or that he would have to sleep on the floor in the living-room and, oh dear, there's only one spare blanket. At least that way you won't have to give a flat refusal.

See you next month!

■ Send your boyfriend problems to Johnny Rave, RAVE, Tower House, Southampton Street, London, W.C.2. For a personal reply enclose a stamped, self-addressed envelope.

Johnny

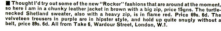

■ Thought I'd try out some of the new "Rocker" fashions that are around at the moment, so here I am in a chunky leather jacket in brown with a big zip, price 15gns. The turtle-necked Shetland sweater, also with a heavy zip, is in flame red. Price 69s. 6d. The velveteen trousers in purple are in hipster style, and hold up quite snugly without a belt, price 89s. 6d. All from Take 6, Wardour Street, London, W.1.

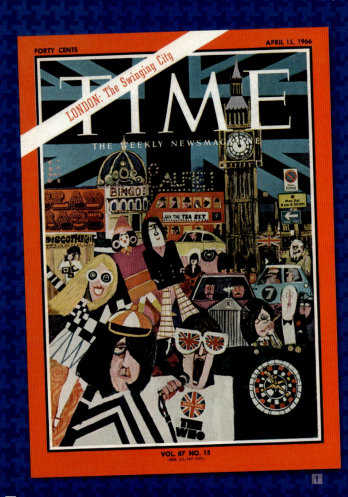

FORTY CENTS

APRIL 15, 1966

LONDON: The Swinging City

TIME

THE WEEKLY NEWSMAGAZINE

VOL. 87 NO. 15
(REG. U.S. PAT. OFF.)

1 Cover of *Time* magazine covering the change of styles to 'Swinging London'.

2 Jimi Hendrix-based illustration for *Rave* by Annie.

3 Batman and Robin designed and painted on the wall of Annie's Victorian terrace in 1972, which was opposite the old Harrow Road Police Station (the steps that Dixon of Dock Green used to stand on and say "Evenin' All).

"The work was very 'hands on,' as there were no computers. At that time, staff at the magazine were expected to do many things. There was a lot of hand lettering by the designers, which was then drawn beautifully by the art workers, who also retouched photos as there was no Photoshop back then. They also stuck down the galleys of type on the pages, which were then photographed ready for the printer. Some headline type was ordered over the phone or done by Letterset. We were often used as models, but in return we gained a great social network and a few other perks along the way.

"I can list my heroes from art school days to the time that I had formed a style of my own and went freelance: at art school, it was artists/illustrators like Paul Klee especially, Andy Warhol, Roy Lichtenstein, Jim Dine and Bob Kane, the original illustrator from 1940s Batman comics. During *Rave* days there was a brilliant freelance black and white illustrator called Malcolm Bird. Then there was the illustrations from The Beatles' *Yellow Submarine*. Alphonse Mucha, Aubrey Beardsley, Granny Takes A Trip (Hapshash and the Coloured Coat), artists Nigel Weymouth and Michael English, and all the American psychedelic artists such as Rick Griffin, Kelly Mouse, etc."

As times changed and the late sixties beckoned, the staff changed, too, and this would have a direct affect on the magazine.

"We all changed and moved on. Mod was no longer the big thing. I remember having to walk through Spitalfields Market and that was awful. I had Biba boots that I'd painted with pixies and mushrooms. I was wearing velvet dresses and had lots of curly red hair. All these guys would be waiting, in their blood-soaked aprons; they'd see me coming and grab hold of me shouting things like 'trash, filthy hippy!' They'd line up and throw me from one guy to the next. It was horrible. Dennis had given up the 'Just Dennis' page. He was tired of being a kind of spokesperson for the Mod bit on clothes. At one point he grew his hair; he'd always had it cropped before but he got his mum to put pipe cleaners in it to make him look more like Jimi Hendrix. His replacement on the page was a guy called Johnny Rave, but we were all sort of disappointed with it.

"*Rave* moved from Tower House to Farringdon Street along with many of the other IPC magazines. Terry Hornett became interested in other projects – actually, he was really dynamic. Colin Bostock-Smith took over as editor and he and Dennis were really in tune with the way the magazine should look. That was when Dennis was given a lot more artistic freedom. Musically they really wanted the same thing so it was a really great time. It was Dennis in his office and just myself and the art worker, Ken, in the small art room/studio. At that point I was freelance drawing for just about all the IPC magazines such as *Woman*, *Woman's Own*, *Woman's Realm*, *True*, *Valentine*, *Loving*, *Pink* and *Girl*, plus some of the supermarket magazines like *Living*, *Family Circle*. I was drawing at night and falling asleep at my drawing board during the day. When the sales of *Rave* dropped, Betty Hale, who had been the editor on *FAB 208* magazine, got involved. *Rave* became more teenybopper. Dennis was furious: none of us thought that was what *Rave* was about. It became about kids' fashion, beauty and problem pages.

"Not long after, I think *Rave* amalgamated with *FAB 208* and Dennis was asked by Terry Hornett, the original editor of *Rave*, to be the art director on a new magazine for men, called *Club*. Michael Roberts, who I had been at art school with and had been doing amazing fashion illustrations for *19* magazine and also working as creative director on fashion shoots for *Nova*, freelanced there. Along with his own illustrated books he became creative director on *Vanity Fair*, designed the Fashionista T-shirts, photographed Vivienne Westwood and continues to do endless things.

"Eventually we left. Dennis went to work for Century Hutchinson doing book jackets. After that he worked for the *Sunday Express* and had an exhibition of his paintings."

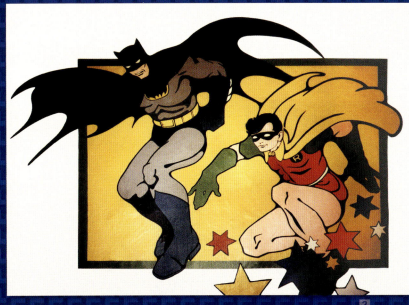

MORE

MONEY FOR CLOTHES & FUN
IF YOU DON'T SMOKE

10 Cigarettes a day cost £30 a year or more
15 Cigarettes a day cost £45 a year or more
20 Cigarettes a day cost £60 a year or more

SO WHY SMOKE CIGARETTES AND RISK YOUR HEALTH?

A selection of adverts from a campaign to discourage teenagers from smoking, which were placed in magazines such as *Rave* and *Honey* from 1966 to 1968.

more money
for clothes
if you don't smoke

10 cigarettes a day cost £2.10.0. a month or more
15 cigarettes a day cost £3.15.0. a month or more
20 cigarettes a day cost £5. 0. 0. a month or more
SO WHY SMOKE CIGARETTES AND RISK YOUR HEALTH?

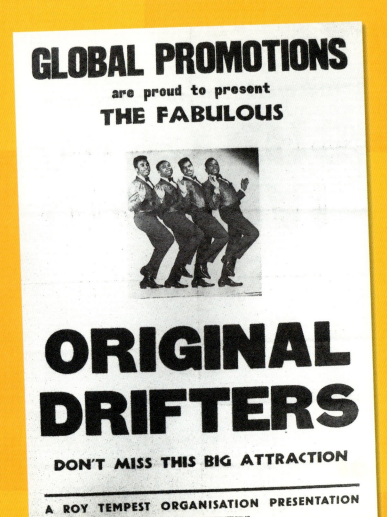

GLOBAL PROMOTIONS
are proud to present
THE FABULOUS

ORIGINAL
DRIFTERS

DON'T MISS THIS BIG ATTRACTION

A ROY TEMPEST ORGANISATION PRESENTATION

HUNG UP:
1960s POSTERS

**" ...I got my
grounding from him. "**

PHIL LUDERMAN

All across the West End of London and throughout every major
town and city in Britain walls were awash with colour and graphics.
For every club night and gig, there had to be a poster. Eye-catching
art of the highest order would often be pasted to a building for a
brief period, only to be pasted over by another, or torn down by
a competitor or fan.

Of course, behind every poster there is a story. The poster's
primary function is simply to inform the viewer of the relevant details
of the night in question, but this didn't always happen.

One fan's story has it that one sixties night in Manchester,
a group of kids had noticed a poster advertising The Temptations at
a venue (the identity of which has been lost in the mists of time).
Of course, it was a treat to see such fantastic visiting US talent and
so the kids duly attended. The fans in question were treated to a
great evening of fantastic dance routines and soulful vocals performed
by five black guys dressed in sharp blue suits. In fact, the young
Mods had enjoyed the performance so much that they decided to
see the group at another venue later that same evening. Once again
they were witness to a highly polished act, although this time it was
performed by four black guys in red suits. Welcome to the world of
the Roy Tempest Organisation.

The promoter Roy Tempest's offices were at 13–14 Dean Street, in the heart of London's Soho. It was from these offices that Tempest built up a reputation as a reliable provider of good quality acts for clubs. Sadly, a few years later, his reputation would lie in tatters and his career would end in a major court battle.

One man who knew Roy Tempest very well was Phil Luderman. Phil had started off as a young scooter-riding Battersea Mod and his love of music led him to an amazing journey. "I was a lift boy at Cecil Gee's in Shaftesbury Avenue. One day I saw this big-finned American car pull up, and it was Marty Wilde. He was like the Pied Piper, and had all these girls chasing him. He came into Cecil Gee's and got into my lift, but even though I was desperate to talk to him, it was against company policy. About a week later Cliff Richard got in, and against what I'd been told I asked if he had any advice on how to get into the music business. He was charming and told me he worked for London Management, a big agency at the time. He told me to give them a call. So I blagged it and told them I was just starting in the music business and Cliff Richard had suggested I rang them. They said they didn't have any vacancies but the guy I spoke to said a friend of his called Roy Tempest was starting up an agency and to try him. So I phoned up and told the agency I'd been doing it for years. In truth, musically I had two left feet and I couldn't hold a tune for toffee. I'd never make a musician but I wanted to be in the business. In those days you were kind of pioneers because nobody had really done it before, so you could blag it. Anyway, he took me on as a roadie to start with, which I didn't take to very well. Then Roy suggested I try being a tour manager. I had no idea that was but I just said 'sure, I'd love to' and that was it.

"Basically you are Mother Hen. You take the artist to the venue, see to whatever their needs are and you pick them up after the show. If it's a concert and you're on a percentage, you get the ticket sales. You find out the company you're working for and ask their percentage and then the percentage to leave at the venue. You just had to wing it really. There was nobody I could ask who had done it before because it was such a new business. I couldn't be seen to ask people where the Twisted Wheel or the Mojo was, so I had maps galore. I did quite a good job, so Roy kept me on."

Phil began to love his job – as both a Mod and a fan he was getting to mix with his musical heroes, whether it be escorting Don Covay to the set of *Ready Steady Go!* on a Friday night to getting Solomon Burke to appear at the Orchid in Purley, the latter of which ended with a phone call from a desperate fan asking if they could meet Solomon. Phil agreed and soon found himself in the home of Paul McCartney and Jane Asher (McCartney being the desperate fan). Sadly, it wasn't too long before Phil started noticing discrepancies in how the Roy Tempest Organisation worked.

"A lot of people didn't like him... ...he wouldn't pay the acts."

PHIL LUDERMAN

"To me, Roy Tempest was originally the best promoter for our kind of music. Straight as a die and brought over some great acts. Roy was Welsh, and from the Valleys, but he decided this business was controlled by the Jews, like the Grades and so on. So he'd put on this pseudo-Jewish accent, which was terrible. Everything was 'Oy vey, vot an act I've got for you,' but of course it was 'boyo' at the end of it! I used to cringe. He was a great salesman though; he'd phone up a booker and say 'Where did you go on your last holiday?' and the guy might say something like 'Bridlington' and Roy would say 'Bridlington? You take my act and you'll be in the South of France next time. You're gonna make so much money.' That was his spiel and I'm glad because I got my grounding from him."

Soon though, Roy's way of doing business started to spiral out of control.

"A lot of people didn't like him because it got to the point where he wouldn't pay the acts. At the time it was all to do with work permits. If you brought an American act over, an English band had to go out there. So these guys had to pay a withholding tax, which meant that if somebody like Inez & Charlie Foxx flew in, and let's say we were paying them $1,000 a month, we would have to hold $200 withholding tax because what they would do was claim tax in America or tax over here once they've proven they're not claiming in America. But Roy used to keep all this withholding tax. What I had to do was physically get the work permit from the Department of Employment in my hand, drive down to Heathrow and find out what time the flight was coming in. Then I'd go through immigration and they would lead me to where the plane landed. As the artists stepped off the plane I would give them their work permits. When I went to meet Inez & Charlie Foxx, who were really lovely people who I'd worked with a couple of times before, at the airport, I watched as they came through the immigration area and were arrested and deported because they hadn't paid their withholding tax."

Phil continued with Roy Tempest until trouble literally came knocking at the door.

"I reckon for the first 18 months Roy was totally legit. I knew something was wrong during a Solomon Burke tour. Solomon had a manager by the name of Babe Shivan, who was part of the Philadelphia Mafia – you know, a real heavy guy. At the end of a tour, Roy would have a meeting with them and pay them all out. They'd get subs from me throughout the tour in advance and they'd get the remainder at the end. Anyway. Roy had found a way of nicking a bit more money. All I can remember, very vividly, was hearing a crashing sound coming from his office, then Babe and Solomon came out. Roy had this beautiful fish tank full of tropical fish. They'd lifted it up and smashed it over his desk. I've still got this vision of Roy sitting there with all these fish flapping around him on the floor."

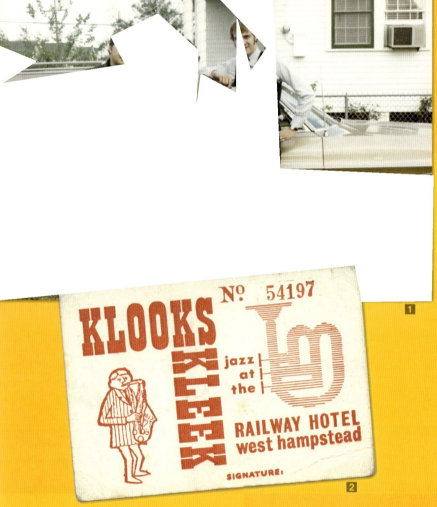

Roy, though was about to change things. In a pre-internet age, most people had no idea what American artists looked like. American soul and R&B album covers rarely displayed a picture of the artist, so as to appeal to white folks and eliminate racial bias. For example, *Green Onions* by Booker T. & The M.G.'s featured a photo of spring onions (or green onions, as they are known in the USA). Of course, artist images appeared in some music papers, but these were often poor quality and grainy. If anybody could capitalise on this situation, Roy Tempest could. Phil Luderman grew more and more disillusioned:

"Motown had started to get popular, so beforehand, Roy could get their artists for around $800 a week, but now they wanted $1,400 dollars. He wasn't prepared to pay that, and the places they were playing wouldn't pay that anyway. He realised that nobody knew what acts such as The Drifters looked like. They hadn't been on television at this point. So why not get four black guys and bring them over and pass them off as a major act. He got the ones who were playing established acts from the USA, but then he'd try and tutor West Indians, living over here, to have American accents then try to pass them off [as the actual band]. I remember William Bell and Percy Sledge would not work for Roy so he found a West Indian guy from Brixton to 'play' them. Some nights he'd be Percy and the night after he might be William. One of my jobs was to put a false moustache on the guy if he was playing Percy Sledge. He would walk on stage sometimes and touch his top lip with his tongue. If he was reassured that the 'tache was there he'd burst into 'When A Man Loves A Woman' or whatever, and if it wasn't there, a William Bell classic would erupt from his mouth."

Roy had been happy to import unknown US groups and present them under a different name. By adding an adjective to an established artist's name he could bypass the law. He could see no wrongdoing in getting The Invitations to perform under the guise of The Original Drifters. However, Motown Records, unsurprisingly, didn't see it that way, and in 1967, having found out that Tempest had brought over a band known as The Velours and presented them under the name of The Fabulous Temptations, they took Roy to court. The judge was less than impressed and ruled in favour of Motown. Luckily, in the early days, Tempest had set up another company that ran alongside the Roy Tempest Organisation, known as Global Promotions, and he continued under that name for a period.

By 1968, Roy Tempest was pretty much finished in the promotions market. Another company now led the way. Henry Sellers and Danny O'Donovan, under their own names, built on the idea that Roy had originally started: supplying Britain with some great US acts – this time genuine acts like the R&B singing duo James & Bobby Purify.

Phil still remembers Roy with fondness though: "I'd left Roy by 1965, one of the reasons being his bad reputation. The other being that I got the chance to become Lee Dorsey's road manager in New Orleans from between 1965 to 1967.

1 Left to right: Marshall Sehorn (co-owner with Allen Toussaint of Sansu Records), Lee Dorsey and Phil Luderman by a Pontiac Bonneville station wagon used as Dorsey's tour bus, New Orleans, 1966.

2 Klooks Kleek membership card. The iconic sax player image was designed by Ted Leach, guitarist with The Central Jazz Unit.

3 The John West Group and Don Rendell played the opening night of the club, January 1961.

4 Georgie Fame and the Blue Flames played the very first R&B night of the club, September 1963.

"The thing that Roy Tempest gave to the world was that he'd created and fed the R&B and soul market over here when nobody else had. Roy supplied the Twisted Wheel in Manchester, the Sheffield Mojo and all those early great clubs. He was pre-Arthur Howes Agency, who were the other major player early on."

Another club that had a great promotion man was Klooks Kleek in West Hampstead, London. When it opened in January 1961, Klooks Kleek was a pure modern jazz club, with great live acts such as Don Rendell, Harold McNair, Ronnie Ross and Tubby Hayes. By late 1963, the club switched musical direction and became a mainly R&B stronghold. Wednesdays were given over to modern jazz, but Monday and Tuesdays were rhythm'n'blues days, while Thursdays became Soul Nite. Dick Jordan ran the club alongside his business partner, Geoff Williams, but Dick was the ideas man when it came to getting in the punters. At the time he worked as a film cameraman by day, and had previously worked for the screen advertising company Pearl & Dean, so he understood the business well.

Dick had once read in a film magazine that the inventor of Kodak film and cameras, George Eastman, had come up with the brand name Kodak because he believed the letter 'K' was the ugliest letter in the alphabet and yet it was an easy letter to pronounce. On a page of print, the letter 'K' will stand out from the other letters. Eastman had thought of the word Kodak because it began and ended with a 'K.' Dick had noticed the 1956 LP by jazz drummer Kenny 'Klook' Clarke, called *Klook's Clique*, and not to be outdone, he realised that if he changed the spelling, he could get his four 'Ks' in the club name. Hence, Klooks Kleek was born.

MIDWEEK JAZZ AT
KLOOKS KLEEK
WEST HAMPSTEAD'S ONLY MODERN JAZZ CLUB

MODERN JAZZ
EVERY WEDNESDAY AT 8 P.M.
at the
RAILWAY HOTEL WEST HAMPSTEAD
FEATURING
THE JOHN WEST GROUP
Plus Britains Top Jazz Musicians as Regular Guests

PRIVATE BAR   ADMISSION 2/6   "CATCHY" ATMOSPHERE

HALF A MINUTE WEST HAMPSTEAD TUBE (Bakerloo)   BUSES: 28, 59A, 159
CORNER OF WEST END LANE AND BROADHURST GARDENS

3

KLOOKS KLEEK
WEST HAMPSTEAD'S ONLY MODERN JAZZ CLUB

Modern Jazz EVERY WEDNESDAY, at the
RAILWAY HOTEL, WEST HAMPSTEAD, 8 P.M.

Opening Wednesday, Jan. 11th, 1961
with the Fabulous . . .

JOHN WEST GROUP
PLUS
DON RENDELL
The First of Britain's Top Jazz Musicians as Regular Guests

- PRIVATE BAR
- FREE CLOAKROOM FACILITIES
- "CATCHY" ATMOSPHERE

ADMISSION ONLY 2/6 :: FREE MEMBERSHIP FIRST NITE (1/- per year)

HALF A MINUTE WEST HAMPSTEAD TUBE (Bakerloo)   BUSES: 28, 59A, 159
CORNER OF WEST END LANE AND BROADHURST GARDENS

3

KLOOKS KLEEK
TWICE A WEEK

EVERY TUESDAY from SEPT. 10th
RHYTHM 'N' BLUES
at the
Railway Hotel, West Hampstead

SEPT. 10th
GEORGIE FAME
and the BLUE FLAMES
(Recognised as Britain's No. 1 R. & B. Band)

SEPT. 17th
GRAHAM BOND QUARTET

ADMISSION 3/-
(1/- life membership covers both clubs)

EVERY WEDNESDAY - Modern Jazz as Usual
WITH YOUR OWN RESIDENT GROUP
BRIAN AUGERS BOYS
PLUS THE PICK OF BRITAIN'S JAZZMEN
2/6 as usual

TUESDAY IS RHYTHM 'N' BLUES DAY

4

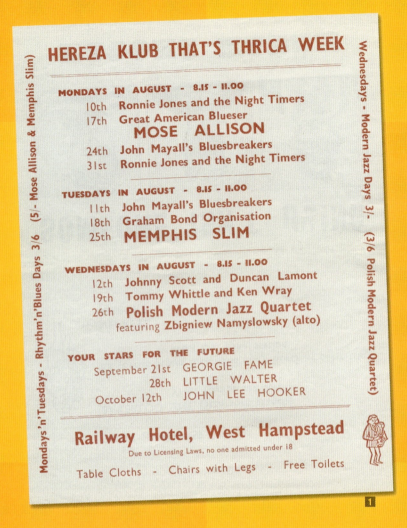

The club's team relished such controversial but humorous gimmicks. Jordan: "There was a period when clubs in the West End would talk about 'atmosphere' and such on their flyers. I was in advertising so I was always into promotion and looking for something a bit different. At the time there was a breath freshener called Amplex with the tag line 'Someone isn't using Amplex,' so we replaced Amplex with Klooks Kleek. Then we had a photo of me on one side and my business partner Geoff Williams on the other. We needed somebody in the middle so I got a copy of Footlights magazine, which casting directors go through to find actors and actresses who are free. I just used a photo from there and changed it a bit."

Another idea was large posters with a facsimile image of Lord Kitchener's recruitment message "YOUR COUNTRY NEEDS YOU!" and in small type underneath "...TO GO TO KLOOKS KLEEK." That was still pretty tame considering some of Klooks' other stunts, one of which included a card with the word "BALLS!" with "Every week at Klooks Kleek!" in tiny letters.

"I used to print thousands of them. We used to leave them on the counter and people just took them," Dick states, laughing. "The most popular, though, were our topless Playboy ones with naked models, from about 1965. They were round stickers with glue on the picture side so that they stuck on the inside of back windows.

Dick Jordan prided himself on his alternative and imaginative methods of club promotion. You could expect the unexpected when it came to Klooks Kleek promotions: "chairs with legs," "free toilets," "nearest airport: Heathrow" and "all the tablecloths are soaked in Watneys" all made it on to the club's promotional flyers. It was probably the only club to provide you with a folded piece of cardboard that read "Reserved – Gone to wee wee at Klooks Kleek," just in case you were caught short and wanted to keep your place at a table.

> ## "...topless Playboy ones with naked models..."
> **DICK JORDAN**

1 Forthcoming attractions for August 1964.
2 Klooks' cheeky dig at Amplex breath freshener adverts.
3 The popular Playboy sticker, 1965.
4 'BALLS!' business cards had to be reprinted instantly as they proved so popular.
5 'Underground ticket' design caused problems for Klooks Kleek.

"We gave them to all of the roadies, who had them in the back of their cars and Transit vans. I often saw them around the West End. I remember Jon Lord, who was playing organ in the Artwoods at the time, asking for some. I gave him a couple of dozen because it was all advertising. But they weren't the only risqué things I did. There was a photographer called Harrison Marks who used to produce a raunchy calendar every year featuring naked girls. I knew him and got about a hundred off him and printed rude speech bubbles on the pictures. Of course it was rude, that's why they sold out in a week!"

Klooks Kleek had a separate bar playing Ella, Bill Evans, Sinatra, etc., the opposite to what was going on in the main club room, which was mostly used by members who'd paid an entrance fee but were perfectly happy spending the evening chatting with friends and enjoying what was not on offer in a pub. But Klooks was more than a pop-up club: members loved the entertaining and cheeky aspect, and cherished the fact that their ultra-violet pass-out stamps would read 'Knickers,' 'Bum,' 'Tits,' 'Balls' or 'Sex.'

It would be in the field of transport, though, that Jordan excelled at really pushing the boundaries. Ernest Marples was Minister of Transport from October 1959 until the Conservatives lost the general election in 1964. Marples oversaw many controversial laws, including the introduction of parking meters, single and double yellow lines and traffic wardens, among other things. "We had these posters and flyers everywhere saying 'MARPLES MUST GO!' [to Klooks Kleek]. It's obviously very dated now but was very topical at the time," said Jordan. "The Underground didn't escape our attention either when we printed replica London Transport tube tickets with West Hampstead in an identical type face, offering a reduced entrance price of 3 shillings instead of 4. I contacted LT's head office and managed to blag 500 tube maps after telling them we had lots of foreign students at our club so were encouraging them to use London Transport. We then stapled the ticket to the map. When our members started using them at stations for a 3s fare, London Transport came to see me and said I had to stop issuing them as they were being widely accepted as kosher. I said they should stop their ticket collectors accepting them and they said 'good point.'"

Dick Jordan's greatest promotional tool, though, didn't end at cheeky flyers. It came in the form of a big win: the club won the Carl Fischer Annual Award for Best Club in the Country two years running. Their DJ, Pat Boland, also won the award for Best DJ in the Country. The fact that Carl Fischer didn't actually exist was total genius.

KLOOKS KLEEK

Playboy!

3

BALLS!

EVERY WEEK AT KLOOKS KLEEK !

4

LONDON TRANSPORT

Issued subject to the Bye-Laws of KLOOKS KLEEK. This ticket saves you 1/– on the fair price of 4/– on any Thursday session at the

RAILWAY HOTEL
WEST HAMPSTEAD

a SINGLE FARE of 3s Railway Hotel West Hampstead

No. 797501

No. 797501

3s   3s

5

"Ah yes, Carl Fischer awards," says Dick proudly. "The name was easy to say, because once again you've got that 'C' or 'K', It sounded a bit Jewish as well. The strange thing is that people would say, 'Well done. That's amazing, top club two years running,' without even having a bloody clue what it was. They just felt proud that they belonged to a top club! We killed it off after two years though, as we didn't want to push our luck."

Klooks also held car rallies, photo competitions and an annual coach trip to Brighton, the latter obviously made far more interesting because the coach carried a sign bearing the words 'Klooks Kleek Sex Club,' accompanied by a pair of knickers taped to the window.

One of the most ground-breaking clubs at this point, though, was the Ricky-Tick club in Windsor, which was run by John Mansfield and Philip Hayward. The 'Tick had also started life as a jazz club, but became one of the pioneering R&B clubs, changing persona at the start of December 1962. The club offered amazing live acts, but the posters advertising said acts were wonderfully unique and the brain child of one man: Bob McGrath.

1 Jimmy McGriff flyer for the last ever jazz gig at the club, October 1968.
2 Klooks Kleek programme, April 1965.
3 The very first Ricky-Tick poster, designed by John Mansfield, printed by a local printer. The Ricky-Tick jazz nights started in 1961 before crossing over in to R&B in December 1962.
4 Guildford Ricky-Tick poster, 1964. Silk-screen print designed by Bob McGrath.

KLOOKS KLEEK

APRIL PROGRAMME

MONDAY

NOW CLOSED

TUESDAY

6   Tony Knights Chessmen
13   Art Woods
20   Alexis Korner
27   Night-Timers

THURSDAY

     OPENING NITE
1   Zoot Money plus Kiko 6
8   Graham Bond
15   Brian Auger Trinity plus
     Hogsnort Rupert's Band
22   Chris Farlowe
29   Mike Cotton

2

1

ACHTUNG!
TRADITIONAL
JAZZ
AT THE
RICKY TICK CLUB
STAR & GARTER HOTEL
PEASCOD STREET,   WINDSOR
EVERY SUNDAY 7.30 TO 10 P.M.
LICENSED BAR + WALLET COUNTER
GORILLAS NOT ADMITTED UNLESS WEARING BOOTS
MAKE SUNDAY NITE
YOUR RAVE NITE
THE BELGRAVE PRESS, SLOUGH.

3

" ...the wonders of Bauhaus design;
everything Helvetica and grids... "
BOB McGRATH

To set the scene, while McGrath was attending Farnham Art School, he was also the vocalist in one of the very early British R&B bands, the wonderfully named Hogsnort Rupert. (Later, another band in New Zealand would use the name Hogsnort Rupert, although there is no connection to any members of the original band.) McGrath recounts: "Hogsnort Rupert was several bands. Originally I started while still at art school with Peter 'Squeaky' McGreggor [tenor sax]. I moved to London as soon as I left there and we formed another line-up with Dick 'Fancy' Forcey on drums and Mick Jones on guitar [who went on to form Foreigner in New York]. There was another musician, who I remember firing when he proudly showed us the wallets that he'd pickpocketed in Hyde Park. We were very poor at this time, living on beans and cocoa. We had no van so we'd carry our equipment on the Tube – one of us holding the train doors open while the others scrambled to take out amps, drums, etc. We played at venues like the 2i's Coffee Bar and Flamingo. I also had a fabulous blind pianist called Brian Goodchild and an alto-sax player called Tony Gerald, who was in a wheelchair. One evening at the Flamingo, Tony who was close to the edge of the stage, heard Johnny Gunnell, the manager, calling from the side trying, unsuccessfully, to get my attention. If you remember there were Shure mics hanging from the very low ceiling above the stage for the horns. Tony leapt up out of his chair, hung onto the mic, and while dangling, screamed 'Cassius Clay has just entered the club!,' and fell back into his chair to enormous applause."

It would be at a Hogsnort Rupert gig near Guildford that John Mansfield saw a poster that would bring them together. "We had a gig at Merrow Village Hall," notes McGrath. "The poster was silk-screen printed in the fabric printing department, which was a place us young Turks would rarely visit, located in the attics of the school and inhabited by elderly Scottish women. I'm sure we didn't invent it, but it was not a common practice then to screen print on paper. We stapled organdy cotton cloth, stretched to a frame much the same way as a canvas is stretched for painting. We cut the artwork from an iron-down stencil with a scalpel knife, which explains the often crude quality. Then ink was then squeegeed through the screen. Shortly after the gig, John Mansfield came calling. He arrived on a battery-powered milk float that he'd renovated. All the way from Old Windsor to Chiswick! Ahead of his time, or what? He came to ask me the secret of the posters we'd done for R&B at Merrow Hall. After a little horse trading, Les Watts and I decided to go down and do them for him. Unfortunately, his milk float ran out of juice on the return journey. Les and I commuted back and forth for a while but when Squeeky and Fancy Forcey left to join the much busier Stormsville Shakers, the lure of free accommodation and a small income printing posters and helping run the Ricky-Tick clubs was too good to pass up."

"...designed quite a few fonts for Letraset..."

BOB McGRATH

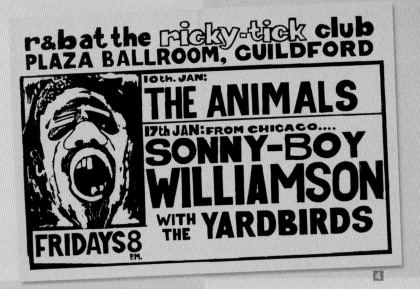

The free room at the venue wasn't exactly luxury, though, and Bob had to endure huge river rats "the size of small pigs" invading the rooms every now and then. But this would be the new home for what became to be known as the Ricky-Tick Posters company.

The club's own posters featured an eye-catching screaming black man's head design. "The screaming black face, which became pretty much the Ricky-Tick logo, I first used on that original R&B at Merrow Hall poster. I think I was inspired by Little Richard's first specialty album *Here's Little Richard*, but it could have been Big Joe Turner, who I was equally obsessed with at that time.

"As I mentioned earlier, I attended Farnham Art School but I did an overlapping day on Mondays at Guildford Art School for a typography course. We were shown the wonders of the Bauhaus design; everything Helvetica and grids, which I still love. Perhaps the loose font style on the posters was a backlash to this. Or more likely just the way the scalpel fell. There was a record shop in Guildford between the train station and the school that had loads of 45s imported from the States, a rare thing then. I think they shipped them as 'ballast' along with old magazines like *Mad* and *Cracked*, which I also devoured. Consequently my time at the typography course suffered with my hours spent hunting there. My time wasn't wasted though, as eventually I designed quite a few fonts for Letraset and other font houses."

Bob was kept busy with the fact that the Ricky-Tick Empire continued to grow. Apart from Windsor, John Mansfield and Philip Hayward managed to secure Ricky-Tick promotion nights at various venues, including Reading, Oxford, Guildford and Hounslow. These too, of course, needed posters. Bob hadn't left his music behind either.

"I formed another band in Windsor, which John managed, and he sent us all over the country – Newcastle, Sheffield, Manchester, Brighton, Cardiff, Swansea and tons of small towns, as well as a residency at the Ricky-Tick on Sundays and the Marquee on Oxford Street on Fridays either side of a live *Ready Steady* radio show. We made very little money but had a great time. I had Milton James on tenor-sax, who went with the Ram Jam Band after we broke up. Johnny Clayton on baritone and alto-sax – he went with Joe Cocker's band; Brian Chambers on guitar, Dave Brown on bass, Rod on keyboards and I'm afraid I've forgotten the drummer's name (maybe John), but I think he left to join The Pretty Things. We backed Larry Williams for his UK tour; sadly, when he recorded he used the Stormsville Shakers because ironically he preferred their/my ex-drummer, Fancy Forcey."

On his travels, McGrath got to meet and play with the best: "It's hard to believe I rubbed shoulders with so many of the greats: Rufus Thomas, Stevie Wonder, Smokey Robinson, Billy Stewart and John Lee Hooker, who we tried to use as a DJ one night in the little booth we had at that time, only to discover his excessive stutter. When I was touring with Larry Williams & Johnny 'Guitar' Watson in Wales, we were in Larry's hotel room in Cardiff, I think, and saw outside his window a street parade in his honour complete with huge 'Long Live Rock'n'Roll' banners. That night at his performance he told them to grow up and get with the times! He and Johnny were about to reinvent themselves as a soul act. The audience pretty much left and the jungle drums alerted the next date, Swansea I think, and nobody showed up at all there. Nice move Larry.

"When we were in Manchester, Larry was interviewed by the local newspaper and was asked how he liked his UK band. 'Oh man, they're baaaad!' The reporter not being hip to current black language wrote 'Larry Not Too Happy with his UK band'. It was so funny we couldn't be upset. Another time, Les and I were assigned as chaperones to Sonny Boy Williamson on his tour of the Ricky-Tick as he was, of course, a bit of a lush and somewhat unpredictable. One morning we went to collect him at his hotel room to find him missing. We panicked and combed the nearby streets. We eventually found him sitting on a 'stoop', playing his harp to a bunch of dancing little kids. Just think how things might have been if there was more of that. The English might have even learned to clap on the right beat."

1 The Who, Ricky-Tick Club, Guildford, 1965.
Silk-screened poster printed in house by the Ricky-Tick Club printing department.
2 Long John Baldry and Graham Bond Organisation, Ricky-Tick Club, Guildford, 1964.
Silk-screened poster printed in house.

Even though the band were gigging all over the UK, they'd rarely make enough to eat most weeks, so they relied on free accommodation at the Ricky-Tick and their income from making the posters.

"When we printed the posters at Clewer Mead we'd lay them side by side across the vast Victorian ballroom floor. Silk-screen printers use drying racks but this didn't occur to us. One guy would operate the squeegee, while another did laps around the dance floor, laying the posters in rows. Hard work, but we'd earn a little extra cash from this to supplement our meagre earnings on the road. I can't be sure of the quantities of the posters but I'm guessing maybe 200 was a regular amount, 500 for some custom orders, like a generic run for The Who, I seem to remember. How many per week? God! Can you remember how much you were producing 50 years ago? Maybe two or three different posters."

Among the people that helped keep Ricky-Tick Posters going was John Mansfield's younger brother, Colin. He was impressed by the production rate and how their posters ended up just about everywhere. "The great thing was that by having Bob and Les residing at the actual club it gave the Ricky-Tick a major advantage. If an agent such as Rik or Johnny Gunnell had had one of his artists cancelled at another venue with only a few days' notice, he'd ring us up and offer them to us at a reduced fee to keep them working. Because it was all handled in-house, they could have posters up advertising the gig 24 hours later. Bob was absolutely brilliant; those screaming Negro faces were such a powerful image. But it was also where they put the posters that really spread the word: they would end up fixed on to trees in Richmond Park! They would find closed shops or hoardings and would put loads next to each other in a block. With the black background and white lettering, it was just visual art. One great place they pasted them was on top of bus shelters so that people on the top deck of a double-decker bus could look down on them."

Bob McGrath smiles as he recounts those days. "I was just recalling the adventures we had when we were clandestinely pasting the posters up. It was, of course, not strictly legal and in fact Philip Hayward did appear at least once in court as a result of being caught in the act. He got off, as he hadn't actually placed the poster on the wall, or more likely snatched it off when he saw the cop. He pleaded to holding a bucket of glue in public and got off on a technicality."

Brian McCabe was impressed with McGrath's talent: "When either Colin or myself designed posters we would use a pencil to write out the lettering or design before cutting them out. Hogsnort [McGrath] would design the thing by cutting it all out freehand. He could cut it out and print it and have it ready for John Mansfield to paste up within a couple of hours. Of course, John was always getting caught putting the posters up. If ever a policeman took his name, John would always say he was Bill Stickers."

EVERYBODY GOES
TO THE DISCOTICK
EVERY SUNDAY 2'6
RICKY-TICK WINDSOR
A RICKY-TICK POSTER • WINDSOR 60/3

Because the Ricky-Tick events were held at various locations, the need for posters grew. Colin Mansfield explains just how they kept up with the demand: "There were two standard sizes of posters. There was Crown, which was 20in x 30in, and Double Crown, which was 30in x 40in. Previous posters were recycled. We did a calendar poster, which had all the events happening that month. There'd be a disco poster advertising Martin Fuggles and his DJ evenings. Then there would be one for individual groups or artists on a particular Friday, Saturday or whenever. All the posters had a heading that stated Ricky-Tick Windsor, or Hounslow or wherever, so that could be reused. So you maybe had a Georgie Fame poster that Hogsnort had done, where there was a profile of a face or silhouette with a bleached-out photo effect, where you've got no half tones. So then you'd have Georgie's face and the band name. You'd staple that on a piece of paper. You've got the heading already there from another poster. You'd staple those onto a blank sheet of paper and sketch in the layout of the other details – date, time, admission price, etc. You'd then staple the stencilled material on top, which is see-through. It's got two layers; a layer of shellac and a layer of a kind of wax paper underneath it. You'd then be ready to cut out your new stencil, taking care to only cut through the shellac layer. The sketched out details would be turned to full letters as you were cutting, which added to their unique, quirky appeal. So other people on our team could make the posters, but McGrath could take all credit for the concept and the way they were done. I learned how to make posters from him."

Bob can also can be cited with another brilliant idea to make money during this period.

"Later at the Ricky-Tick, we adopted this same printing process right onto T-shirts. I'd seen these printed shirts coming out of California, with Hot Rod designs, but I'm pretty sure we were the first in the UK to do it. Of course, pretty soon it was hard to find a T-shirt that didn't have something printed on it! Shame we couldn't copyright it. We sold the T-shirts in a room near the entrance, where Philip's girlfriend, Brenda, ran a little shop called the Bou-Tick. The word 'boutique' was very in at the time. Among other things, we bought in button-down shirts from the Wren Company in Connecticut. These were very rare at the time – only available (as far as I know) at the Ivy Shop in Richmond and the previously mentioned Austin's on Shaftesbury Avenue, where Georgie Fame and all the cool black modern jazz guys went. Ben Sherman had quite a success copying them."

❝ Previous posters were recycled. I learned how to make posters from him. ❞

COLIN MANSFIELD

Sadly, by 1965 the lease on the Clewer Mead house where the Windsor Ricky-Tick nights were held was coming to an end. During this period, Italian film director Michelangelo Antonioni had his heart set on featuring the club for a scene in his new film *Blow Up*, released in 1966. Although filming began at the club, the actual scene is confusing. The exterior shots were filmed outside the Marquee. The black walled corridor that actor David Hemmings walks through is the actual club, and shows some of McGrath's brilliant posters. The actual interior footage of the club, though, was a complete mock-up. Of course, Bob was involved in this too.

"After the Ricky-Tick closed its doors and my band broke up, I moved to Canada and made my living in advertising as an art director. Just before I left England, a lucky break came when, after searching for locations, the 'Tick was chosen as the location for the film *Blow Up*. However, by the time Michelangelo Antonioni had recovered from his bout of flu and returned from Italy where he'd been recuperating, the Ricky-Tick at Clewer Mead had closed to be demolished. As I was very much involved in the design of the original, I was hired to recreate the club at Elstree Film Studios. Since I was non-union they had to pay me as special consultant at three times the usual rate, which gave me enough money to move to Canada."

After the Ricky-Tick closed, Philip Hayward wanted to carry on in the entertainment world and moved on to a club called Pantiles in Camberley. John Mansfield, however, had decided on a new venture and got new premises at Oxford Street in Windsor. The L-shaped building, which had originally been called Wetherall's and had dealt in army surplus, was huge and on three levels. John, however, proceeded to set up a record shop downstairs, although after a year or so, he'd changed to dealing in old furniture and pianos. His brother Colin rented a room on the first floor in order to continue designing and printing. Bob McGrath's legacy lived on, as Colin carried on producing concert posters after McGrath had left to start a new life in Vancouver.

"I was very much involved in the design of the original..."

BOB McGRATH

1 DJ Martin Fuggles, Ricky-Tick Club, Windsor, 1965/66. Silk-screened poster printed in-house.

2 Impact Printing promotional poster, 1970. Silk-screened poster printed by Impact Printing of Windsor, which evolved out of the defunct Ricky-Tick printing department, which finished in late 1967.

Colin recalls: "I was going to go to art college when I left school but got involved helping John in his new ventures. In the end I didn't go and I started producing posters. I started on my own but was very soon joined by my cousin Brian McCabe, who'd just done his Pre Dip at High Wycombe Art College, a friend from school, John Luckie, and another friend, Nick Dunn. This was the start of Impact Printing.

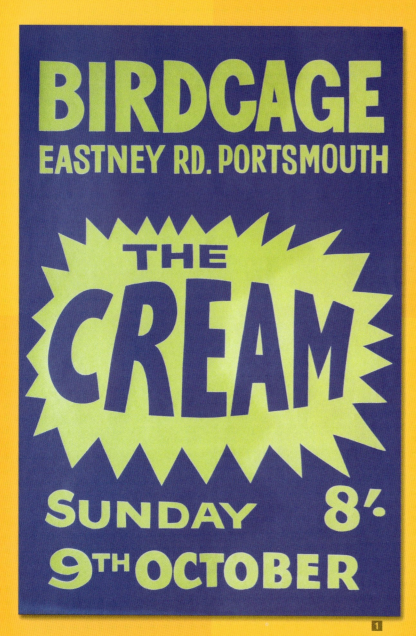

"...pushing boundaries
all the time."

BOB LEWIS

"The first thing we did was to improve the way we actually printed the posters. We built our own vacuum table to hold the sheets of paper while they were being printed. The screens had a quick-release bolt arrangement and they were counter-balanced so that when you lifted the screen, it stayed there! No more holding it up on your head! We made two stacks of racks, which allowed you to print unlimited quantities as long as you could get them dry quickly enough. Anyway, with the improvements we were able to produce much higher quality results and more accurate two- and three-colour prints. We still cut by hand for the next few years, and got bloody good at it. We could cut lettering as small as 5mm for IMPACT PRINTING WINDSOR 68379. Isn't it amazing, I can still remember our phone number 50 years on! We did posters for a lot of the people that the Ricky-Tick had supplied for, but also lots of new customers like universities and colleges, plus 'appearing here' posters for bands like Peter Green's Fleetwood Mac, John Mayall's Blues Breakers and Jethro Tull."

One legendary Mod club that secured the services of Impact was the Birdcage in Eastney, Portsmouth. Colin chuckled as he remembered the day that the club's manager Rikki Farr paid them a visit: "We were out in Windsor and all the agents were from London and were trying to get us to do their posters. We had a good reputation at the time but all these agents were like, 'Listen boys, do us a good turn and we can put a lot of work your way.' They always wanted to try and get you to do their stuff for nothing. They had all their spiel and thought we were bumpkins living out in the sticks.

"The building we were in was huge and on three levels. Our office where we did our designing was on the first floor. The thing is, you couldn't see it because halfway across that level was a kind of studwork wall and the room was full of junk furniture. Our entrance to the office actually had a wardrobe in front of the door. This was because my brother John was always playing practical jokes on us and would block up the entrance so we couldn't get out. We opened the door, which opened inwards, and there was a wardrobe without a back on it. So you had to walk through the wardrobe and open the door at the front to get out. We thought that was brilliant, so we got some packing trunks, put them on top, and screwed it back against the door to fix it there permanently, and that was our entrance. You had to step over the drawer at the bottom and went through the wardrobe to get in to our office!

"Anyway, one day Rikki Farr came down from London to meet us. As I said, the building was on three floors. Rikki asked somebody working downstairs where Impact Printing was and they just replied 'upstairs.' Well, we could hear him coming up the first flight of stairs, then the next, coming back down again and shouting 'Impact Printing?' We are in our office shouting 'Hello!' He does this about three or four times until somebody told him to walk through the wardrobe. He's got this folder-type case with him, and he's wearing a leather jacket with all the tassels, thinking he's THE MAN kind of thing. Anyway, he tripped up coming through the wardrobe and tipped his documents all over the floor. So all of his 'I'm Mr Cool' kind of thing had gone. We just sat there laughing and watching him pick all his stuff up."

Brian McCabe laughed about this too: "Impact Printing was on one of the upper floors of John Mansfield's junk shop. We opened the door to leave one evening and were faced with a wooden panel covering the doorway. Smashing through this, we discovered that John had placed a heavy Victorian wardrobe across the doorway. For a long time afterwards we would give directions to Impact starting with Queen Victoria's statue on Castle Hill pointing down Peascod Street and ending with going through the door of the third wardrobe on the left." The Birdcage Club could eventually boast some fantastically iconic posters, courtesy of Impact, although Colin remembers just how primitive the whole process actually was: "When I took over doing it I used to joke that we took up the level of technical development just a few decades after William Caxton. There used to be posters hung on strings across the room and you'd put a string up for the next poster and hang them all over it. You would push the printing press around because it was on wheels. You lifted the screen up and rested it on your head while you peeled the poster off. We took it from that to about the 18th century. We did end up a lot more modern with proper racks to hang the posters and doing photographic stencils. The rest of the world did photographic stencils while we were just hand-cutting. I would say we were probably the best hand-cut stencil people probably in the world at that time, because nobody else did it."

Bob Lewis joined Impact to learn the trade and got a three-month trial. He'd been a regular at the Ricky-Tick in his Mod days and had loved the posters. Bob remembers working while the music of The Yardbirds blasted out and says with admiration, "Colin Mansfield was the main designer and Brian McCabe was fantastic. I watched Brian working on this screen and it's got a bloody great blank space. I said to Brian, if you pour colour on that it will just come through. He said 'Watch this,' and dripped candlewax onto the nylon chiffon. I thought it would burn through and fuck it up but it didn't. When he printed over it, he had this weird pattern. The guy was pushing boundaries all the time. Colin and Brian were my teachers. They were great, show me anywhere that could teach you that fast."

While Bob appreciated the money, it wasn't always easy-going. "It was cash in hand. There was a promoter called Freddie Bannister who ran the Bath Festival. He'd have a big list of posters he wanted and we'd have a week to do them. We'd work 12-hour days for about a week. One poster roughly took eight hours from start to finish, but you were always working on other things so you never stopped. Most people wanted runs of a 100, apart from Bath Festival, who wanted at least 500 of everything. That was bloody murder. You'd get halfway through a screen print about 3 o'clock in the morning and the screen's going dry. We had this stuff called screen re-activator. Believe me, that stuff was lethal! You'd spray it to loosen up the screen but the fumes got to you and knocked you sideways!"

As Colin had mentioned the rest of the world was using photographic stencils and Impact would follow.

"We would get pictures from the *Melody Maker* or *NME*," McGrath said. "We'd cut them out and there was a bloke called Mick Redding in Maidenhead who would blow the pictures up. The guy projected the image onto a big screen and had a slop bucket full of chemicals that he'd wipe with a broom... When the image was enlarged you had all the dots. You've only got the two colours, black and white. So you'd maybe do it lemon yellow on dark green or lemon yellow on purple. You get a velvet paper and pick an ink that will go with it. After colours, the idea was to make an odd shape if you could because most posters were flat lines in one colour. So you did something weird with the colour to make it stand out. You had to make it look ridiculous on one level because people would be driving past it. All the advertising posters surrounding it would be flat, square with nothing going on. So you'd leave spaces. I remember talking to an art teacher at a North London poly. He asked me 'Why did you leave space there?' I said, because people will look at it and wonder why I left a space there. It draws attention to it."

McGrath worked at Impact for around nine months but became frustrated that he only got to print and not do his own designs, so he set up his own company called Argus Printing, in Slough. Although it was very successful, he remembers that the bottom fell out of the printing game when a guy called Les Watts, who had worked for Ricky-Tick Posters, set up a rival company, undercutting both Impact and Argus. By 1973, both companies no longer existed.

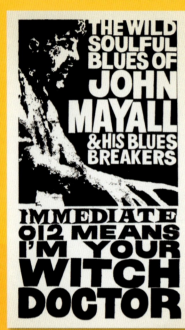

A ROUGH GUIDE TO 1960s POSTERS

Alexander Budnyj runs Briggs Rock and Pop Memorabilia in High Wycombe and Damian Jones runs Pop Classics in Reading. Both are leading experts on concert and promotional posters.

Alex: From the late fifties to the early sixties concert posters and promotional posters were generally of a simple boxing style design [lines of writing without images]. The first exponents of changing that sort of style, and it was probably done on the basis of cost, were the Ricky-Tick, who did these simplistic, almost crude silk screens. They'd sometimes use curtains as templates. Sometimes they'd use basic paints. The only exception, of course, was the Royal Academy of Art in London, which was doing fantastic posters and the artists tended to do them for exotic jazz concerts – Americans who had come over here, who most people hadn't heard of, and some of those designs are works of art in themselves. By late 1964/early 1965, you do see a period of student-designed silk screens used to advertise concerts for mainstream bands. The Moody Blues and The Yardbirds logos are very similar; it must have been the same person who designed both logos. You start to see bands' designs coming through on the posters. There's a poster I've got of The Who at the Royal College of Art, and it has an image of a cowboy and the word 'Pow!' It's one of the first examples I've ever seen of pop art with The Who. Because a lot of the concerts occurred in colleges and universities, students began using their own art departments to create the promotional posters.

So there's this interesting period between 1965 and 1967 where it's really experimental, and of course there's the end of 1966 where it becomes more psychedelic, which changes everything.

Damian: The Ricky-Tick was a cottage industry producing posters, and posters that they could sell as well as use for advertising. The colleges weren't doing it for a profit but the Ricky-Tick was a commercial business. Obviously there was a demand for it, but it wasn't initially set out that way. It was just that people were nicking the posters, so they'd overprint a run and sell them off.

1 John Mayall poster designed for the Gunnell Agency, 1965.
Designed and printed by the Ricky-Tick in-house printing department.
2 Sounds of '66 night, independent production, 1966.
Printed by the Ricky-Tick in-house printing department.
3 The Who at the Roundhouse for an LSE benefit, 1969.
4 This poster was once behind the bar of the famous Mothers Club in Birmingham during 1968.
Most of the Mothers Club posters could be purchased during concerts.
Silk-screened poster printed in-house by the Mothers Club printing department.
5 T-Bones, Chelsea College, 1965. Designed by Chelsea College art department.

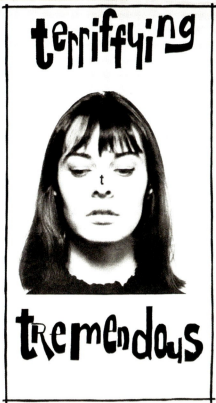

Alex: At the time, universities and colleges were government-subsidised so they could get bigger bands in, and it didn't really matter if they broke even, and that went on until about 1973. The Labour government brought [subsidies for providing entertainment for students] in, but they also finished it, which is a sad thing because you may well have ended up seeing The Who, Led Zeppelin, Pink Floyd or pretty much any big band of the time, except for The Beatles, who'd given up touring, at a university gig. Even the Stones were still doing one or two universities in the early seventies.

Alex: As far as European posters go, Günther Kieser was probably the finest exponent of posters at that time. What is strange is that nobody ever really copied his style. The way they were printed, compared with British posters; it was far ahead of the game. They were proper litho posters and not basic screen prints. Everybody else in Europe, though, was very basic.

Damian: What you have to remember is that collecting sixties posters is a very niche market, whatever the genre – be it Mod bands, soul bands, or whatever. Anybody who dips their toe in it gets very paranoid about if they've got an original or not, so posters that should sell for good money often don't. The people who collect the high-end bands, usually collectors overseas who want things like The Who, The Rolling Stones,

Pink Floyd, Led Zeppelin, The Beatles and the big bands, don't start collecting the lower league bands. There are people with curio interest who may pay £20 to £50 but they'll never pay big money. The only people who like them are people interested in the history. The most expensive posters aren't necessarily the rarest or the best, they just feature the biggest bands.

Alex: There are posters out there that you might only see one of, but it's worth £20, whereas you get one for a big band and it could be worth a fortune. If money wasn't involved, my favourite type to own would be those college posters from about 1965 to around 1968. Sometimes you've got bands like The Temperance Seven and then a great Mod band like The Action or something.

Alex: The most interesting posters tend to be the ones of bands from that period that you've never seen before and it's been designed by a student at a college or university gig, and he's just trying to display his talent as a designer, and he's silk screened something and put in a lot of effort to do it.

Damian: If somebody found 30 to 40 of a big-name poster in a pile the price would diminish. It's supply and demand: a poster previously worth £8,000 might only be worth a grand. There's a case in point of The Who at Torquay. If there was one of them it would be a £5,000 or £6,000 poster, but there's loads so it's worth £400–£500. High-end collectors want it to be the only one.

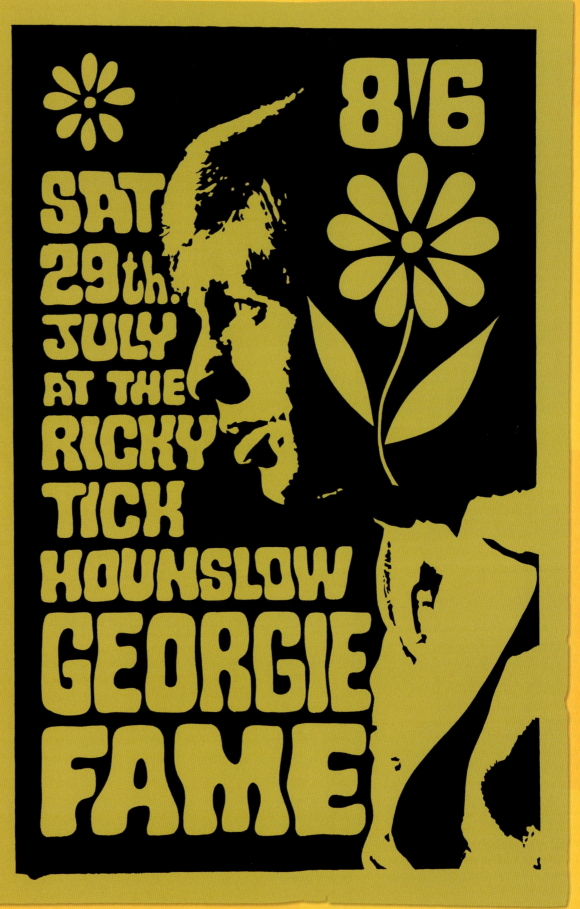

Alex: In terms of value, to make a poster valuable, that band must have been big in the USA. For example, The Kinks and the Small Faces: you can find a great poster for them, but nobody cares in the USA. History has not been kind to them. There are some American acts that did gigs in the UK whose posters are a worth a bit from a collector's completist point of view. Aretha Franklin, when she came over here in the sixties – we've had flyers but never seen a poster for [gigs]. That's because a lot of those American artists did very few gigs over here during that period. Janis Joplin did one gig over here in the sixties at the Royal Albert Hall, supported by Yes. That one is worth a lot of money. Rare, big-name posters can go for anything from £2,000 to £10,000, but it depends how many are out there.

1 Georgie Fame, Ricky-Tick Club, Hounslow, 1967. Silk-screen print designed by Bob Lewis.
2 Led Zeppelin, Canterbury College, 1971. Poster designed by Dave Arnott at Screendream Print of Redhill. Dave Arnott's work is recognisable by the hand-cut font that was unique to him. 'Danke Baedeker' is a tongue-in-cheek reference to Hitler's use of the Baedeker guides to plot raids on towns and cities of cultural and historical importance. In the 1960s and 70s the use of Hitler in this context was not unusual as he was considered a 'joke' figure. While not connected to Mods, it exemplifies 1970s pop art and shock tactics long before punk came along.
3 Led Zeppelin merchandise poster, sold at the concert, rather than a promotional one. Designed by Impact Printing in 1972, with a clear evolvement in quality from the Ricky-Tick posters.
4 Jimmy Powell and Chris Farlowe, Chelsea College, 1964. Designed by Chelsea College art department.

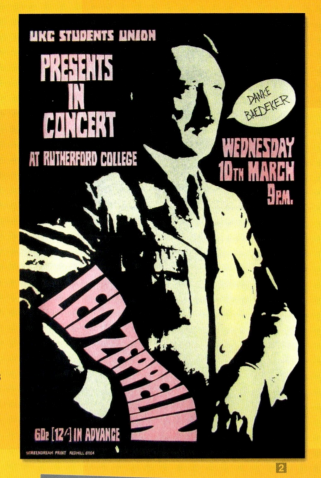

BARNEY BUBBLES AND THE ART SCHOOL CONNECTION

" He was a really buzzing bloke... People used to gravitate towards him... "

NICK TWEDDELL

1 The Muleskinners.
2 Blow boy blow! Nick Tweddell on the harp.

Twickenham Technical College (now Richmond upon Thames College) on Egerton Road was built in the 1930s' British-modern style. The corridors and the classrooms were all laid out in a kind of grid pattern and painted green and cream, divided by a tan stripe. In the art department, all the lockers were on the same floor, down a big corridor, and this would prove to be a meeting places for students catching up between classes to chat and arrange their social lives. The chat usually revolved around art and music. Their social lives usually revolved around the pubs in Twickenham.

One group of students spent their days by the river or at Eel Pie Island, which was a wonderful old, decadent, ruined hotel. Sketch books at the ready, the beauty of the surroundings captured on paper. Their evenings a mixture of laughter, drawing, drinking, playing guitars or strumming banjos, usually at their favourite haunt the Albany pub in Queen's Road, Twickenham.

Pete Brown, Ian McLagan, Nick Tweddell, Mick 'Chippy' Carpenter and Dave Pether were all united by a common factor. They were The Muleskinners, and they preached the blues to all who would listen. Regular disciples in the crowd on most nights were David Hills, Roy Burge and Colin Fulcher.

Fulcher was cool: he was a Mod, a talented artist and he sure loved the blues.

Nick Tweddell, The Muleskinners' harmonica player, recalls: "We were all in different groups at the time. Colin Fulcher was a year above us and Mac [Ian McLagan] was a year below. It was a four-year course so we were split up by time and groups. When I went there I was more of an illustrator. I wanted to be a painter but I got stuck in the graphics group simply, I guess, because there were fewer in that group. You didn't get a choice, it was ridiculous. So when Pete, Colin, Dave and myself got together it was through the music and through the pubs. Chippy wasn't at art school. He was an engineer and had his own business and I really didn't meet him until The Muleskinners got together really. We hooked up with Colin really because we shared similar interests and because he was a year above us, we sort of looked up to him a bit. He was a really buzzing bloke, and like a little whirlwind. People used to gravitate towards him because he was spinning, if you know what I mean."

Fulcher was in fact a very shy and introverted guy but he managed to cover that up with his love of clothes and by being a bit of an exhibitionist. His creativity came out through various forms of art, including photography and film making. His group of friends would get starring roles as he made flickering 8mm films of cowboys and gunfighters somewhere in the countryside.

Tweddell: "The odd thing about art school in those days, Twickenham Art School, was that it was partly a 19th century art school so we did drawing from plaster casts. They had a cast room there like the V&A. We had a full-size statue of the *Venus de Milo* in plaster of Paris and you'd be in there for hours doing minute drawings of an ear or a hand. So it was a classic art school but it was also a technical college, so we did painting – oil painting, life painting – but also more technical things like litho, printing and all those things on the graphic side of it. So it was a weird mix. It didn't know if it was an art school or a technical college.

"These days with computers and things, you can put your ideas down on paper really quickly, but in those days it was a pretty slow and laborious process and everything was done by hand. You had to be quite neat and tidy. Colin, for all his kind of weirdness, was very neat and precise. He was very good at lettering by hand. One of Colin's favourite techniques was like a splattered spotty effect with paint. He used to use a toothbrush, mask off sections and flick the paint on. We all did it, it was kind of 1930s litho with spattering to get half tones.

"What made Colin what he was, in part, was this love of music, which went hand in hand with the whole art thing. To be honest, I don't think we saw a difference between it. Whether we were sitting down playing our guitars and singing or doing a bit of sketching or drawing, it all amounted to making stuff. That was the weird thing about the sixties, is that it all came together. There was a whole ring of art schools around London at that time: Twickenham, Ealing, Highgate, Kingston, and then of course the Royal College and the Slade. The people at these places were liking music, they were liking trad. and folk. It gave you that freedom, that elbow room, not just to be sitting in a classroom but to be mixing, talking about art and music. They encouraged you at art school to think creatively about everything."

In 1965, Fulcher won the British Poster Design Award in the double/four-sheet category with a poster he'd made for The Muleskinners. The stunning poster features fellow student Lorry Sartorio in a photo taken at Fulcher's home in Whitton, Middlesex, around July 1964. In the photo, Lorry is wearing a denim jacket and a white T-shirt, onto which Fulcher has applied dry transfer lettering that spells out the phrase "Them Muleskinners. Knockout R&B Here Tonight," accompanied by a Mod target with a heart at its centre.

2

Tweddell: "He would have used a photocopier and put a photo in and made it very over-exposed to burn out the image, so it was almost just black on white. Posters were often pretty crummy then. In those days, a lot of bands just sent venues a general poster and wrote on it 'appearing here Saturday night' or whatever. But we thought that was a bit uncool, so we just had this poster made up with 'Them Muleskinners. Knockout R&B Here Tonight.' I had a big stack of them under my bed. I think they were screen printed, and they were big because they were A3. They were all wrapped up in brown paper so he'd definitely had them printed somewhere. We certainly didn't pay him for designing them because we were all mates. We must have dished out thousands of them, but sadly it seems there's only that tatty one remaining."

By 1965, Fulcher was a senior graphic designer for the Conran Group. It was also during this period that he organised happenings, parties and other events under the name A1 Good Guyz with his two friends from art school, David Wills and Roy Burge, while they were living at Leigh Court in London.

In 1967, Fulcher adopted the name 'Barney Bubbles,' because he was operating a light show that created a bubble effect by mixing oils and water on 35mm projection slides. Travelling in a psychedelically painted ice cream van to various underground locations, Fulcher's lightshows were for groups including The Gun, at venues including the Roundhouse, Jim Haynes' Drury Lane Arts Lab, the Electric Cinema and Middle Earth.

"In 1967, I was up there one day and we were all into Indian mysticism then, especially me, and I'd written this song called 'I Am The Maker Of All Things.' Richard Neville was up at the flat because Colin was working for *Oz* magazine [Oz was an underground alternative magazine first published in 1963 in Sydney] I was singing this song and it was all a bit druggie, Indian-y. He said we should record it, and at the time flexi discs were just appearing but he thought it would be a great idea to do an *Oz* magazine based around this record. We recorded it and he paid the money for it. As far as I know, all the flexi discs were pressed but nobody had ever released a recording in a magazine. It was covering new ground and you had to have special licences to do it. Most of The Muleskinners were there and Martin Sharp, who did a lot of artwork for *Oz*, and he played the bongos and was meant to be on the record, but he never turned up so Chippy played drums on it in the end. Colin took loads of photos but I don't know whatever happened to them."

Bubbles and Wills art-directed *Oz* magazine Issue 12, dubbed *The Tax Dodge Special* and published in May 1968. Also in 1968, Ian McLagan (who had gone on to a successful career with the Small Faces) would invite Nick Tweddell and Pete Brown of The Muleskinners to help design the inside sleeve for the Small Faces' *Ogdens' Nut Gone Flake*.

Tweddell: "We still used to see Mac a bit but not as much because he was off out and about with the Small Faces. He had a flat at some point up off Kensington High Street. He was living there on his own but the other Small Faces used to pop in. Pete and I were still living at Kew Gardens in '68.

"I was working for the BBC as a scene painter because they still used painted scenery back then. Pete was doing graphics and I think he was working at a studio in Putney. Mac got in touch with us and said he wanted this piece of artwork doing for their new album. Pete did a lot of the work, he did the painted layout of it. I did the black and white drawing, which was cut in half. That drawing was made up of little tiny dots and it took me a while. I designed the arch-type shapes around it and the colours based on an Edwardian style by the likes of Alphonse Mucha, who also did posters back then. Well, those were the shapes we were using and that sort of look.

"We didn't get paid... ...we didn't want money."

NICK TWEDDELL

"I also collected these Victorian scraps, sheets of flowers and butterflies. During the Victorian era they used to cut shapes out and put them on screens. They were really beautiful things and quite hard to get. They were stone litho, printed on these sheets and punched out. I had quite a collection of them. Pete did those coloured circles, it wasn't a rainbow but that kind of thing. He also did the guy smoking a dodgy pipe. That was the only part of the album we designed – I have no idea who created the rest of it. I know that Mac said they were going to visit a tobacco company and look through their archives of tobacco labels. It was obviously a spliff tin of tobacco but I think the original was called 'Ogdens' Nut Brown Flake'. I guess they gave that to a technical illustrator who redid it, and it is beautiful artwork. We didn't get paid, but then we didn't want money. We did it for Mac."

Bubbles' later work would include designing Hawkwind LP covers, among many others, often while avoiding credit for his work or adopting pseudonyms. By 1977, he had joined Stiff Records as designer and art director and would work on sleeves for The Damned, Elvis Costello and Ian Dury. He also directed several music videos including The Specials' 'Ghost Town,' Squeeze's 'Is That Love' and Fun Boy Three's 'The Lunatics (Have Taken Over the Asylum).'

Sadly, Barney Bubbles committed suicide in November 1983 by gassing himself, trapping the fumes in a plastic bag he had placed over his head. He had suffered from bipolar disorder and depression, and was having severe financial worries.

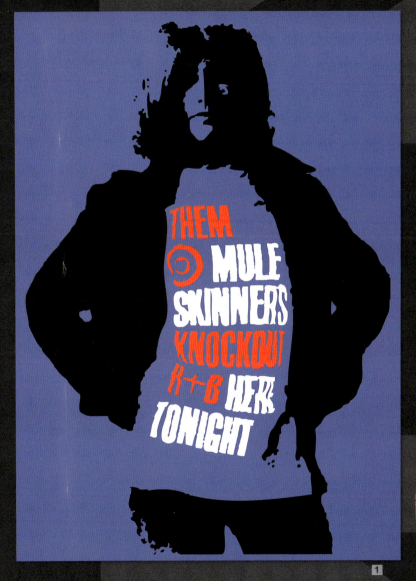

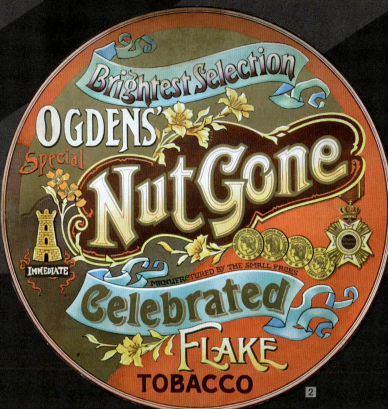

1 As originals are rare and ripped, Nick Twedell has made an exact replica of Barney's famous Muleskinner picture.

2 Front cover of *Ogdens'* LP.

3 Inner sleeve of *Ogdens'* LP.

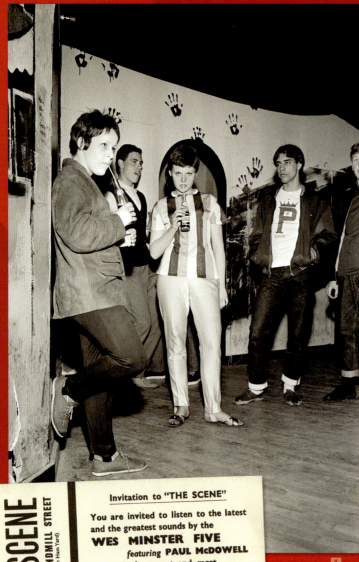

THE ART OF
THE MOJO CLUB

❝ This is the New Scene... ❞

ANDY ELLISON

Beautiful MOJO club

One thing that made clubs in the sixties individual was the way that they were decorated. The Scene Club in Ham Yard was famously painted all-black — jet-black walls meant the focus was then given over to the music. Later in the club's life, when it re-opened as the New Scene club, Andy Ellison of the band John's Children had transformed it. Ellison remembers: "I painted the Scene Club with a guy called Martin Sheller. Martin was the King Mod from the East End and he'd been to the Sir John Cass Art College with our drummer, Chris Townson. So Martin became the harmonica player in our first band, The Few, and he later found fame as lead singer in The Regents, who had a hit with 'Seventeen' in 1979. Anyway, we got the job to paint the club all white, both inside and outside. And I remember daubing in black writing just by the door 'This is the New Scene babe.'"

The Flamingo, too, changed its interior in 1967 when it was 'hippiefied,' becoming the Pink Flamingo.

Clubs such as the Birdcage often had their interiors decorated with pop art-type slogans. One club that took this style to another level was the King Mojo in Sheffield, which could claim some great artists among its regulars. In fact, the first mural to appear at the King Mojo was from Mojo Club owner himself Peter Stringfellow, who created a design of African warriors with mirrors for eyes that reflected the club lights, creating wonderful effects.

Later it was club members themselves, Paul Norton and Dave Senior, who would go on to paint the walls of the club with some great pop art and 1920s gangster murals.

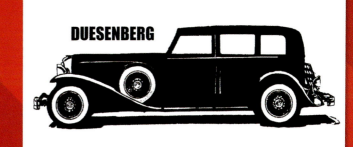

KING
MOJO
CLUB
(SHEFFIELD)

Telephone 23516

MEMBERS No. 1129

Name DAVE MANVELL

Date Joined 26 AUG 1967

Date Expires 31st AUGUST, 1968

Members must conform to the rules as displayed on the club premises.

Phone Sheffield 23516

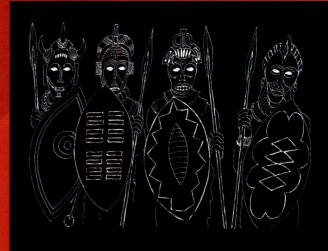

1 The Scene Club, Soho, May 1964.
2 Murals inside the Mojo. All work by Dave Senior.
3 The first mural at the Mojo was by Peter Stringfellow.

SMASHING FUN: HOW THE WHO INCORPORATED ART AND MUSIC

> **"...Mod thing is dying. "**
>
> PETE TOWNSHEND

1 Pete Townshend in action. Destruction in the name of art, or just fun?

As the heat appears more intense, the noise becomes almost deafening. Condensation drips off the ceiling and runs down the nicotine-stained walls. The pink light bulb dimly captures the action on stage. Roger Daltrey's voice wails and spits out venomous lyrics, as Pete Townshend swoops over the audience with arms held out, going through his 'Birdman' routine. He then scrapes his guitar against the mic stand, the strings howling in protest as the audience gazes on. Suddenly the guitar is violently thrust upwards and the air is filled with a heavy buzzing noise. The head of the guitar has punctured the low ceiling, and as Townshend pulls it downwards the shattered guitar head reveals itself. The mutilated equipment is then thrust upwards over and over again as the splintered mess whines out distortion. The instrument is bounced around on the stage before finally being thrown to the floor. Townshend then casually picks up a newly acquired 12-string guitar and continues to play.

This was the scene witnessed at the Railway Hotel in Harrow on the evening of September 8, 1964. The club had a fantastic atmosphere; the windows were blacked out, the radiators were turned up and it was dark and smoky, the area lit by only two pink light bulbs and the stage itself made up of old beer crates. The crowd, though, were young, hip and outrageously Mod.

The event is historic, as it was the first time The High Numbers had performed the destructive stage act, something they would become famous for in later years.

The Railway Hotel evenings had started out as R&B nights promoted by Richard Barnes and Lionel Gibbins. The High Numbers began their 12-week residency at the end of June that year and had only recently recorded their first single 'Zoot Suit'/'I'm The Face.'

That fateful evening in early September, Townshend had never imagined that the Rickenbacker 360 that had cost him £169 at Jim Marshall's shop would eventually end up a smashed wreck, lying on the stage. The whole thing had been an accident, with Townshend fooling the audience into thinking it was intended stage performance. When the audience returned the following week full of expectancy, they were disappointed.

In fact, the concept of guitar destruction was put on hold until an evening the following year. By now, The High Numbers had reverted back to their earlier name of The Who. Kit Lambert and Chris Stamp were now managing the boys, and were looking for a new promotional angle.

On April 8, 1965, the band found itself in Reading, Berkshire. The Olympia Ballroom in London Street was familiar territory, since they had played there three times previously as The High Numbers, as part of Leo De Clerck's 'Leo's Cavern' nights. They had also played there once as The Who. The band's new single, 'I Can't Explain,' was riding high in the charts. Kit Lambert had invited Virginia Ironside, a writer for the *Daily Mail*, and writer Nik Cohn along to witness the band in action. He had already asked Townshend to destroy his guitar during the routine in order to impress the writers and drum up some publicity. Townshend obliged and duly smashed his guitar, closely followed by Keith Moon, who smashed his drum kit. Sadly, Kit and the journalists were delayed at the bar and ended up missing the act of wanton destruction. On finding out that his orders had actually been carried out, Lambert was naturally horrified. It was 1966 before The Who made instrument destruction a regular part of their show.

Over the years, Townshend has given various reasons for destroying his guitars on stage. At times he has said it was intended as an artistic performance, auto-destructive art. This may partly be true, as Townshend did study at Ealing Art College and attended classes hosted by Gustav Metzger, who developed the concept.

Townshend and his guitar would feature on one of the most iconic posters of the 1960s, the famous 'Maximum R&B' series, which were made to advertise the band's 16-week residency on a Tuesday night at the Marquee, starting on November 24, 1964. A friend of Townshend's, Brian Pike, had the fantastic idea to add a giant arrow stretching upwards from the 'O' in 'Who.'

Siggy Jackson was in charge of the promotion for the Marquee back then and had granted The Who a chance by giving them a gig on Tuesdays, which was a notoriously dead night. Kit Lambert and Chris Stamp were determined to beat the Tuesday night stigma, and so had 15,000 posters put up around London. Around that time there was a notorious practice of 'fly mean' covering up or tearing down promotional posters, unless you paid them in a kind of protection racket. Therefore, £10 was duly paid and the posters remained intact.

The first night was poorly attended but by the third week the Marquee was packed, and soon the Tuesday night was the most popular event at the club.

"We think the Mod thing is dying. We don't plan to go down with it, which is why we've become individualists," Pete Townshend told *Melody Maker* in the June 5, 1965 edition. "Pop art is something society accepts, but we represent it to them in a different form. Like Union Jacks. They're supposed to be flown. John [Entwistle] wears one as a jacket." In the same interview they describe their new single 'Anyway, Anyhow, Anywhere' as the first pop art single.

Townshend had in fact decorated his flat in Chesham Place with pop art pictures torn out of a book stolen from his art school. Kit Lambert had noticed them and encouraged Pete to use them. The band having already draped Union Jack flags over speakers, somebody then came up with the outrageous idea of making a jacket out of one of the flags. Townshend wore this on stage, while John Entwistle went on to have a jacket constructed out of the Royal Standard. If that wasn't enough to rock the establishment, the band also began wearing military medals and insignia.

In the *Melody Maker* issue dated July 3, 1965, Pete Townshend gives an account of his feelings in a feature entitled 'Well, What Is Pop Art?' when he is quoted as saying, "We stand for pop art clothes, pop art music and pop art behaviour. This is what everybody seems to forget – we don't change off stage. We live pop art."

Townshend often mentioned Peter Blake as a huge influence during this period. Peter Blake recalls: "I first met Pete Townshend at *Ready Steady Go!*. I was there for some other reason and they were sitting in the foyer, so we sat and talked. I think their look was very specific at the time. I think he would have had a genuine interest in art anyway, which would have included pop art. The actual pop art direct influence would be because the two managers [Lambert and Stamp] actually had picked up on it and decided they wanted a change in the look of The Who. They called them the pop art band and obviously went through books, pulling out particular motifs, so things like wearing badges, the Union Jack and targets, and they would have found some of that in what I was painting at the time."

**❝ We stand for pop art clothes...
We live pop art. ❞**

PETE TOWNSHEND

1 Pete Townshend in his London home, 1967.
2 The Who in their medals and symbols, 1966.

Paul Weller, who would later state that hearing 'My Generation' by The Who was the inspiration for him becoming a Mod: "My interest in pop art probably came from The Who, through their graphics or their clothes at the time, and through my love of the sixties. I like the concept that you can take ordinary everyday things and put them in a different place or environment so they become something else and you see them differently. I can see links between that and a lot of music as well, in terms of lyrics. Townshend did it, and I suppose Ray Davies to some extent. I definitely did, but yet again, copying from those two writers."

In June 1967, The Who found themselves on their first tour of North America. The Mod image was long gone but the destruction was still there. The biggest test to them winning over the American audience was when they were booked to appear on the final night of the Monterey International Pop Music Festival in front of a capacity audience. Also joining them on the bill that night was Jimi Hendrix. The band were no strangers to Hendrix, who had in fact supported them in January that year at a tribute concert for Brian Epstein at the Saville Theatre, London. That night Hendrix had gone on first and during his last number smashed the amplifiers up. Townshend was quoted as saying "he blew us away." The Who were determined not to be outdone during this crucial concert in Monterey, and Townshend and Hendrix were involved in an argument over who was going on first, as neither wanted to follow the other's act. In the end a flip of a coin was left to decide their fate. The Who won and went on first.

The final tune in their set was a ferociously paced version of 'My Generation' which as it came to an end, saw Townshend ramming the guitar against the mic stand and speakers before fully smashing the guitar to pieces on the floor. With smoke canisters helping shroud the stage, the band exited, leaving only Moon to kick over the drum kit. Hendrix would need to pull off a mighty impressive show to top that. And he was about to rise to the occasion. During his performance of 'Hey Joe,' he played his guitar with his teeth and behind his head. It was during the end of his cover of 'Wild Thing' that he really went to town, though. Dropping to his knees with the guitar laid in front of him, Hendrix writhed in a simulated sexual frenzy before squirting lighter fuel over the instrument like some rabid ejaculation. Then, after gently kissing the guitar, he proceeded to light a match, before the instrument bursts into flames. He then picked it up and violently smashed it against the stage floor, leaving the air filled with feedback.

The Who returned to London but in July, 'Pictures Of Lily' entered the US singles chart and the band returned to the USA. On July 7, they played the Malibu Beach and Shore Club, in Lido Beach, New York, at the beginning of dates prior to joining Herman's Hermits on tour across the USA and Canada. It was during this period that Keith Moon would enter an even more destructive stage and unveil his new pride and joy, a drum kit that became known as his 'Pictures Of Lily' kit.

"...'Keith Moon Patent British Exploding Drummer'..."

JEFF HURST

The drum kit started life in the mid-sixties, when Premier Drum's advertising manager commissioned their advertising agency, Cunningham Hurst Limted, to design a special kit for Moon. Their latest hit was 'Pictures Of Lily,' and it was agreed that a 'picture' of 'Lily' would somehow feature in the drum kit design.

Jeff Hurst, the owner and creative director of the agency, undertook the job himself, thinking it would be fun: "I came up with the phrase 'Keith Moon Patent British Exploding Drummer,' having been to a couple of Who concerts and watched Keith's antics on stage, and so I made it a major feature of the design. At the time there was a wave of quite odd art and design coming from the West Coast of the US, mainly from San Francisco. I then drew all the panels for one drum, and got Keith to come and give his reaction to it. To quote him in *Beat Instrumental* magazine: 'It's a knockout!'

"Work then started on producing the entire kit, which was highly work intensive. I started on the drawings for all the different drum sizes and then it was all reproduced on line film and laid over the fluorescent colours in each place, which is how this fantastic colour effect came out. I even gave Keith a pair of fluorescent drumsticks, which looked great when he used them. We also had six T-shirts made, one each for the boys, one for the chairman [of Premier] and one for me."

The kit was delivered to the agency where each drum had to be carefully dismantled in order to install the new decorative panels. Keith and his roadie came along to help, and at last the drums were all ready. By now, even the chairman of Premier, Mr Fred Della-Porta, came along to see it.

Keith then got the three other members of the group to come and have a look at his new "engine" (his word). Jeff has a very vivid memory of the day The Who pulled up outside his agency in Paddington Street.

"The four of them came in a Rolls Royce. Left outside, bumped up on the pavement because there's no parking. Along came a lady traffic warden, and starts writing out a ticket. I can't remember which one of The Who it was, but one of them, it wasn't Keith, ran downstairs, opened the boot of the car, took out a smoke bomb, struck it and stuck it underneath the car and came back up. Our offices overlooked what was going on. All of a sudden this smoke starts billowing out from under the car. The warden was alarmed and rushes into a newsagents next door and phones the police. So they and the fire brigade all arrive and block the road off. So I told the guys it looked like they were in serious trouble. They said 'Don't worry about it. We'll come and get the car tomorrow. Where's your fire escape?'

"So they legged it down there – it went down to Nottingham Place, which was next door, then legged it up to Marylebone Road to hail a taxi home. They just abandoned the car outside and obviously it got towed away."

The band had seemed impressed with Jeff's designs, although he believes that Townshend wasn't so endeared to the new band logo. Pete Townshend, whose own logo was not featured in the designs, confessed in the end, "Yeah, they're OK."

The drums weren't the only new addition to the US and Canadian gigs. While the band were in Georgia, they found a firework shop and decided to stock up on smoke bombs. It was here that Moon discovered the fireworks known as 'Cherry Bombs' (a small explosive that was much more powerful than the English version, 'Bangers'). From that moment no hotel toilet was safe as Moon left a trail of Cherry Bomb-shaped destruction in his wake.

With the band licking their wounds after Hendrix upstaged them at Monterey, they were intent to pull out the stops when they were invited to perform on *The Smothers Brothers Comedy Hour* on September 15. Filmed at the CBS TV Studios, Los Angeles, the show would be transmitted two days later. Unbeknown to the rest of the band Moon had bribed the pyrotechnic guy to load more Cherry Bombs in his bass drum. At the climax of 'My Generation,' the explosion was so fierce that it caused a momentary breakdown in transmission. In the ensuing chaos, Moon was left with a piece of cymbal shrapnel in his arm and Townshend's hair was singed. The drums did, however, survive enough to be used until late 1968.

Distressingly, Jeff Hurst never kept the original design drawings, which would be worth a small fortune now. He didn't really make that much money at the time either but he has no regrets. "Sadly, I didn't formally copyright, and Premier have reproduced many kits with my designs on them. We always charged our clients for artwork, photography and typesetting for advertisements, but we only charged for the production of the drum and not for the design work. We probably got it all produced for around £1,000, but I had great fun doing it, so now I just say 'sod it.' Anyway, the kit didn't last long as a kit because Keith wasn't exactly gentle with it while touring the States. Later he got rid of it entirely and, I believe, had a completely chromium kit from Premier."

"Jeff kept in touch for a while, but lost the account to a smaller agency, mainly because we could not continue to spend as much time on the account because the agency began to get very large clients such as Honda UK."

In later years, Townshend would blame the 'Smothers Brothers incident' for leaving him deaf in one ear. Meanwhile, Keith Moon's practice of blowing up toilets with explosives led to him being banned from several hotel chains around the world for life, including all Holiday Inn, Sheraton, and Hilton hotels.

1 Jeff Hurst goes through the designs with Keith Moon. **2** One of Pete Townshend's many destroyed guitars.

"Oh Christ, not another target!"

THE MOD TARGET

"...the iconic motif of The Who."

THERESA KERR

1 Jasper Johns.
2 *Target With Four Faces*, Jasper Johns, 1955.

"Oh Christ, not another target!" are the oft-said words tumbling out of Mods' mouths the world over, as the target has become *the* cliché symbol for all things Mod... or not Mod, depending on your view.

The dartboard-style icon began to be associated with the Mod culture in the 1960s, mainly through the fact that Keith Moon had worn one on his top in various photo shoots and during a *Ready Steady Go!* performance in 1965. It certainly gained a bigger amount of attention during the 1979 Mod Revival, as an easy way to announce your affiliation with the movement of Mod.

Theresa Kerr was running the boutique Hem and Fringe with her husband, Patrick, in a shop in Moreton Street, Pimlico: "I made up the designs, and I don't remember how it happened but Pete Townshend's wife, Karen, worked for us as a machinist, so of course The Who used to come in. We had a young designer called Michael English and he designed the targets for The Who. We printed the T-shirts with the targets for the band and they became the symbol, the iconic motif of The Who."

The actual target, or roundel, was of course nothing new, and had been featured in heraldry and coats of arms since at least the 12th century. During the First World War, the French Air Force introduced the red, white and blue roundel on their aeroplanes to prevent their own troops shooting each other. During August 1914, the British attempted to use the Union Jack design on its planes but from a distance it could easily be mistaken for the German Iron Cross symbol. So, in December, the Royal Flying Corps (which would later become the Royal Air Force) adopted the French-designed roundel, simply reversing the colours.

Various artists have been associated with using the roundel or target in their art, from the 1930s designs of Ukrainian-born French artist Sonia Delaunay to the English abstract painter Sir Terry Frost. More commonly, American artist Jasper Johns is linked to the icon, through his pieces such as 1955's *Target With Four Faces*, which show the familiar target with visible brush-strokes loosely applied and four women's faces in plaster cast.

During Peter Blake's period as a teacher at St Martin's School of Art, he produced *The First Real Target* in 1961. In this piece, Blake took Jasper Johns idea even further when he purchased a Slazenger real archery target from a sports shop. Using acrylics and painting without obvious brush strokes, the item appears far more 'real.' The painting is often seen as a witty swipe at the question of originality, with reference to the work of Jasper Johns and artists like Kenneth Noland.

Blake: "I think what I was doing really was because a lot of abstract artists were using that symbol but nobody actually called it a target. They all said it was a circular motif or used different wording, and they were all obviously painted. I thought, what I'll do is just buy a target and call it *The First Real Target*. In a way it was an actual target but it was also a comment on the fact that nobody had admitted it was a target."

It was through the use of pop art that bands such as The Who became associated with the symbol and yet Peter Meaden, the man responsible for originally getting The Who involved with the Mod scene, famously insisted that pop art was nothing to do with the Mod scene and that the band had sold out at this point. Whichever way you see it, it cannot be denied that the red, white and blue roundel target has become synonymous with the Mod movement. It certainly provides various brands trying to sell their wares with an obvious focal point.

1 Keith Moon, pop art icon.
2 The Artwoods LP, Decca, 1966.
3 *The First Real Target*, Peter Blake, 1961.

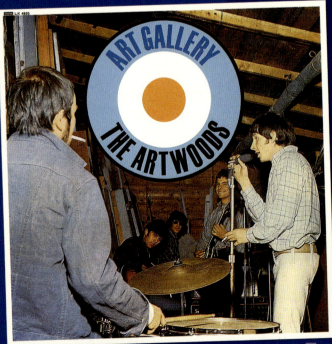

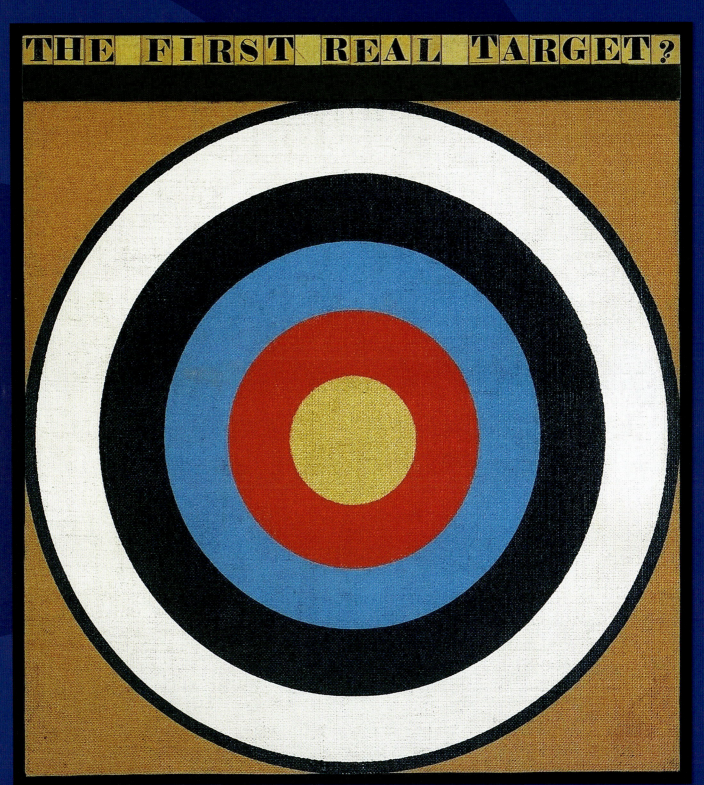

1 *Triptych*, Sonia Delaunay, 1963.
2 Film poster for *Quadrophenia*, 1979.

THE 1970s AND THE BIRTH OF *QUADROPHENIA*

> ❝There was no musical heritage at home.❞
>
> BRETT 'BUDDY' ASCOTT

As the 1970s dawned, Mod seemed to have faded away. Of course, there were the boys and girls up north keeping parts of the dream alive. Dance floors at the Twisted Wheel in Manchester and the Catacombs in Wolverhampton were still filled with pill-fuelled kids strutting to rare sixties soul. There were even the scooter gangs. Across the country, skinheads grew their hair and became known as 'Suedeheads,' and attention to image seemed just as important.

It is fantastic to imagine that during that time, somewhere there was a perfectly preserved French-cropped, bespoke-suited, dedicated Mod unaware of the world changing around him, like a Japanese soldier in the jungle who doesn't know the war is over. But in the grand scheme of things, Mod was pretty much as dead as a dodo. For by 1973, the country was gripped by glam rock, as bands like The Sweet, T. Rex and Slade began to dominate the charts. Platform shoes, huge lapels and wide flares were the order of the day, but not everybody was impressed.

Brett 'Buddy' Ascott, who would go on to drum with The Chords, was one of those people. "There was no musical heritage at home. When I was growing up in the early seventies there was glam rock and heavy metal, neither of which appealed to me. I started looking back to The Who, Kinks, Beatles, and Stones... anything contemporary left me cold. Although, strangely I did become a big Bowie fan later.

"It all started for me when I bought The Who's 'Join Together,' which came out in '72, and I just kept on playing it. Anyway, about a year later I turned it over and it's got a live version of 'Baby Don't You Do It' written by Holland/Dozier/Holland on the B-side. I suddenly thought 'What's this? This is amazing. It can't be the same band.'"

On October 26, 1973, The Who released the double album *Quadrophenia*. It is the only Who album ever to be entirely composed by Pete Townshend. The front cover and photo of a Mod sat astride a chromed GS scooter is credited to Graham Hughes, while the booklet that accompanied the album is credited to American photographer Ethan Allen Russell, and recorded at 'The Kitchen' in Battersea with Ronnie Lanes Mobile Sound acting as a control room.

The album told the story of a sixties teenage Mod and his struggle to be noticed. The lyrics tell of an outsider who doesn't fit in with either his parents' viewpoints or that of his peers. The booklet provided the listener with glimpses of the fashion from a decade previous.

Ascott: "A friend of mine at school lent [*Quadrophenia*] to me. I was 14 at the time, and I just thought 'this is terrible. It's prog rock.' I really thought the music was shit but I loved the imagery in the booklet that accompanied it. From the age of 18 I thought that I wanted to be a drummer, although I never had any drums, drumsticks, nothing. That led me to investigating Keith Moon and The Who.

"I just became a diehard Who obsessive. I went out and bought *Meaty Beaty Big And Bouncy* [a 1971 compilation album of Who songs]. Then I borrowed *Quadrophenia* again from the same kid, and that time I heard it different. Suddenly it was amazing. The lyrics, which were full of angst, frustration and anger, suddenly made sense to me."

Geoff 'Goffa' Gladding was born in the East End but grew up in Enfield, North London. He too was one of those people for whom the *Quadrophenia* lyrics made perfect sense.

"I've been a massive Who fan since as long as I can remember. I first saw them live on November 6, 1971, at the Rainbow Theatre as part of the 'Who's Next' tour. I was 14 at the time. There was no Mod inclination from my family at all. At this point I was wearing black Sta-Prest trousers for school, Salatio loafers, red socks and white Brutus shirts, which were much cheaper than Ben Sherman's at the time. Tonik [a fabric produced by French textile company Dormeuil] for jackets or trousers, although I don't think I ever had a suit. This was the smart approach. Going to 'Davis – A doorway to a man's world' in Tottenham. Sozzler's in Edmonton, too. They were the kind of shops I went to for my clothes, so it was pretty smart."

Although Goffa's style is often seen as connected to reggae and soul scene, rather than the Mod scene, he was very sure about on his real musical loves.

"I loved the Small Faces. I had no sense of soul music at that point whatsoever other than I quite liked that Motown beat, but I didn't really know what it was. All through the early seventies I was just a Who fan first and foremost and when I got a bit more money I was able to go to see them play in Paris in 1976."

The Who and the influence of *Quadrophenia* would play a big part in how Mod would one day make its return. One underground scene that was thriving in 1974 was that of pub rock, which was about as far away from glam rock as you could get. The music was largely based on sixties white-boy R&B. Pubs such as the Hope & Anchor in Islington would reverberate to the sounds of Ducks Deluxe, Brinsley Schwarz and, more importantly, Canvey Island's finest, Dr Feelgood.

In 1975, Dr Feelgood played at the Guildford Civic Hall. Alongside their set of raw, jerky, stabbing, intense R&B, the band was something to behold on stage. The intimidating glares from frontman Lee Brilleaux, who could play a harmonica like no other, and the strutting menace of guitar player Wilko Johnson was a completely unique at the time.

In the audience that night was a 17-year-old by the name of Paul Weller. Paul had his own band, The Jam. The band had been playing their local pubs and clubs with a set list of old rock'n'roll and R&B numbers, and a handful of original numbers. Now that Weller had seen the Feelgoods, things were about to change forever. Around the same time he heard The Who's 'My Generation,' and his fate was set. Paul began to absorb the culture to which The Who had been linked a decade before.

An all-consuming passion took over and soon Weller was buzzing around Woking town centre, wearing a fishtail parka, on a black and yellow Lambretta GP150, complete with mirrors and a whip aerial. He began to devour all the information he could on the youth cult. Not only would it dictate what clothes he wore, but the music he listened to and the way he wrote songs. Weller's about-turn would have a major effect on the band and saw long-term friend and founding member of The Jam Steve Brookes leave, because he was unhappy with the band's burgeoning musical and sartorial direction.

Within a year, though, everything would change again when punk rock exploded and bands like the Sex Pistols, The Clash and The Damned terrorised Britain with three-minute vocal assaults. Pure energy, hard-edged melodies and a nihilistic swagger. Paul Weller at last sees bands his own age creating pure excitement.

1 *My Generation*, John Davis, 1972-3.

2 *Dr Jimmy And Mr Jim*, John Davis, 1972-3.

John's artwork first appeared in a series of The Who paintings

featured in the book *A Decade Of The Who* (1977).

Sadly, John died in a car crash in 2006.

The paintings are now owned by Paul Kelly.

My Generation

SPEEDY VESPA AND MY GENERATION '76

❝ ...we couldn't afford to buy all the Mod gear, so we had to improvise... ❞

DAVID DRAGON

Britain, 1976. God, that summer was hot. The mercury hit 28°C (82°F) for 22 days in a row. Britain baked, ice creams melted and summer revellers were happy tapping their feet to the third British win at Eurovision, Brotherhood Of Man's 'Save Your Kisses For Me.' It was a great year for underdogs, as Southampton beat Manchester United 1-0 in the FA Cup – when that trophy actually meant something – and James Hunt was crowned Formula One champion. At the cinema, crowds cheered on *Rocky* in his first outing in the ring but were left shocked at the intensity of *Taxi Driver*. It wasn't all fun in the sun, though, as the long, hot summer ended with riots between the police and carnival-goers in Notting Hill, highlighting racial tensions.

While punk rock bubbled away underground on the live circuit, the charts were drowning in The Wurzels, Abba and Showaddywaddy. Among the releases in November that year was an EMI compilation that certainly wouldn't trouble the charts, but instead harked back to a bygone age. *My Generation* featured tracks by The Action, Downliners Sect, The Gods, The Yardbirds and Rod Stewart, among many others.

David Dragon illustrated the album cover – one that took inspiration from the Mod and pop art scene now almost a decade old – and he seemed ideally positioned to capture that period. "In '63 going into '64 I went to Southampton Art College. I could generally be described as an 'art school Mod,' as Pete Townshend once called us types. Being students, we couldn't afford to buy all the Mod gear, so we had to improvise and do the best we could.

"During that time, I was introduced to lots of new music I'd never heard before. Back in Southampton a group of us had frequented an old merchant sailor's pub, a real dive, but it had lots of blues on the jukebox. That is where I first heard 'Smokestack Lightning' by Howlin' Wolf, and I'd never heard anything like that before. Of course, The Beatles and the Stones were coming up, but the Stones were always more popular among the art school crowd because people thought they were a bit more authentic, whatever that means.

"In our class at Southampton were two people who called themselves Mods – this was late '63 to the beginning of '64 – but they were different from how Mods went on to be known. Within a year, Mod would have moved on and changed. They were really flamboyant dressers. The guys would wear suits with shirts that I seem to remember as quite frilly, big ties. They were the only two that dressed like that. All of the other guys dressed like the Stones really."

" ...you can't make money out of art. "

DAVID DRAGON

Dragon, though, very nearly bypassed art altogether.
"I stumbled into going to art college really late at school. In those
days you had to have five GCEs to get any kind of decent job.
I passed three but had to do a retake of two others, so I retook two
subjects I failed and thought I'd better have a third option. It didn't
have to be that academic. I'd only done art in the first year at school
so I went along to the art teacher, a guy called Chick Jack, and told
him I wanted to do art. He'd never seen me before and couldn't
believe that I wanted to sit an Art GCE at Christmas, bearing in mind
it was already September. So he asked me to bring in the stuff I'd
drawn at home and I ended up doing a crash course with him until
I sat the exam at Christmas. And I got it. Mr Jack then asked if
I'd ever thought of going to art college. I replied 'No, because you
can't make any money out of art.' He asked 'Who told you that?'
He replied that he had [made money from art] and that he used to
draw comic strips. So he asked me to take my mum and dad to his
house for a chat. So that was it... I was heading for an office job
and suddenly did this handbrake turn and went off in a completely
different direction.

"I did a year and a half foundation and then went to
Canterbury to do graphic design, which was a small college but had
a great reputation for graphic design. There were only 24 of us in
our year. I did three years at Canterbury. When I went to Canterbury
it was a bit of a culture shock because it was a much smaller place
and it didn't have the diversity that Southampton had... it was far
more white middle class. There wasn't the mix and I really struggled
in that first year and thought I may not see it through.

"If the course wasn't suiting you in the first year you could ask
for a transfer. A few people from our group went, but luckily for me
a guy called Gordon came into our group. I'd always had an interest
in music, and he introduced me to a lot of music I wasn't aware of,
including the classic John Mayall album, the 'Beano' album, as it
became known. He had a mate who was really into Mod. I was already
into The Who and the Small Faces by then, but they switched me
on to a whole lot of stuff, so I not only got an art education but a

Dragon's influences were Peter Blake and the American painter
Robert Rauschenberg. He'd also discovered David Hockney and fallen
in love with his California series of paintings. Canterbury, however
was quite traditional and pop art was frowned upon, so Dragon found
himself having to sneak it into his work when he could.

"I got a diploma in art and design – Dip AD, it was called, and it
replaced the NDD, National Diploma Design. The old NDD course was
very hands on, it was all about the craft. Then they tried to upgrade
it so you had to write a history of art, you had to write a thesis and
all this would go towards your end mark. The old NDD didn't bother
with that, it just concentrated on actually doing it. I think the old
way was better because the people who did that, their craft ability
was better than ours. Graphic design at this point had really just been
invented; I bet up until the time I went to college it was still referred
to as commercial art. There were three people called Fletcher,
Forbes and Gill. Two of them were English and one was American
and they were the first of what we know as a design group. Up until
then you would have been called a commercial artist. Not only was
music changing but the job I would end up doing was going through
a huge shift as well."

Luckily, Dragon got to realise his dream of designing record
sleeves. He'd gone home to Southampton for the weekend and visited
the local library. He picked up a copy of *Campaign*, an advertising
and design magazine. The friend he was with spotted a job
advertisement for Decca's design department, and so Dragon wrote
off to apply for the position and got the job.

Starting in the summer of 1969, Dragon soon discovered that he
wouldn't always be designing album covers for his most-loved bands,
as his first job was to design a cover for *The World Of Reginald Dixon*,
the latest offering from the Blackpool Tower organist, who's career
went on to span more than 50 years.

It was a competitive world and it quickly became apparent that
the best jobs, stuff like the blues releases, such as Savoy Brown LPs,
mainly went to a talented guy called David Anstey. Eventually, though,
Dragon was offered John Mayall and an early Thin Lizzy album.
However, he soon found that he'd actually much rather taken on
the classical material, because it meant starting from scratch,
without the involvement of management. The pop releases always
seemed to have too many instructions.

In 1973, Dragon moved to EMI just as it was setting up a new
and improved art department. Three years later he suddenly found
himself being asked to design a cover that would take him straight

"*My Generation* was an album consisting of Mod-type music that [EMI] had in its back catalogue. It came in the standard way. The label manager would brief it in, he gave me the track listing and it was entirely down to me as to how I approached [the design]. So I thought I would do it around the Mods and Rockers riots theme, as that's the thing that people remember most from that period.

"I'll tell you what inspired my illustration: there was a Belgian artist called Guy Peellaert who had a book called *Rock Dreams*, in which he interpreted either a song, genre or band. He used photographs, but he airbrushed them and made composite pictures so they were not necessarily a real event that had happened, but they would conjure up a mood. So that is what I based my idea on.

"I knew I wanted two Rockers in the foreground and these Mods going past in the background. So I started by taking photographs for reference. I got some of my workmates to pose for me. Brian Palmer posed as the Rocker on the left, but it was just for the stance, as he had longish hair and a moustache. A guy called Adrian Sadgrove posed for the Rocker on the right and he did look like that, his hair wasn't exactly a quiff but it was similar to that. I think we got hold of a leather jacket and Brian smoked anyway so I got him to have a drag on a fag and we put sunglasses on him. I had the scarf and got Adrian to wear that and put the same leather jacket on him. So after I took the photos I started with the 'Mods' and the people on the scooter were actually sat astride a wall out of the back of the studio.

"The 'rider' of the scooter was Chris Baxter, EMI's Tape Marketing Manager, who is also the same person I used for the guy's face just behind him on the right and also the guy in the target T-shirt. Steve Newport is the model for the guys either side of him and the girl is based on Sara Batho. They all worked at EMI. All the other stuff I had to source photos for. These days referencing stuff is a doddle because now you just type in 'Lambretta' on the internet and up pop 200 images. A lot of the things in that picture, though, are based on my memories, such as the 59 badge the Rocker is wearing. I mean, really only 10 years had gone by from the originals at this period so it was relatively fresh in my mind.

"You would roughly have two to three weeks to produce something like this. Sometimes longer, but it was usually pretty tight. I do remember for the type lettering I was going to base it on the Wimpy burger bar logo, kind-of fat, plastic lettering, but then the album got shelved for a few months. I'd kind of forgotten about it until the label manager came in and almost casually said 'Oooh you know that *My Generation* album? We're going to put it out now.' Then I decided to change the design, because by then the style of repeating the band's names [performing on the compilation] with the picture inset and not such a big title had become popular. I was pleased with the way it came out, and that pen and ink style was something I'd always done. Although when the actual album came out I was disappointed. The picture appeared a lot darker and had 'thickened up.' These days you could make adjustments on a computer when you scan it in. You were kind of at the mercy of the printer in those days. You might see a proof but they really didn't like you to change it."

Throughout 1976, Dragon had witnessed the music world change and one very obvious indication that something was afoot was when Chris Baxter gathered the staff and proceeded to put a record on the turntable. The Sex Pistols' 'Anarchy In The UK' was met with absolute horror by the staff, except for Dragon, who found it different. As the popularity of punk rock grew, he found himself working on the cover for *The Roxy London WC2 (Jan – Apr 77)*, a live album of punk recordings taken from gigs at the Roxy in Covent Garden. He also designed a few post-punk singles for bands such as X-Ray Spex, The Stranglers and Dr Feelgood.

A few years later, Dragon's 'Mod' services would be drawn upon again, although this time under a design pseudonym, due to a temporary petty ban on those in the EMI design department giving themselves a design credit. David Dragon was to become 'Speedy Vespa.'

"Gordon Frewin, the label manager, came in. They realised that the Mod Revival was underway and wanted to put out a Motown compilation to accompany it. So I wanted to keep the graphics really, really simple. I remembered The Who's 'Maximum R&B' poster with the arrow, so I just thought I'll use the target with an arrow. I actually thought that EMI wouldn't go for it because it was so simple but Gordon loved it because it was effective. Anyway, the album sold well so I was asked to design *Volume 2*. I decided on the Union Jack yet again because of The Who, but I did hesitate slightly because of the National Front, racist connotations that were connected to the flag at the time. But it seemed in context with what we were doing.

"At the time we were doing what is known as mechanical artwork; in other words, you'd draw everything in black and when it went for printing you just marked it up for which colours you wanted. It was all drawn by hand, even the circles were done using compasses. For the lettering type there was a series of acetate overlays. You'd order the type from the typesetter, cut it out then stick it on the boards. So these types of covers just really took a couple of days."

In 1981, Dragon left EMI to go freelance. He took desk space in a studio in Kilburn and soon began a long-standing working relationship with designer Ken Ansell, which continues to this day. Together they have designed album covers for artists such as XTC including the psychedelic homage *Oranges And Lemons*, as well as UB40's *Labour Of Love* and *Baggariddim*.

In 1983, together with Ansell and also Adrian Miles, Dragon founded the Design Clinic. The name was later amended simply to Clinic. The company continued to produce album covers, but grew rapidly into a design and advertising company, working for clients that included Virgin Retail, Virgin Atlantic, Sky, Barclays, ITV and Network Rail.

Although still an avid functioning artist, Dragon smiles as he says, "I retired from the company in 2007. Clinic celebrated its 30th anniversary in 2013. My last hurrah in the music industry was an illustration for the DVD release of a rockumentary based around Oasis' last world tour, entitled 'Lord Don't Slow Me Down.' Like them, I quit on a high."

Covers to two of the most influential albums for the Revival generation, featuring some of the original 60s soul numbers.

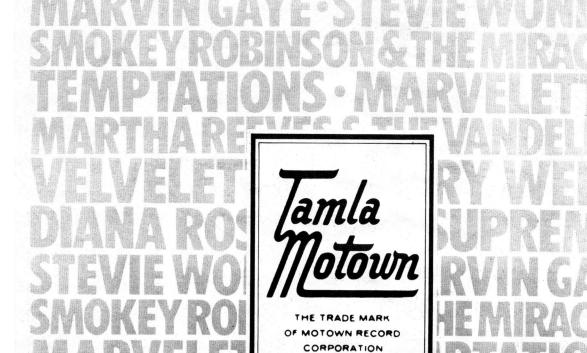

MARVIN GAYE · STEVIE WONDER
SMOKEY ROBINSON & THE MIRACLES
TEMPTATIONS · MARVELETTES
MARTHA REEVES & THE VANDELLAS
VELVELETTES · MARY WELLS
DIANA ROSS · SUPREMES
STEVIE WONDER · MARVIN GAYE
SMOKEY ROBINSON · THE MIRACLES
MARVELETTES · TEMPTATIONS
MARTHA REEVES & THE VANDELLAS
MARY WELLS · VELVELETTES
DIANA ROSS · SUPREMES
MARVIN · WONDER
SMOKEY · MIRACLES
TEMPT · ETTES
MART · AS

Tamla Motown

THE TRADE MARK
OF MOTOWN RECORD
CORPORATION

Presents

20 MOD CLASSICS

STEVIE WONDER · DIANA ROSS & THE SUPREMES · MARVIN GAYE · SMOKEY ROBINSON & THE MIRACLES
MARTHA REEVES & THE VANDELLAS · TEMPTATIONS · MARY WELLS · MARVELETTES · VELVELETTES

Now available on one album, twenty original classics from the Mod era.
Includes Marvin Gaye's 'Can I Get A Witness', Diana Ross and The Supremes' 'Come See About Me',
Martha Reeves and The Vandellas' 'Heatwave' and 'Dancing In The Street'
and The Temptations 'My Girl'.
STML 12125

For the latest information on Motown's artists and records send a s.a.e. to
MOTOWN MUSIC MESSENGER, PO BOX 4NJ, LONDON W1A 4NJ.

EMI

Licensed Repertoire Division, EMI Records Ltd., 9 Thayer St., London W.1. 01-486 7144.

STOP PRESS - Now Available
'Do I Love You (Indeed I Do)'
by FRANK WILSON TMG1170
This rare 1965 single
available commercially
for the first time.

HOW PUNK TURNED TO MOD

> **" ...it was what rock'n'roll should be... "**
>
> **BARRY CAIN:** *RECORD MIRROR*

> **" The East End...
> ...was a dead zone. "**
>
> **GRANT FLEMING**

Barry Cain was a music journalist for the *Record Mirror*. After a Clash gig at a cinema in Harlesden, which changed his life, he started covering the punk explosion in his reviews. He would also be the last person to interview Johnny Rotten the day before Rotten appeared on *Today*, a live tea-time TV show hosted by Bill Grundy. Rotten's band, the Sex Pistols, famously swore on camera, after Grundy encouraged them to "say something outrageous." The next day, the band, and the punk revolution in general, were splashed across the front pages of every newspaper in the country.

Cain also met The Jam early on: "The first time I saw The Jam was at a party run by a guy called Jeff Deane, who was their PR guy at Polydor. The party was in South London, and they'd just signed The Jam. All of a sudden these three guys walked in, pissed, and they drunk the place fucking dry. I just thought, what a bunch of cunts. I looked at Jeff and he said 'this is the band – The Jam' and I said what a shit name. He told me they were supposed to be good. They'd only signed for about 6k, or something ridiculous. That was my first experience of them.

"The next time I saw them was at the Hope & Anchor in Islington, in March '77. That was the first time I'd seen them actually play and I fucking absolutely loved them. They were one of the best bands I'd ever seen. Their songs were just so good, and the fact that Weller was only 18 then... to me it was what rock'n'roll should be. You should be some teenager screaming and pouring out your hopes, dreams and nightmares to another bunch of kids. I thought, yes mate, you've got it. You've got it in one. People had been telling me about this band that wore suits and covered fucking 'Heatwave' and the *Batman* theme, and I thought, what the fuck's that all about? But I never thought in any sense or form it was derivative because everything is tinged with this punk thing so everything was new. It was like Motown kissed by The Clash."

Record Mirror, March 4, 1978

'My mum goes mental'

SOUTHEND AND STRATFORD MODS: complete sixties fashion . . . right down to Lambrettas, Quadrophenia . . . but with a crush on The Jam

The caption underneath the photo says it all: "Southend and Stratford Mods." Peering out from the photo is the ice-cool stare of 17-year-old Grant Fleming, resplendent in his homemade Jam T-shirt. The stare could be a result of too many late nights out watching bands in sweaty clubs or too many late nights out fuelled by cheap speed. The reader can never be sure, but either way the image is a snapshot of the times-a-changing. Appearing in the *Record Mirror* on March 4, 1978, the photo accompanies an article dedicated to "super fans."

Fleming was one of the new breed of kids who'd revived the 'Mod' tag. The article relates the story of how he and other Mods from Stratford and Southend, including Andy Swallow (17), Steve Wait (18) and Alan Suchy (17), follow The Jam to various gigs around Britain, with the hope of one day following the group to Europe.

Fleming recalls: "In that article I'm wearing a stencilled 'This is the Modern World' T-shirt. You could almost date that as being the forerunner to the Mod Revival because I was with some kids from Southend there who were Jam fans before I was. That was after a gig at the Marquee, but it wasn't a Jam gig. That could be seen as a starting point for it, around March '78."

Fleming, though, already harboured Mod traits from years before, which he would now rekindle. He'd been an early Suedehead, when he was just nine years old.

As the 1970s dawned, Fleming was swept along by glam rock and started following David Bowie, as well as seeing bands like The Faces and The Who live. Football was his other big love and he found himself being drawn into the world of terraces gang culture.

"I was just into common fashion and then punk came along, but I was quite involved with the West Ham lot. I suppose you could say that hooligans are always quite conservative to anything a bit wild and crazy. In 1977, when I was around 16, my friend, Al, got a car and we went off on a mad week's holiday, sleeping in the car, and we saw some punk gigs in Brighton and suddenly we're into it.

"I really liked Generation X for their pop art stuff. I actually wrote to Tony James to ask about their T-shirts and he wrote back with a really nice letter. Later on, when I was in bands myself, I used to stencil designs based on his advice. I guess I was reluctant to go too far because it weren't our world. I know there was a lot of working-class kids involved and you can't just say it was an art school thing, but it was a West London thing in a way. The East End at that time was a dead zone."

"...I've turned Mod!.. "

GRANT FLEMING

On May 9, 1977, The Clash played at the Rainbow supported by The Jam, Buzzcocks, Subway Sect and The Prefects. It would be a night that would change Fleming forever.

"The Jam and The Clash were at the Rainbow. Now, prior to the gig I met up with Al and another bloke, Johnny. We met at Liverpool Street, at Dirty Dicks pub, around 6 o'clock. Outside the nearby police station on this particular day there was a street market and there was a rail of mohair jumpers. Not the kind they were selling at Seditionaries, but mohair jumpers nonetheless. Anyway, we've had three of them away, quite literally. We ran into the station and put them on, so now the three of us have got our uniform. I swear this is the moment. It's a stupid thing that only a kid would say, but this was the turning point. The Jam played and we were two or three rows from the front and they were phenomenal. Now you are seeing The Jam, this is what you've heard and the pictures you've seen. During the interval I've turned to Al as I ripped my mohair jumper off and said, 'That's it, I've turned Mod!,' and the next moment they ripped theirs off, too.

"From that moment it was suits from jumble sales, looking for Tonik, and it really was a mission to be as obsessive as Weller, if not more so. I think the legacy of particularly East London being a stronghold of original sixties Mods meant that even subconsciously we were thinking this is our thing. Punk went mainstream, but this could be ours. I guess subconsciously we were thinking this is more us than punk will ever be. That's not to say that there were not others having similar ideas, 'cos there was. There was a point where suddenly we all came together and that would have been The Jam gigs. They were the catalyst, there's no question about it. That's where the scene locked horns with people from different areas."

Undeniably, the Mod Revival had grown from the punk crowd's despondency when they realised that punk never really lived up to its promise. The Jam were suddenly seen as a focal point for these disaffected youths. Another dominating factor was a generation of Who fans for whom The Who had meant everything until punk came along.

Geoff 'Goffa' Gladding, long-time Who fan, had taken to punk wholeheartedly. "When Punk started happening I totally embraced it. At the time I was a student in York and the only punk there. I went over to Leeds Polytechnic to see the Sex Pistols, The Damned, Johnny Thunders & the Heartbreakers and The Clash on the 'Anarchy' tour. I was a homemade punk – ripped-up shirts and narrow trousers, which unbelievably at that point were really hard to come by. So I went to charity shops, added a few safety pins and hair that was a lot shorter than everybody else's. In late '76, I bought a pair of bondage trousers from Seditionaries in the King's Road. They were slightly damaged and needed repairs, so I got a discount and a receipt signed by Vivienne Westwood! It was too difficult to nick from there but I did thieve a few things from a shop further along the King's Road, including a shirt that had straps all over it and another one with buckles down the side on which I stencilled 'Heavy Duty Discipline.' What the fuck's all that about...?"

In 1977, Goffa went to the Nashville Rooms in West Kensington to see the punk rock band 999, but would also witness his old world colliding with his new one.

"There wasn't that many people there and who should turn up? Keith Moon, with his minder. He was dressed up, bizarrely, in an all-white dinner jacket. I was wearing this leather jacket, which coincidentally, I had nicked about a week before from the Red Cow in Fulham. I was a bit pissed and fell into conversation with Keith and cheekily said, 'Keith, it's fantastic to meet you. I'm a massive Who fan and I first saw you play in 1971. So I can remember this meeting, can we swap jackets?' He said yes and gave me this white dinner jacket, which he signed on the shoulder 'To Goffa from Keith.' I then proceeded to wear it for the next few months to all these punk gigs. It just got torn to pieces and I ended up chucking it away."

Life changed again for Goffa when he came home from university, having flunked his degree. He started to hang around with several old school friends. One of them had a girlfriend whose brother was in a band. Sam Burnett, who had previously played for The Scooters and then The Modern Boys, was now playing guitar for Back To Zero. The band had a Mod look... Goffa was once again hooked.

WEDNESDAY 13th JUNE

BACK TO ZERO

THE NUMBERS

PLUS

SIX MORE PROPHETS

"MOD GIRL POSES IN NON - MOD GEAR AT THE SAVOY."

Julian '79

at the 'Coalbin'

Dublin Castle - Camden Town

1 Bob Manton (lead singer with The Purple Hearts): "Tony Lordan was one of the first people we got to know as a band. He designed the Lambretta type logo for our band name. He was later in his own band, Department S."

2 Bob Manton: "I think we told designer Rob O'Connor what art direction we wanted for the LP, but basically left it up to him. The LP cover is 'Warholesque', which I didn't even notice until someone pointed it out to me years later."

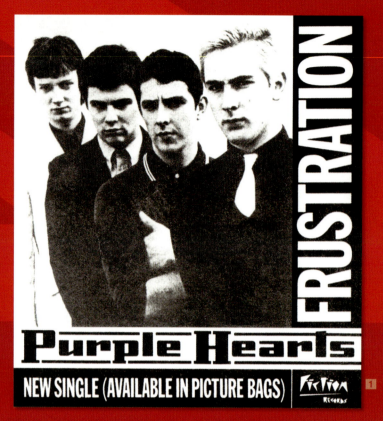

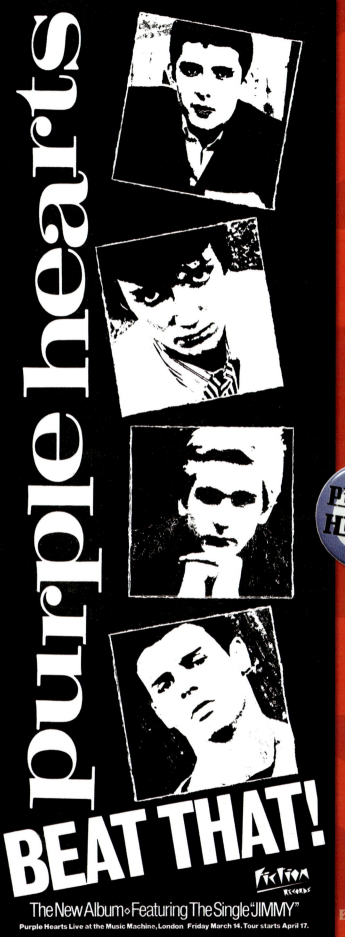

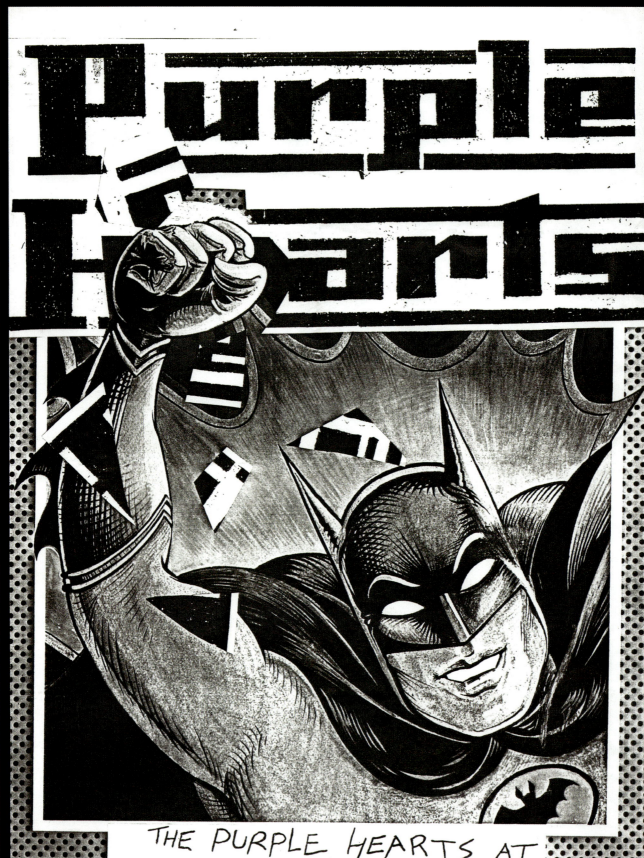

POP ART ←

"Obviously we think of ourselves as mods, and that's like a state of mind, but it don't mean we gotta sleep in our mohair suits, we don't wanna be tied down by an image, we'd rather be thought of as a group for teenagers, for anybody."

THE PURPLE HEARTS, regarded by many as the best, hail from Romford in Essex.

The Purple Hearts

Bassist Jeff (year, just Jeff) describes their epic single-to-be, 'Jimmy', thus:
"It's a Pop - Art - Teen - Confusion - Anthem!"

PEPSI

P · H
ACTION TESTED

Carnaby St.

RotoSound music strings

screaming out its message to all and sundry. 'Purple Hearts' it proclaims, 'The Sound Of The Eighties'

ICI

DÉCOUPAGE

MONTAGE

They cover three oldies — The Monkees' 'Steppin' Stone', David Bowie And The Lower Third's 'Can't Help Thinking About Me' and wicked Wilson Pickett's gut-wrenching 'If You Need Me.' But it's the eight originals that make up the bulk of their live set that leave no doubts as to what decade Purple Hearts are living in.

Pop Art

PURPLE HEARTS AT: BARKING FOOTBALL CLUB APR 22+29
UPSTAIRS AT RONNIE'S APR 24
MUSIC MACHINE MAY 7

"The Purple Hearts are the gap between Newton's Third Law and Einstein's Theory of the toilet seat!"

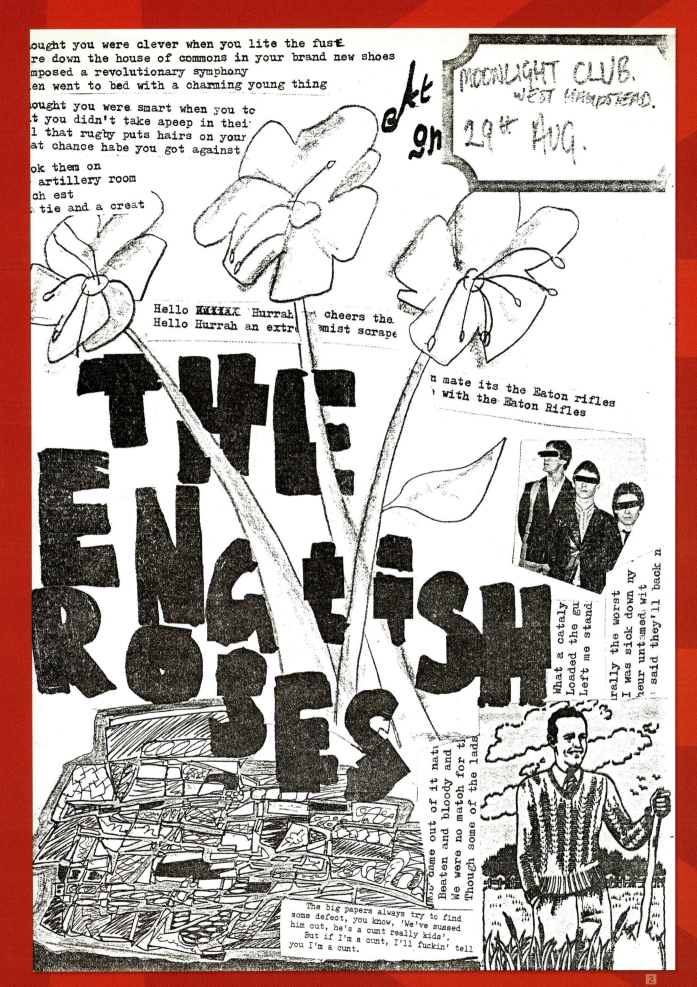

2 The Jam played secret gigs under various guises including 'John's Boys'. The flyers here and on pages 148 and 149 show gigs across three nights in a row under different names.

I'm up on the hills with the little boy soldiers
Reconnassience duty up at 5.30
Shoot shoot shoot and kill the natives
You're one of us and we love you for that
Think of honour, Queen and country
You're a blessed son of the British Empire
God's on our side and so is Washington

**: Don't you think that's because
people like you get up on stage and
speak out?

**: No, that would make me out to
be a martyr which is absolute bullshit
because I'll write a song like 'Tube
station' and the next minute I'll get
in a fight. Which is a little bit
hypocritical. I don't like getting in
fights because I hate violence. I
don't want kids fighting each other.
I just want them to come to gigs and
enjoy themselves.
     Certain aspects of life and society
make me hate everything. We all go
through the same old things and never
learn our lessons. Sometimes this
feels a little silly, like a total
parody of life and that makes me feel
bitter towards people and bitter
towards meself because I don't learn
either. I'm nothing special.
     BW: What about the

Saying find enclosed one son one medal and
to say he won

Woking Boys at the

30th Aug.
BridgeHouse
CANNING TOWN.

Dressing to

Come on outside XX I'll sing you a lullaby
Or tell a tale of goodness prevailed

KILL MEN

These days I find that I can't be bothered
to argue with them well what's the point
Better to take your shots and drop down dead
Then they send you home in a pine overcoat
With a letter to your mum

We ruled the world we killed and robbed
the fucking lot but we don't feel bad

It was done beneath the flag of democracy
You'll believe and I do yes I do

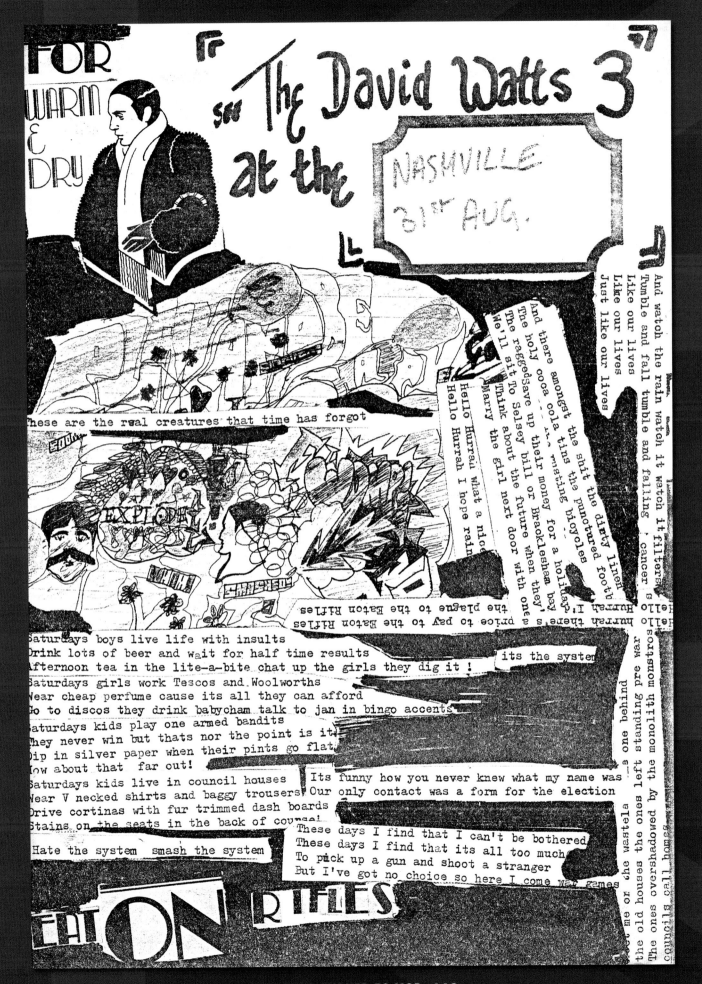

CLASSIC ALBUM:
ALL MOD CONS
THE JAM

❝ I did get involved with the design... ❞

PAUL WELLER

The Jam had just returned to British shores from America after a disastrous tour supporting rock band Blue Oyster Cult. At the time, Paul Weller was suffering with writer's block, but the band was contracted to deliver their third album to Polydor. Chris Parry, the band's A&R man and producer, rejected the demos and suggested they return to their home town of Woking to write a whole new set of songs.

The result was a masterpiece. Weller's fury and bitter indignation would spill out through the lyrics of 'Mr Clean,' 'Billy Hunt' and the chilling tale of 'Down In The Tube Station At Midnight.' Elsewhere you find the beauty of 'English Rose,' a love song that shows the sensitive side of Paul's nature (although at the time he was too embarrassed to credit the song in the track list). Released on November 3, 1978, and containing 11 originals and a cover of The Kinks' 'David Watts,' *All Mod Cons* reached number six in the UK album chart.

The front cover displayed all three band members, standing against a white wall in a completely empty room. Weller states: "I did get involved with the design, but more with the collage on the inner sleeve. Not because it was pushed on us, but because the art director, Bill Smith, would ask us if we had any ideas. We didn't really know. I mean, we knew what we wouldn't want, but we didn't know what we did want. The cover design was probably Bill's concept, but it wouldn't have been ours."

It was the inner sleeve that had the biggest impact on the band's legions of fans, though. On one side were the song lyrics, printed over a blueprint of a Vespa scooter; on the reverse, a collage of various photos and objects that would become influential reference points to an army of fans seeking clues to all things Mod.

Weller: "I would have brought in loads of bits and pieces. Not all of it would have been mine, but a lot of it. There's The Creation single 'Biff Bang Pow.' I didn't know about The Creation until we did our first John Peel session. He played whatever track it was of ours and then said 'Shades of The Creation there from The Jam.' So that made me go out and try to find their records. Alan McGee first saw that [reference on the album sleeve], and that's where the idea for Creation Records came from. Which is nice, y'know, the way things all go around. There's the images of London, Battersea Power Station, the 100 Club, because that's where we played a lot. My old Sheerwater Comprehensive badge – I guess there's a certain amount of irony to that. The 'Roadrunner' single is on there 'cos it's a great tune. What I like about a collage is that it says an awful lot about people and you can put it in quite a small place."

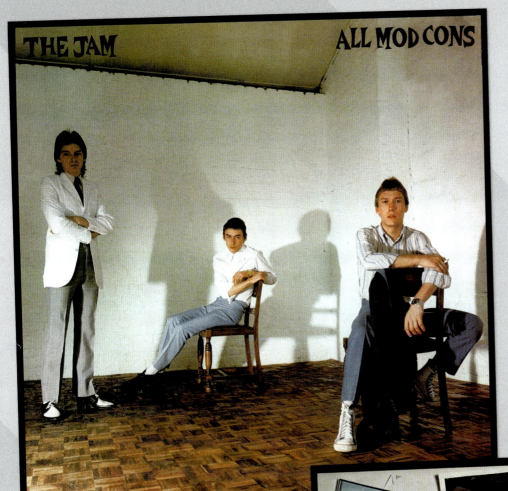

The Jam — All Mod Cons

Cover design courtesy of Bill Smith, who along with Jill Mumford came up with the ironic idea of an empty room for *All Mod Cons*. Meanwhile, the inside cover of the collage of Mod-related ephemera would influence and direct the bands fans to moments of Mod's history. Photography was by Peter Kodick.

> **"...we knew what we wouldn't want, but we didn't know what we did want."**
>
> PAUL WELLER

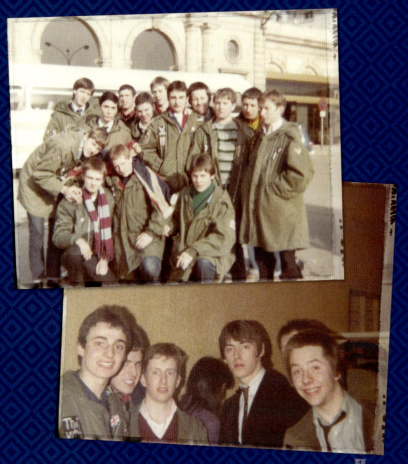

"A POCKET FULL OF SPEED"
THE MOD PILGRIMAGE

> **❝...a pocket full of speed...**
> **...my eyeballs are bulging. ❞**
>
> BRETT 'BUDDY' ASCOTT

1 Grant and his mates take Paris by storm and link up with Paul Weller.

2 Grant's original hand-drawn and typed flyer.

The Jam's February 1979 gigs in France (in both Paris and Rheims) were events that would prove pivotal to the emerging Mod Revival. The shows are seen as the moment when the scattered-all-over Jam fans finally got together and realised that they were part of something very special. The gigs would bring together kids from Shepherd's Bush, Stratford, Barking, Dagenham and other areas of London, as well as kids from further up the country, such as Newcastle.

Brett 'Buddy' Ascott: "I'd just joined The Chords when Billy Hassett told me about the Paris gig. Now, I was a huge Jam fan because they were a surrogate Who for me, so I was well up for it. I'd only been abroad twice before at this point. I got to Charing Cross and there were all these Mods there. It wasn't such a huge surprise, as we'd seen a load of Mods at the first gig at the Wellington. As we got on the train, somebody said 'You know when you get to Dover, they'll search you for drugs.' I've got a pocket full of speed, so I decide to take the whole lot. I get on the boat and my eyeballs are bulging.

"When we got to the venue, John Weller [Paul's father and the band's manager] got us in to the sound check. Afterwards, he said he'd put us on the guest list, then he gave me the clipboard and asked me to get everyone's names. I'm off my head at the time and that's where I met Grant [Fleming] for the first time. I asked his name. 'Grant,' he replies. I say 'Grant what?' He says, 'Just Grant, they'll know who it is!' I thought, you cunt, so I wrote 'Just Grant you cunt!' on the list."

Grant Fleming: "I saw The Jam at the Hammersmith Odeon and The New Hearts were supporting them. Then they played a gig at the Marquee and that's the gig where I got talking to Weller at the bar. He was telling me about them going to Europe and the whole Paris thing. I asked for the dates and he said if I gave him my number he'd call me and give them. I'm thinking, of course you will, pop star. A couple of nights later, the phone goes and my sister says, 'There's a bloke called Paul on the phone.' It was him, so I thought he's given me the dates so I've got to go now. So after that I designed the 'Mod Pilgrimage' flyers and organised the trip. That was one of the amazing little things that would happen with Weller. They would make that connection with the fans. That's what made them different."

MOD PILGRAMAGE '79

GO TO FRANCE TO SEE

IN PARIS AND REIMS

```
MEET AT CHARING X  0630   Monday 26  Feb
DEPART  CHARING X  0700   Monday 26  Feb
        Travel by Hovercraft and Train arriving in PARIS at 1420  Monday 26  Feb

    Go to gig at LE STADIUM, PARIS at 2000  Monday 26  Feb

DEPART PARIS  0902 or 1106  Tuesday 27 Feb
ARRIVE REIMS  1032 or 1241  Tuesday 27 Feb

    Go to gig at CINEMA OPERA, REIMS at 2000  Tuesday 27 Feb

DEPART REIMS  0618 or 0708 or 0958 or 1228  Wednesday 28 Feb
ARRIVE PARIS  0803 or 0840 or 1131 or 1400  Wednesday 28 Feb
    Then change Stations to connect any of following trains:

DEPART PARIS   0820 or 1010 or 1420  Wednesday 28 Feb
ARRIVE CHARING  1340 or 1540 or 1940  Wednesday 28 Feb
        X

FARE: LONDON-PARIS RETURN   £18-50 (Tickets must be bought by 23 Feb from any main
                                   British Rail stations or agents ie. Liverpool ST.)
      PARIS-REIMS  RETURN   £10-40 (To be bought in Paris)
                           ------
                           £28-90

PASSPORTS NOT NEEDED. TAKE A PHOTO WITH YOU AND GET A IDENTITY CARD AT DOVER FREE
                                        (VALID 60 HRS)

PARKAS ESSENTIAL FOR DOSSING, TAKE UNION JACKS FOR SUPPORT.
```

"MOD" PARKA
GENUINE AMERICAN
FISHTAIL PARKA
AS WORN IN THE 60's
U.S. Army Surplus
Not new but in good condition

WITH
FREE
SEW-ON STRIPES

ONLY £12·50 + 1·50 p p
State chest size and height
SEND CHEQUES OR P.O.S TO:
PRINTOUT PROMOTIONS
28A ABINGTON SQUARE, NORTHAMPTON

MODS AND
THE MUSIC PRESS

"...every single music journalist was a failed middle-class, English graduate..."

IAN PAGE [SECRET AFFAIR]

1979 would be the year that the music press would make – then break – the so-called Mod Revival. As the year started, a January edition of *Melody Maker* ran with an article on Paul Weller, entitled 'A Mod At 20,' in which Weller spoke of not being able to write "kid's anthems" now that he'd kissed his teenage years goodbye, and that by writing songs about everyday situations he likened them to pop art. He is pictured in a parka and college scarf. Meanwhile, near the back of the music paper are the small ads featuring adverts for Afghan coats, 'Kansa' fringed moccasin boots and embroidered cheesecloth kurta tops. The old hippies were still clinging on.

Ian Page, lead singer of Secret Affair, which had formed from the ashes of the new wave band The New Hearts recalls that period well: "At that point most journalists were into bands like Foreigner, you know, that adult-rock orientated world that was before punk. All of the music papers took an enormous bite of the bullet to say, right we'll go for it, so they invested an awful lot of intellectual capital in saying 'we're going for the new wave and the punk.' They probably took the view that it's the job of a newspaper in general to be contemporary. In fact, they went completely over the top – all of a sudden it was 'Robert Plant is a wanker' type stuff. That was a ridiculous thing to do. Almost every single music journalist was a failed middle-class, English graduate – not all of them, obviously. Punk was a middle-class movement. It wasn't working class, it wasn't for working kids. At the time I never succeeded in explaining that Mod's origins lay in the fact that its fan were the first post-war generation that could get jobs and have money in their pockets, and didn't have to go through rationing, so they could go out and buy clothes. It was an entitlement for working-class kids to say 'I'm as good as you.' But the middle-class men and women in their twenties in 1976, went out, bought their skinny jeans and their motorcycle jackets, and suddenly Giovanni Dadomo was cool. When previously he'd been some creepy middle-class kid with no identity. Then we come along – and I really am working class – followed by genuinely working-class people, and we decide to put on suits. A sense of identity. Now they're going crazy! It wasn't a personal thing against the band. It was a big fear. 'Oh no, they're making us look like fools!' Which we weren't.

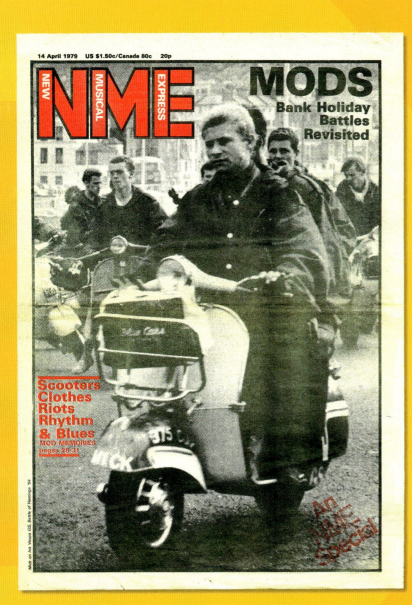

14 April 1979   US $1.50c/Canada 80c   20p

NEW MUSICAL EXPRESS

NME

MODS
Bank Holiday Battles Revisited

Scooters
Clothes
Riots
Rhythm
& Blues
MOD MEMORIES
pages 29-31

An NME Special

> ## " ...it was a snotty little closed club... "
>
> DAVE CAIRNS [SECRET AFFAIR]

"I think Dave [Cairns] and I were as influenced by new wave ideas and ideals in Secret Affair. I always thought there was something New Wave about us, even in Secret Affair, with our high energy and intensity. We rejected the complacency, I suppose, of Super Groups, but secretly we all thought Jimmy Page was one of the most amazing guitarists in the world."

Dave Cairns was Secret Affair's guitarist and saw first-hand how the punk dream failed: "When we first put our band, The New Hearts, together at college we were wearing button-down shirts and original Tonik jackets that you could still get, and then we'd mix them up with skinny jeans and a pair of Converse shoes. It was just the look we wanted. I think we found out pretty soon that where punk is supposed to be a great opportunity to open doors for you, we found out it was a snotty little closed club, and the doors were shut in our face. Really with the Mod Revival, the fans started coming along to see us as Secret Affair, which was just a continuation of something that was occurring long before the press were in on it. The first Secret Affair show we did was in February 1979 supporting The Jam at Reading University. That was the only gig we did with The Jam. A lot of the audience were coming in as Mods, and The Jam's audience was changing."

In April, *NME* ran a couple of amazingly insightful features on original sixties Mods. The front cover featured an iconic black and white photo of Mods entering Hastings in 1964. The first article, 'The Young Mods' Forgotten Story,' was written by original Hackney Mod Penny Reel; the second, 'Land Of A Thousand Dances,' by Paul Rambali. Both tell stories as if purely fictional, but each is steeped in hard fact and these two pieces remain some of the best written about the original Mod era to date. The third part of *NME*'s Mod bonanza was based around the new Mods, and featured the latest bands interspersed with quotes from some of the current faces on the scene.

By May, *NME* was running previews of the forthcoming film *Quadrophenia* and reporting on the Mod nights at the London Music Machine, as well as reviewing the recent Who gig at the Rainbow.

June would see *Record Mirror* give the revival a major boost, when it ran with a Mod cover (seen over) and a guide to the best new Mod bands. The biggest and most interesting Mod special came courtesy of *Sounds* magazine and featured five pages of quotes from new Mods attending a Secret Affair gig at the Bridge House and an informed guide of all of the new bands, entitled 'Who's Who In Mod.' Garry Bushell, one of the few music journalists to champion the Mod Revival, wrote the lead article, which explained the rise of the trend.

RECORD MIRROR

June 2, 1979   18p

MODS & SODS

THE CHORDS
THE JAM
and others

BEE GEES

Picture by GEORGE BODNAR

MOD ART 156

NOVEMBER 10 1979 20p

sounds

Pic by Iain McKell

Mods vs. The World
THE GREAT DEBATE: PAGE 31

MOD ART 158

"Mod ain't very interesting at all now. "

GRANT FLEMING

All was not well, however, as many scenesters were becoming disillusioned with the hype. There were even a few restless natives at the Bridge House. Grant Fleming is quoted in the *Sounds* magazine article as saying: "Mod ain't very interesting at all now. I know it was inevitable that it'd become commercialised so I can't really moan, but I just don't feel aligned to it now." His contribution continues and ends with, "Our crowd is still the same, we're Mods, but we don't feel part of the mass movement."

Tom McCourt is also quoted: "I'll tell ya, Mod used to be personal, now it's just a fashion."

As a mass underground fashion trend, Mod, at this point, is roughly six months old. *Quadrophenia* is yet to be released and yet many are already filled with dread at the prospect of Mod becoming just another 'street fashion.'

While August sees many features covering the 'March Of The Mods' nationwide tour, which featured Secret Affair, The Purple Hearts and Back To Zero, the backlash gains pace, with many negative reviews of both Mod-related records and gigs, whiled Two Tone music starts getting more favourable reviews.

On November 10 that year, *Sounds* magazine, which had so far been mainly positive towards the scene, held a 'debate' called 'Mods Vs. The World,' with an eye-catching front cover and a three-page article led by *Sounds* writer Dave McCulloch, accusing Mod as being "harmful because of its continuation of the out-dated idea that rock'n'roll is merely a business." The following week, *Sounds* featured a front cover with Secret Affair's lead singer Ian Page, entitled 'Mod Manifesto,' which presented a letter written by Page, as he had been absent at the so-called debate but nevertheless had come in for abuse. Ian's dad delivered the letter to the *Sounds* offices himself. While addressing most accusations thrown at the revival, Page was quick to point out that McCulloch earned his living from writing about music, thus making it "a business" himself.

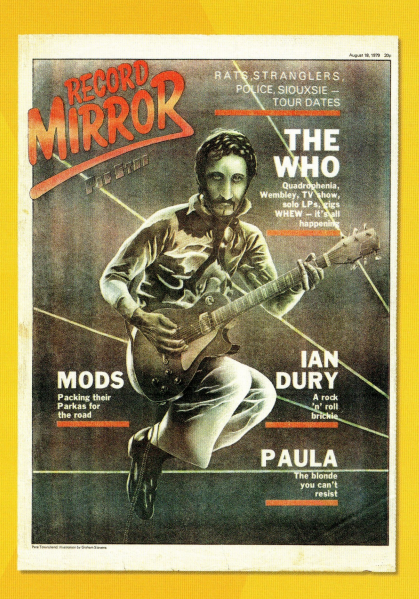

" ...Mod used to be personal, now it's just a fashion. "

TOM McCOURT

MOD ART 160

"...the only paper that would really support us. "

IAN PAGE [SECRET AFFAIR]

Far more interesting was the *NME* issue that came out the same week. It not only featured Ian Page and Dave Cairns on the cover and in a two-and-a-half-page interview inside, but it also carried a fantastic five-page article, 'The Ace Face's Forgotten Story' by Steve Turner, which gave a full transcription of an interview Turner had done with top sixties Mod Peter Meaden in 1975 while researching the book *A Decade Of The Who*. For many it was the only glimpse into the mysteries of the person who had made The Who Mod. This, combined with the *NME*'s sixties Mod special from April, became the treasured keepsakes for those wanting to know more about the original movement.

On the whole, throughout 1979, most journalists mercilessly ripped apart the Mod Revival. *Sounds*' Garry Bushell always seemed to be fighting in the Mod bands' corner, but generally the daggers were usually out for any band that dared align themselves with the movement. Two Tone bands, meanwhile, seemed to get a much fairer treatment.

Dave Cairns [Secret Affair]: "When you look back on the ska days of Two Tone and Madness, it was very easy to market all of that as just one sound and one genre. So it was very easy for the music press to switch into that and think this is an easy job to work behind. With the Mod Revival, they lost that connection to Mod culture and saw it purely as a musical force, which it wasn't. Therefore when you picked it apart, and bands sounded really different, they found it too difficult to deal with. So there was a sea of change and they decided to go with Two Tone."

Ian Page [Secret Affair]: "*Record Mirror* ended up the only paper that would really support us. *Melody Maker* was very old school and had the likes of Pink Floyd on the cover. *Sounds* had staff that hated us and didn't like us, and even though *NME* put us on the front cover, they were vile to us all the time."

Bob Manton [The Purple Hearts]: "I've no complaints about the music press, we got a lot of good coverage and even some of the criticism was at least entertaining to read. I think *Sounds* was very much a supporter of the scene because of Garry Bushell, the *NME* less so but they did a fantastic article on the original Mod scene written as a story."

'Goffa' Gladding: "It was a little bit of a fault of the bands to model themselves as Mod bands, in a lot of ways. If you look at bands like The Purple Hearts, The Chords, Secret Affair... all those bands would absolutely stand on their own two feet as really good quality if you don't want to pigeonhole them somewhere. The way it turned out, with that kind of Mod label, there's no doubt that it limited their success."

Grant Fleming disagrees with this statement: "You're talking about a time when we were tribal, and you had to pin your colours to a mast. So for any of those bands to step outside and say 'we're not this or that,' it could be fatal. Chris Pope of The Chords was always kind of 'we're not a Mod band' and that possibly held them back in one area as much as it allowed them to progress in another. It was swings and roundabouts. The reason The Jam transcended it all, was because they didn't just come from the scene, they'd helped to *create* it."

"...you had to pin your colours to a mast. "

GRANT FLEMING

1 The *Ogdens'*-inspired 7" cover from The Exits, Lightning Records, 1978.

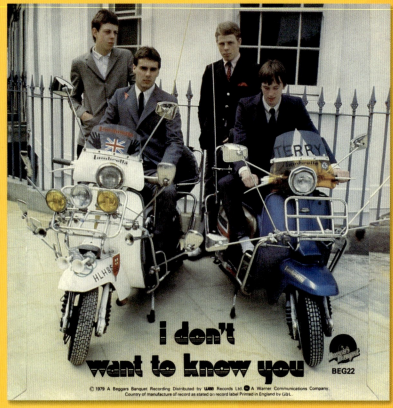

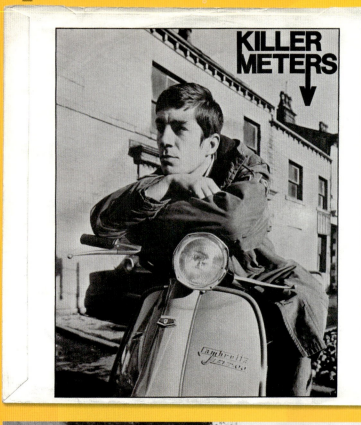

1 Rear cover of 'You Need Wheels' 7" by Merton Parkas, Beggars Banquet, 1979.

2 Rear cover of The Killermeters 7", Psycho Records, 1979.

3 Substitute 7", Ignition Records, 1979.

4 Arthur Kay 7", Red Admiral Records, 1979.

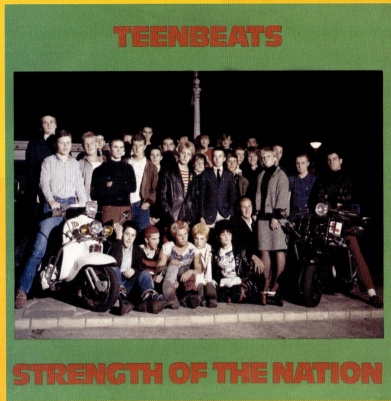

TEENBEATS

STRENGTH OF THE NATION

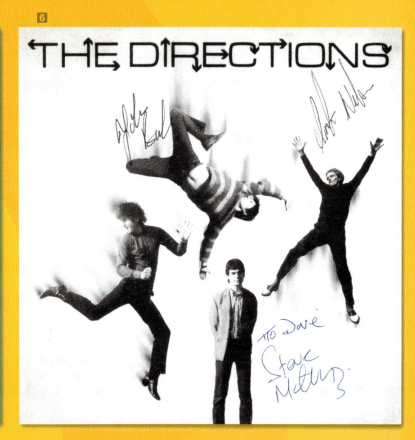

THE DIRECTIONS

DON'T LET GO

SEVENTEEN

BANK HOLIDAY WEEKEND

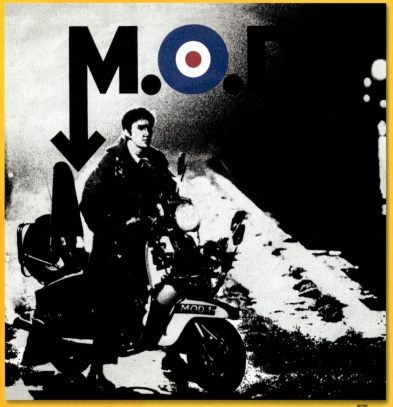

M.O.D

5 Teenbeats 7", Safari Records, 1979.

6 The Directions (signed), Torch, 1979. (2,000 copies made but 800 ruined in a flood).

7 Seventeen 7" (the band found later success as The Alarm), Vendetta Records, 1979.

8 M.O.D 7" (actually David Essex under a pseudonym), Vertigo Records, 1979.

1 London Boys 7" EP, Decca, 1979 (design included the Mods Terry Rawlings & Garry Crowley).

2 The Circles 7", Graduate Records, 1979.

3 Compilation LP, Safari, 1980.

4 The Chords LP (cover based on the Spencer Davis Group second LP), Polydor, 1980.

5 The Purple Hearts 'Frustration' 7", Friction Records, 1980.
Sleeve design by Rob O'Connor and illustration by Brett Ewins.

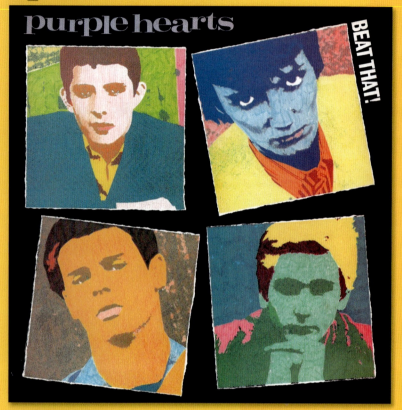

1 The Purple Hearts LP, Friction Records, 1980.

2 The Aces 7", ETC Records, 1981.

3 Merton Parkas 7", Well Suspect Records, 1983.

4 Small Hours 7" EP, Automatic Record Co, 1980.

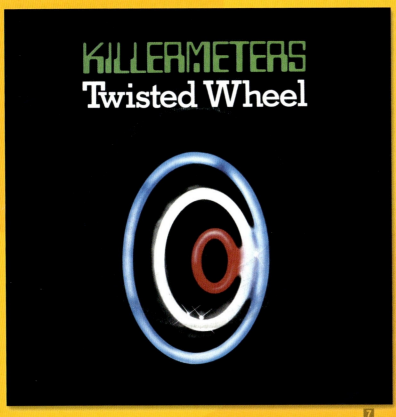

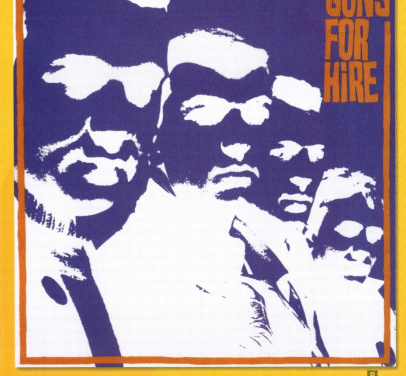

5 The Sussed 7" (Mod cash-in record). Graduate Records, 1980. Artwork by Richard Bedford.

6 The Akrylykz 7", Red Rhino Records, 1980.

7 Killermeters 7", Gem Records, 1980.

8 Guns For Hire 7", Korova Records, 1980.

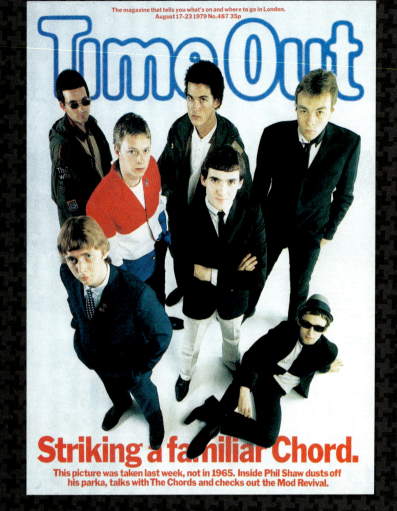

The magazine that tells you what's on and where to go in London.
August 17-23 1979 No.487 35p

Time Out

Striking a familiar Chord.

This picture was taken last week, not in 1965. Inside Phil Shaw dusts off his parka, talks with The Chords and checks out the Mod Revival.

A FAMILIAR CHORD:
TIME OUT ARTICLE
AUGUST 1979

> **"We had no money,
> we couldn't afford stuff..."**

BUDDY ASCOTT

1 Sadly the roller isn't theirs! The Chords (minus Billy Hassett), October 1980.

2 The Chords, 1979. In both pictures Buddy is wearing homemade pop art shirts.

Looking resplendent in a tri-colour jacket, 20-year-old Buddy Ascott stared up at the camera lens. In what would prove to be their only 'front cover' appearance, The Chords did a pretty good job at capturing the spirit of 1979 in one single colour photo: unsmiling, confident and focused with a look of determination and defiance that spoke volumes of what they stood for.

That August 1979 edition of *Time Out* magazine featured two articles aimed at Mods, one on the new scene was entitled 'Remodelling,' while an article by Dick Hebdige called 'Putting On The Style' is an academic overview of subcultures, from Teds and punks through to the latest Mod Revival.

Phil Shaw, an original sixties Mod, opens the first article by drawing comparisons between the new Mods and those of his own memories, but soon finds that this new species are a kind of bastardised vision of what Mod once was. Noting a lack of leather maxi-coats and in their place a sea of green parkas, Shaw comes across as almost sympathetic to the newcomers' naivety until he realises they are in fact a different breed. He begins to realise that this generation has come through the nihilism and imagined chaos of punk. They have their own bands, and he mentions The Jam, Secret Affair and many others. While he does his best to convince the reader and himself that these youngsters have a fascination with their 1960s counterparts, he does at least end the article on The Chords' recent outing to see the 1979 version of The Who at Wembley, and of their disappointment in what they saw.

The second article, 'Putting On The Style,' attempts to dissect why each generation attempts to create a new style, and it ends with a fantastic piece about a scooter charge at the gates of Buckingham Palace in 1966, with Hebdige explaining that the person who told him the story has a questionable ability to tell the truth but helps perpetuate the mythology of Mod by telling such tales.

Overall, the *Time Out* pieces give an overall feeling of encouragement towards the Mod Revival, while many other journalists would not be so generous. The cover photo alone would prove to be an outstanding image of the time. This was helped by the eye-catching tri-coloured jacket that Johnson's shop at 406 King's Road had provided.

Lloyd Johnson [owner of Johnson's boutique]: "We opened up the shop in the King's Road and I did lots of Ivy League hook vent suits in shark-skin mohair that we'd got from up north. We used to get all types in that shop and obviously the new Mod bands like The Chords, The Jam, Merton Parkas, The Lambrettas and The Mods.

"In fact, The Mods' manager was always in there buying stuff for [the band]. I remember he had a scooter in his front living room. Anyway, we decided to make some jackets like The Who wore, but I didn't want to do a Union Jack jacket. I made up a red and white block stripe and then we found a load of Mary Quant checkerboard fabric in black and white tweed. Then I wanted to do something representative of that sort of pop art Union Jack jacket, so I did one in a French flag, red, white and blue. I made up one in the colours of the German flag and the Italian one. I think we basically limited them to one of each size: small, medium and large."

Buddy Ascott remembers: "We had no money, we couldn't afford stuff from Johnson's as we were always fucking broke. Even when we signed to Polydor we were only on £25 a week. Johnson's was a shining beacon of hip clothing but it wasn't cheap. Then we did this interview with *Time Out* magazine with a lovely journalist called Phil Shaw, and he told us we had the front cover. It may have been the same day, but he phoned me up and said 'I want you and loads of Mods behind you.' Before mobile phones and the internet came along, how did you assemble 50 Mods at the drop of a hat? Answer is, you don't! After phoning some mates I managed to get three of them and the band. So it just ended up looking like a seven-piece band instead of the band with 20 or so Mods behind us. Polydor heard about the photo shoot and got us down to Johnsons. I felt like the fucking king of the world! I walked in there, and I can still see it – that jacket was on the left-hand side – and I said 'that's mine.' I loved that jacket and I just had to have it. It was probably 60 quid or something and I'm on 25 a week. I was just thinking about The Who and their Union Jack jackets."

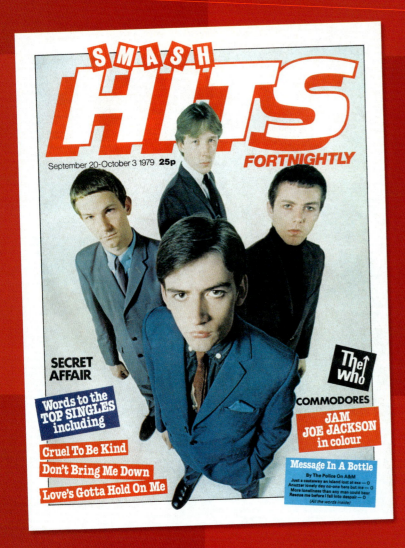

September 20-October 3 1979 25p

SMASH HITS FORTNIGHTLY

SECRET AFFAIR

The Who

COMMODORES

JAM JOE JACKSON in colour

Words to the TOP SINGLES including
Cruel To Be Kind
Don't Bring Me Down
Love's Gotta Hold On Me

Message In A Bottle
By The Police On A&M
Just a castaway an island lost at sea — O
Anuzzer lonely day no-one here but me — O
More loneliness than any man could bear
Rescue me before I fall into despair — O
(All the words inside)

TIME FOR ACTION AND THE GLORY BOYS

"...kind of edgy street kid... ...a bit smart... ...a bit sharp..."

IAN PAGE

Although Secret Affair are hardly mentioned in the early press reports on the new Mod craze, their name was soon being touted along with the words "band most likely to break through." They'd been desperate to distance themselves from their contract with CBS, as their previous incarnation, The New Hearts. After the disappointment of punk and new wave failing to live up to their promise to change the world, both Dave Cairns and Ian Page found inspiration from other sources. They shared a love of the 1960s, and of films, and they got to combine both, when they visited late-night screenings of cult films at the Gate Cinema in Notting Hill and the Electric Cinema on the Portobello Road. One of the films to capture their imagination and become an inspiration was the 1970 film *Performance*, directed by Donald Cammell and Nicholas Roeg. In the film, James Fox plays 'Chas,' a sharp-dressed East End gangster, while Mick Jagger, in his film debut, plays a reclusive rock star. The film is a dark, acid drenched, violent drama that eventually received cult status. It seemed the perfect foundation on which to base the new band's image. Page's admiration for Mick Jagger, mixed with a love of cool sixties London underworld chic, started the ball rolling, but they needed a name to go out and preach their vision to the world.

Ian Page: "Everything that Dave and I did was by conversation. We spent a lot of time driving around London in his mum's Mini. Everything started from the name, really. We'd written quite a few of the songs, and because we'd written 'Glory Boys' we had a mental description of what our people were like, if you know what I mean. This kind of edgy street kid that looks a bit smart and looks a bit sharp and all the rest of it. We were already working on sixties stuff by doing a cover of 'Going To A Go Go' by Smokey Robinson & the Miracles. We were drawing on that element of Motown to mix into our sound. White R&B mixed with black R&B is what we were after. We discussed at great length what the name of the band should be. We were looking for symbolically influencing sixties stuff, movies like *The Thomas Crown Affair*. I think that's where we got 'Affair' from. Also we had a thing we often talked about, Dave and I, with song lyrics and song titles, which was the idea of trying to come up with phrases that people might see in other parts of their life, so they sell each other. Also, we wanted the kind of sense of specialness, you know these street kids, these Glory Boys.

"So we were driving around Soho Square, trying to get out of our record deal. As we were looking for a parking space we kept shouting out names to go in front of 'Affair' because we didn't want to be 'The' something. Then we came up with 'Secret' because one of the most common *News Of The World* newspaper phrases would be 'Vicar's secret affair with...,' and that sort of thing. We realised people would keep seeing that phrase again and again. But also 'secret affair' means anything, it's not just about sex but it's also just about secrets, and secrets are cool, and it also gave us imagery to play with, such as secret agents. That's why we called our label I-Spy. So the notion that we were a secret affair, and that you had to be in on it, was very Mod. It's a positive kind of elitism. So having got that, we thought, where do you most likely find out about secret affairs? Well, you spy them through the keyhole like the butler saw. That's how our keyhole symbol came about. We were conscious we didn't want any targets or arrows."

The band had managed to change labels, from CBS to Arista, and it's there that they were given their own subsidiary label, I-Spy.

Cairns recalls the happiness of that first association: "They were a brand new team, lots of money, and with hungry young people. New Hearts were at CBS, old fashioned and a big company. We made the mistake of signing to CBS because their CO Maurice Oberstein came to see us eight times on the trot, unheard of. But it doesn't mean because he signs you, that he's going to be looking after you. He just sends it downstairs – he knows we're a good band – and a bunch of idiots try to turn us into a boy band. They had no idea it was meant to be a new wave act. They just went in the opposite direction. As newly formed Secret Affair, we got a front page on *Sounds* magazine, courtesy of Garry Bushell, very early, and it fell between still being signed to CBS and joining Arista Records. It almost created a problem for us. CBS didn't want us because they didn't understand what we were doing but suddenly we're on a front cover and now they expect us to be bought out by another label. No matter how hip an act you might be, selling out the Marquee and having a *Sounds* front cover, a record company wants to buy you fresh. A lot of great bands that could have been, we've never heard of since because they were stuck on a label attached to a debt. So while it was great, it was also a millstone around our necks."

The *Record Mirror* cover (*see Mods And The Music Press*) dated August 18, 1979, featured an illustration by Graham Stevens, of Pete Townshend leaping into the air with his guitar. The magazine featured an article on *Quadrophenia* and Mods but lurking among the pages were three small black box ads on separate pages, which built up the promotion for the 'Time For Action,' Secret Affair's debut single, released on August 17. These were just part of the band's clever marketing campaign.

"...the keyhole was an icon in visual art."

IAN PAGE

Ian Page: "The imagery for the I-Spy record logo derives from the Motown label and the Decca logo, as they both had wraparound frames. We knew that the keyhole was an icon in visual art. So we convinced people based on this notion that the first street poster campaign in London for the single would just be a white keyhole with a black background and underneath it would just say 'Time For Action,' but not the name of the band. So people would see it and think 'what's time for action? Is it a protest movement? Is there a revolution coming?' Everybody else's posters were kind of 'The Sick Bags Live At The Roxy,' with safety pins, grainy and ugly people. Now pasted over one of those would be this very slick, black square with a simple white keyhole and 'Time For Action.' It contrasted with the artwork around it. The record company we were with at the time, initially, were very responsive to that kind of thinking. Just like in the early days of punk where record companies were saying to punk bands, 'We don't know what you're doing. We're still wearing shiny jackets and perms and listening to Foreigner. We'd better listen to you,' for the first year we were with Arista, they did that and let us have creative control. All the artwork and visuals came from us."

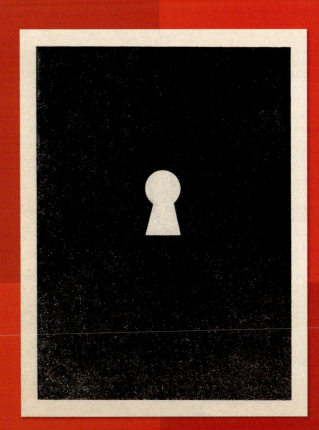

SECRET AFFAIR

"GLORY BOYS"

I-SPY RECORDS

But something threatened to dampen that longed-for impact: a Chris Westwood review of the single, published in the same issue: "Thing with Mods, see, is hypocrisy – 'I never reckoned much to the punk thing' and all that mouthwash, perhaps two months ago after slithering out of their bondage strides: these people wouldn't have even picked up their guitars if it hadn't been for the dread, dead punk. But here they are – gnawing through their contracts (they only just cut their milk teeth) and pushing out reasonably paced, reasonably tight, reasonably insinuating records of totally unremarkable quality: records which would live and die within two weeks of release were it not for this kind, motherly 'scene' to which they attach themselves with leech-like relish. I apologise, but I see nothing in it."

No mention of the song, the lyrics, tune or even band. On the same page, Westwood also reviews The Jam's 'When You Are Young'… but not without having another dig at the Mod scene. Despite poor reviews, 'Time For Action' entered the charts on September 1 and reached number 13 in the charts, eventually selling a quarter of a million copies.

With a follow-up of 'Let Your Heart Dance' reaching number 32 in the charts in November, the album *Glory Boys* was released at the end of that month. Garry Bushell gave it a five-star review along with a full breakdown of the album, summing it up with: "And there you have it. An album of startling strength, ripeness and self-assurety, which virtually single-handedly justifies the New Mod Explosion and places Secret Affair firmly in the vanguard of today's hungry new wave of bands. It is an excellent testimony to their strengths and abilities. A dance album that sparkles with righteous anger, tight instrumentation and snappy singsongs. It's the New Dance."

The cover shot for the acclaimed album features all four members of the band staring out from a rain-soaked window, directly at the viewer. Dave Cairns was happy that they got to work with a photographer they trusted: "We had the photo shoot set up at Fin Costello's converted double garage in Islington. He did all his shoots there. He had a huge portfolio, mainly of heavy rock acts. There was a pub called the Crown in Islington, and his house was opposite. You'd see the bands sat in the pub waiting to go over for the photo session. I can't recall why he wasn't available for the second album because we would have used him. Fin Costello worked with us, not the other way round, and we really liked him."

"For the single, instead of taking a half-page ad in the *NME*, which Arista suggested, we said no, we want to do it a different way. So we had these little box teasers. Sometimes they would go alternate pages [in the magazine]. Sometimes there would be a long gap and one right at the end. It was a very cheap way of advertising, and they loved that, but it also meant we got to use the budget more effectively because we were able to do it for weeks. So then it made sense, to us anyway, to say 10,000 limited edition in a plain brown wrapper, and then you get the whole 'the secret is out' when it culminated. The epiphany of understanding came in the end when people went 'Oh, that's what it's all about!,' which had a much greater impact than just 'Secret Affair. Out Now.'"

"...single-handedly justifies the New Mod Explosion..."

GARRY BUSHELL

1 The band's UK debut LP. Photography by Fin Costello and graphics by GRAPHYK.
2 The band's US version of the cover on Sire Records, signed by lead singer Ian Page.

Although the final result didn't turn out exactly how Ian Page had originally envisioned it, he remembers the amount of effort they put in to getting the album cover just right: "One of the sixties figures I'd always admired was Andrew Loog Oldham. So a lot of the ideas I put forward at the start came from what I knew about him. I thought he was very cool. If you look at the first two original Rolling Stones albums, they're both supremely arrogant, because if you look, there's a really cool photo of the Stones but it doesn't have the name of the band and the albums don't have titles. That was Oldham's idea, and Decca were going crazy saying he couldn't do that. But he was trying to find a way of being non-Beatles, in a way. His notion was that [the Stones] were already successful, he didn't have to tell people who they were, they'd just know. I tried to explain the Andrew Loog Oldham approach to [the record company]. I didn't want the *Glory Boys* album cover to say the band's name but they made us have Secret Affair written on the front and while I knew what I wanted, I had to take into account that I was talking to a very cooperative bunch of people. The outrageous compromise we got, though, was having the title *Glory Boys* with the two outrageous speed pills as the 'Os.'

"We had the distorted look, because Gered Mankowitz had done a photo shoot with The Rolling Stones called 'Between The Buttons' using experimental sixties photography, smearing the edges of the lens with Vaseline to make it look a little bit freaky. On our cover, we are actually standing behind a pane of glass, and Fin Costello had sprayed it with water, the idea being that you are seeing us through a window because it's a 'secret affair.'

"We went for a photographer who knew about light. You look at those Rolling Stones albums and you can see how they've been lit, and our *Glory Boys* cover was painstakingly lit and angled. We spent a whole day doing it. The reason it has the white trim is because almost all the albums of the sixties had a white trim, a gloss vinyl finish and a white cardboard back. Fin also took the back shot standing on a step ladder using a semi-fisheye lens. But, again, it's influenced by The Who's *My Generation* album cover, of them looking up at the camera.

"If you look at any of the early Rolling Stones albums when Loog Oldham was the manager, he always wrote some strange poetic prose on the back sleeves so that's why we put the lyrics of the 'City Of Dreams' poem on the right-hand side of the sleeve."

Secret Affair would go on to have three more hit singles: 'My World,' 'Sound Of Confusion' and 'Do You Know,' plus would put out two further albums: *Behind Closed Doors* and *Business As Usual* before splitting in mid-1982. In 2002, they reformed and although they have changed line-ups along the way, Ian Page and Dave Cairns continue to perform today.

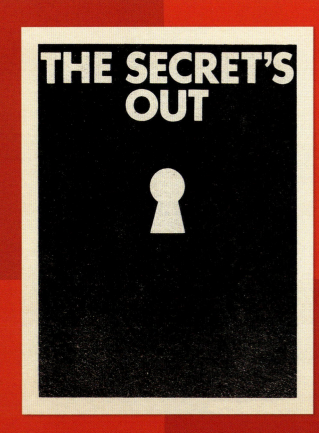

**MY WORLD
SECRET ♁ AFFAIR
THE NEW SINGLE**
SEE 5

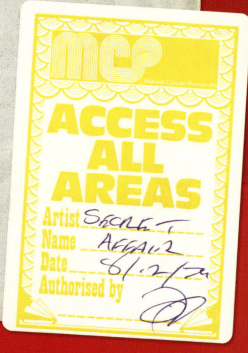

ACCESS ALL AREAS

Artist *Secret*
Name *Affair*
Date *8/.2/14*
Authorised by

MOD ART 174

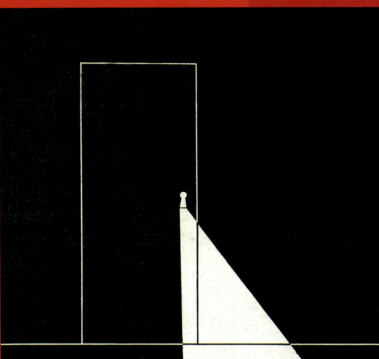

SECRET AFFAIR

THE WORLD TOUR
April
6th Dunstable, Queensway Hall
7th St. Austell, New Cornish Riviera
8th Bournemouth, Stateside Centre
9th Brighton, Top Rank
11th Manchester, Free Trade Hall
12th Hull, Withensey Pavillion
13th Sheffield, Top Rank
14th Stoke, Victoria Hall
15th Cardiff, Top Rank
16th Blackburn, King George's Hall
17th Newcastle, City Hall
18th West Runton, Pavillion
19th Birmingham, Odeon
20th Bristol, Locarno
21st London, Hammersmith Odeon

The Album
GLORY BOYS
I-SPY 1
The Hit Single
MY WORLD
SEE 5

I-SPY RECORDS

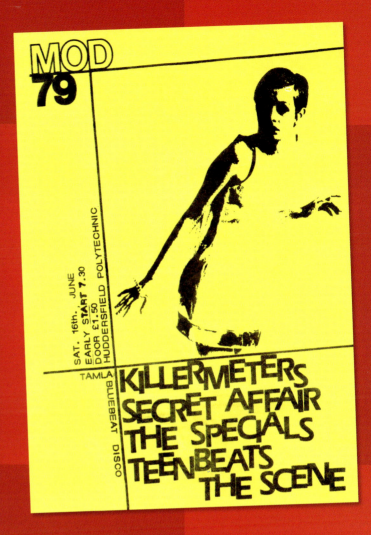

MOD 79

SAT. 16th, JUNE
EARLY START 7.30
DOOR £1.50 HUDDERSFIELD POLYTECHNIC
TAMLA BLUEBEAT DISCO

KILLERMETERs
SECRET AFFAIR
THE SPECIALS
TEENBEATS
THE SCENE

TIME FOR ACTION

SECRET AFFAIR
THE SINGLE
TIME FOR ACTION
—IN A BROWNPAPER BAG—
ON
I-SPY RECORDS

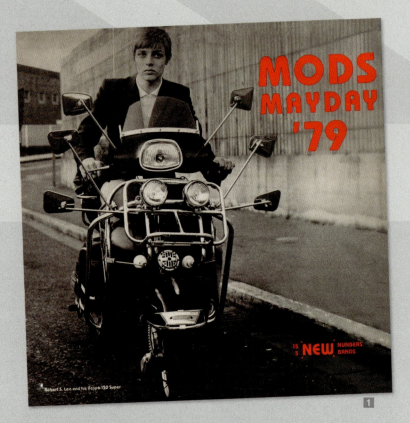

MODS
MAYDAY
'79

15 5 **NEW** NUNBERS BANDS

Robert S. Lee and his Vespa 150 Super

1

CLASSIC ALBUM: *MODS MAYDAY '79*

❝...I considered myself a Mod rather than a revivalist...❞

ROBERT LEE

1 One of the LPs with the spelling mistake on the cover. That original batch was one of the first collectable records during the revival period.

2 Robert Lee sat astride his pride and joy at the time.

The Bridge House in Canning Town was a strange pub to be a music venue. Not only was it nowhere near a tube station, but its long stage was directly opposite the bar, making it difficult for any audience to be more than 10 or 12 people deep, and the areas to either side of the bar gave only a limited view of the proceedings. That said, its rollcall of bands who went on to greater things included U2, Depeche Mode and Paul Young with the Q-Tips.

Terence Murphy had taken over the pub in 1975 and began to revive it as a live music venue. Terry and his friend John McGeady handled band promotion, whilst Terry's son Glen ran the pub business. Glen later found fame as an actor, playing George Green in the ITV television series *London's Burning*. In what proved a shrewd move, the pub began its own independent record label, Bridge House Records Limited, in 1978.

One evening in April 1979, Secret Affair were booked to play. Terry advertised the evening as a Mod night – and a regular weekly event was born. Every Monday, an average of 400 youngsters arrived at the Bridge House, to hear the bands Terry was promoting that week.

On May 7, 1979, the venue hosted an event featuring the hottest new Mod bands, while a live album was recorded to document the rising scene. Secret Affair, Beggar, Merton Parkas, The Little Roosters, Small Hours and The Mods were all lined up to play but, at the last minute, The Little Roosters failed to show. As luck would have it, a little-known band called Squire had driven up from Woking in their van and found themselves filling in, and on the album.

Merton Parkas, having signed a record deal for their first single 'You Need Wheels' with Beggars Banquet records, played but found themselves off the record. The whole album was recorded by the L.M.S. 16-track mobile studio owned by ex-Small Face, Ronnie Lane. It was then cut at Trident Studios in Soho and released on June 29 of that year.

Of the initial 2,000 sold-out copies of the live album, the first 500 had a spelling mistake on the front cover. Instead of '15 new numbers' they read '15 new nunbers,' and once the mistake was spotted these copies began changing hands in certain circles for £20 each – £16 more than the asking price of £4.

Secret Affair were easily the most well-known of the bands on the album. Having already signed to the Arista label, the band were presented on new subsidiary label I-Spy Records. Brian Morrison, the band's publisher, negotiated a deal whereby from September of that year *Mods Mayday '79* would be distributed by Arista, and therefore reach a wider audience.

The cover of the LP was striking: a simple black and white photo of Bridge House regular Robert Lee sat astride his Vespa 150 Super. Robert has vivid memories of those days: "In early '79, the Mod scene around Essex and East London was a completely different animal to what it would become later that same year, with the release of *Quadrophenia* – so creating the Mod Revival. A title that never sat too well with me, personally, as I considered myself a Mod rather than a revivalist, not realising then what lay ahead and how I would end up becoming a part of the forthcoming revival. The scene at that time owed a lot to the new wave ethic of following live bands, as these were generally unsigned and could only be heard at gigs. The Bridge House in Canning Town was typical of this ethic, in that it supported a lot of unknown and unsigned bands, normally on midweek nights that would have been difficult to sell anyway. Monday evenings must have been a difficult night to sell and presumably vacant given that early 1979 Mod Mondays was born with Secret Affair being the main attraction. I first attended the Monday night gigs after hearing from a friend about Secret Affair, and became a regular attendee along with a lot of others. At this time, there weren't vast numbers involved and, due to the fact this was the only venue we knew that was catering exclusively for our musical taste, it was common to see the same people every week regardless of which band was playing. For me personally, Monday nights became the main event of the week; a chance to catch up with like-minded people and compare and hone my attire and of course show off the scooter. It was close to being a youth club in that everyone knew or recognised each other, with the added bonus of live music."

The effect of the *Mods Mayday '79* LP on Robert's life, was mixed. "The May Day event and the recording of that day have since gone down in Mod folklore as being a pivotal point in the Mod Revival, and the fact that my photo was used and is now considered to have been an influential part of the scene makes me very proud – but that wasn't always the case. When I was first asked to pose for a few photos to help promote the forthcoming release of the album I, of course, agreed without question, never expecting much to come of it.

"Then, a couple of weeks later, I arrived at the Bridge House and was invited upstairs to view the photos, only to be shown the album. To say I was gobsmacked would be an understatement. I was truly lost for words, and when I went back downstairs to the bar and was greeted with the site of promotional posters complete with my photo all over the walls, I felt about 10 feet tall. To this day I cannot remember who was playing that night, the whole night is a blur.

"The euphoria didn't last that long though and, quite literally, within weeks of the album being released the scooter was damaged outside the Bridge House – most likely by the ever-growing crowd of younger Mods who were too young to get in and would hang around outside wanting to be part of the scene, which seemed to include sitting all over my scooter. From that point I was allowed to park behind locked gates at the pub, but that only prevented any further damage while I was there on a Monday. There were other places where I had bits either broken or stolen – most annoyingly in my own local area where I had previously been under the radar. The acknowledgement and attention from complete strangers was a buzz to begin with but that, too, soon became a bit of a pain. After all, I was just an 18-year-old Mod who had posed for a photo. I was totally unprepared for the attention I found myself receiving.

"This attention wasn't confined to the scene, as you would expect, but it seemed to spill into everyday life with people nudging each other and pointing, and when Mod became unfashionable within the music scene a year or so later I became a focal point for the inevitable piss-taking. I can remember reading an article in *Sounds* that ran a poll headlined, 'Bore of the year,' and, yes, Mod came out top – complete with a photo of my scooter to help emphasise their point. So I could now add embarrassment to the list of emotions that I had experienced within the space of a year. It really did feel like I had taken the proverbial drink from the poisoned chalice."

The legacy of the album, however, is not all bad. "The one positive that I can now take from the album photo is that it has given me the opportunity to meet some fantastic people in recent years, who I would otherwise not have met, and their enthusiasm and claims that it influenced them have helped me lay my demons and bad memories to rest."

NEWS OF THE WORLD:
MOD FANZINES

"I thought fanzines were great...
...written by fans for fans...
...no other kind of agenda. "

PAUL WELLER

If ever there was one thing that kept the Mod scene going it was fanzines. As most proper music magazines had little or no interest in the movement, it was down to the Mods themselves to relay what was going on in their scene to the rest of the country.

As we've already seen, fanzines were hardly a new idea. In fact, they weren't that different from those R&B monthlies and soul fanzines of the mid-1960s.

Fanzines reached a whole new level during the punk era, when the movement's DIY aesthetic created a whole new underground press featuring the most unlikely wordsmiths. The first UK-based punk fanzine, *Sniffin' Glue*, started life in July 1976. Written by Mark Perry, it paved the way for anybody who had a felt tip, a typewriter, a stapler, a Pritt Stick and access to a photocopier to get on board the fanzine train. Grammar and spelling was irrelevant; it was energy and enthusiasm that really mattered.

While many of the early punk fanzine, such as *48 Thrills*, had a positive reaction to The Jam, *Sniffin' Glue* was less complimentary, stating that the band were indeed too polished. Paul Weller took exception and he burned a copy of the fanzine on stage at the Marquee.

Despite his protest, Weller could see the importance of fanzines in helping to promote bands: "I thought fanzines were great because we weren't getting much action from the *NME*s or the *Melody Maker*s for quite a long time really, and if we were, it was fairly critical and disparaging. Shane MacGowan did one called *Bondage* and there was *48 Thrills* by Adrian Thrills, among others. They were really behind us. The Mod fanzines came later on, and they weren't my cup of tea at all really. I'd moved on at that time, but having said that, I still loved the whole idea of a fanzine because it's written by fans for fans and there's no other kind of agenda."

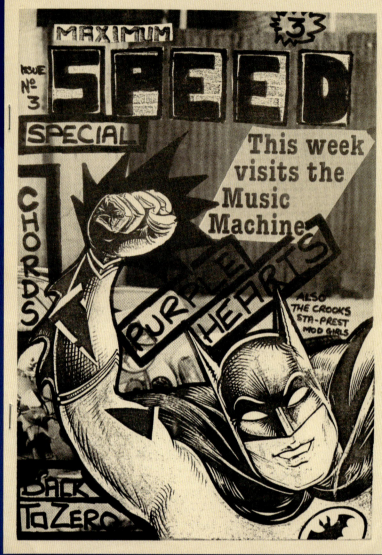

Jamming! was the creation of 13-year-old Tony Fletcher, the first issue hot off the high school printers in 1977. By the the fifth issue that came the following year, *Jamming!* was featuring interviews with the likes of Paul Weller and John Peel, and Fletcher had to upgrade to professional printing and wider distribution. From 1979–84, *Jamming!* was printed and partly distributed by Better Badges. It would go on to feature interviews with a range of artists that included Pete Townshend, Dexys Midnight Runners, The Jam, The Damned, Crass and Tom Robinson, among many others. The magazine finally folded in January 1986 after 36 issues. Tony Fletcher would go on to become a successful author, writing the widely acclaimed and bestselling biography *Dear Boy: The Life Of Keith Moon*.

By the time the Mod Revival was truly underway in 1978, *Sniffin' Glue* and many other punk fanzines were already consigned to history. There was nothing out there to promote this new musical direction, that is until Geoff 'Goffa' Gladding, Kim Gault and Clive Reams started *Maximum Speed*.

Having flunked his degree and finding himself living back at home in London, Goffa found himself helping to promote a friend's band, Back To Zero. Although they started out playing to around six people at venues such as the Hop Poles in Enfield, the audiences slowly grew.

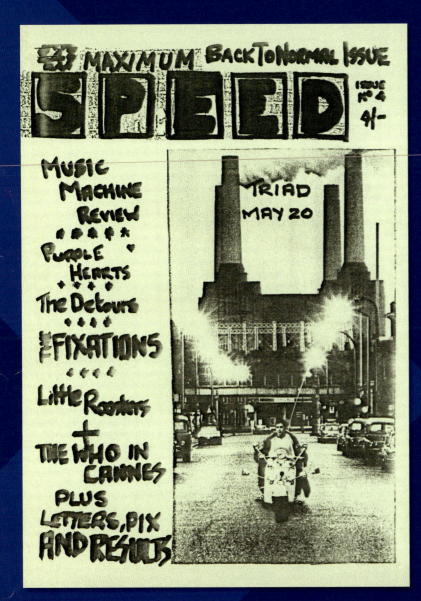

Goffa recalls: "Clive said we need to give this band a leg up by promoting them. How about we do a Mod fanzine? We'd obviously seen punk fanzines such as *Sniffin' Glue*. This seemed to be the only way to get your kind of thinking out to a bigger audience. So we did the first edition, which was pretty much nonsense, and Clive did it mostly on his own, by and large. We got about 50 printed by a local firm. If you look at the second issue, though, it's a bit more professional and higher quality. It was a real labour of love."

The initial result was a very crude-looking fanzine. Sold for 20p, *Maximum Speed* had a single staple in the top left-hand corner holding together nine single-sided A4 pages. That said, they managed to cram in a review of The Purple Hearts in Southend, a preview of *Quadrophenia* – "borrowed" from another publication (although, in felt tip, they already warn that the film will be the beginning of the end for the scene) – a short biography of Back To Zero and a handwritten advert for a Brighton Mod meet-up in May. They also feature clippings about sixties Mods and photocopied passages from the 1964 book *Generation X*.

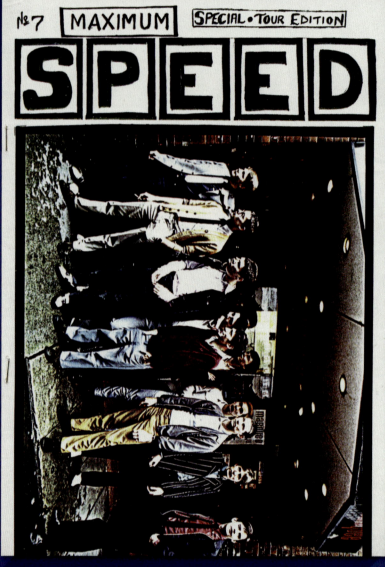

By Issue 3 you can see the quality creeping in, as by that point the fanzine was held together with *two* side staples, boasted a glossy cover and contained 12 one-sided pages of good quality, including photos.

"...amazed how *Maximum Speed* took off..." "

GEOFF 'GOFFA' GLADDING

By June 1979, *Maximum Speed* had become a fortnightly release. The print-run had risen to 1,000. The fanzine was still growing (16 single-sided pages) and contained great interviews from such luminaries as Billy Hassett of The Chords and Paul Weller. Profits were put to good use, as the trio of writers began holding their own concerts under the banner Maximum Speed Promotions. The three also began managing Back To Zero, and helped them negotiate a record contract for their only single 'Your Side Of Heaven,' produced by Chris Parry, producer of The Jam records at Polydor and founder of Fiction Records.

MILLIONS LIKE US / BEAT THAT!!
FICS 003

YOUR SIDE OF HEAVEN / BACK TO BACK
FICS 004

NOW ITS GONE
b/w DON'T GO BACK
2059 141

PLUS......QUADROPHENIA......TEENBEATS......LONG TALL SHORTY......LAMBRETTAS......SOUTHEND......AND MUCH MORE......

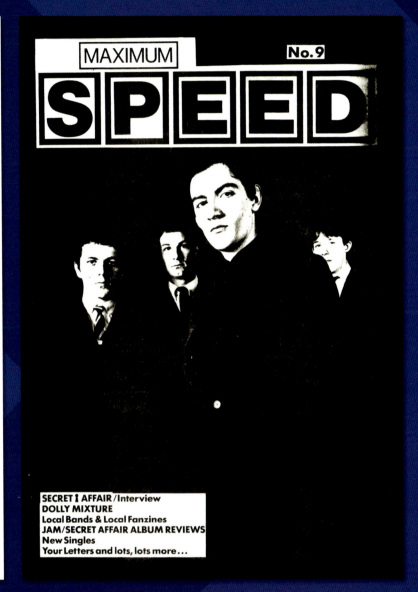

SECRET ⚡ AFFAIR / Interview
DOLLY MIXTURE
Local Bands & Local Fanzines
JAM / SECRET AFFAIR ALBUM REVIEWS
New Singles
Your Letters and lots, lots more...

Sounds magazine eventually picked up on the trio's accomplishments, and a small article about the fanzine appeared in one of the June editions. A month later, *Sounds* asked the trio to compile a dossier of current Mod bands, in the feature entitled 'Who's Who In Mod?.'

Goffa: "I was amazed how *Maximum Speed* took off and how music papers, particularly *Sounds*, picked up on it. We would go around the back of Carnaby Street on a Wednesday lunchtime. There was a newsagent that would get *Sounds* in early, and a group of people would gather there to buy it. For a period of a few months the first thing we wanted to know was if we were in it. They would say things like, 'Billy Idol had come to a Maximum Speed Promotions gig at the Cambridge pub in Edmonton,' in a little gossip column."

It was Issue 7 before *Maximum Speed* finally featured double-sided pages. Goffa explains the long, drawn-out process of getting a copy together: "To do a front cover for the fanzine we'd go to Polydor and get a photo of Dave Cairns or whoever. Then you think, shit, I need more. So you go to Polydor again and get another two photos. Then you cut around three of them so you can get the effect you need. Then you photocopy them. Type the thing out... shit, it doesn't fit! So then you had to retype it, as there was no Photoshop back then, but in truth I loved it, loved it, loved it."

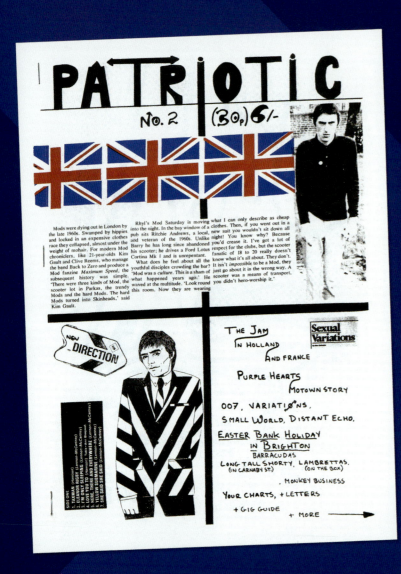

Looking through *Maximum Speed*'s back catalogue, you get a feel for the mixture of personal and sometimes puerile articles, combined with an informed awareness of the scene. Write-ups, such as Grant Fleming's hilarious account of The Jam in Paris, would never make it into an officially released magazine. Many of the articles included some of the scene's great characters and you could follow the adventures of people such as Barney Rubble or The Crank, adventures that inevitably involved drinking, stealing, fighting or shagging. Sometimes all four.

On a more serious note, *Maximum* helped many of the bands through gig and album reviews. Among the bands that they championed were Secret Affair, The Chords, The Purple Hearts, Squire and Merton Parkas, but also lesser known bands such as The Little Roosters, The Fixations, Speedball and Six More Prophets. They never really promoted The Jam, who they affectionately named The Jim Jams, as they knew the band got plenty of press in the music weeklies anyway during the Mod Revival.

By Issues 7 and 8, the fanzine is sporting a full-colour glossy cover, and you can give up waiting for the long-promised piece (either an interview or article – it changed all the time) on Pete Townshend, as it would be appearing in the next issue. *Maximum Speed* continued to be sold at various gigs and was now also available by mail order and stocked by record shops such as Rough Trade and various Virgin Records outlets. By the time Issue 9 was released, circulation was up to 9,000. Issue 10 was advertised as featuring insights into Paul Weller's love of poetry, a Small Hours article and, of course, the Pete Townshend spectacular... sadly none of these appeared as Issue 10 never materialised. The fanzine, much like the Mod Revival itself, had been fuelled by the fire of new ideas and music, only to burn out by the end of the year. However, the *Maximum Speed* writers ensured their legacy would live on when, in their final issue (Issue 9), they reviewed six new fanzines that were helping to spread the word.

"We never minded when other fanzines started," says Goffa. "We weren't looking into being the only one on the block. We were genuinely doing it because we loved it to bits and we loved the music more than anything. It was never meant to be a stepping stone to anything else."

Goffa's writing skills were never in doubt. The magazine *Fab 208* had already invested in his talent by getting him to write a short article entitled 'A Day In The Life Of A Mod' in a Mod-themed issue that November. The following year, 1980, would see him writing about various bands for *Sounds* magazine, including The Circles, Secret Affair and The Chords, but reading his articles, you can almost feel his disdain for how the scene went downhill so quickly.

> **❝...genuinely doing it because we loved it... ...proceeded to write this really slag-off review. ❞**
>
> GEOFF 'GOFFA' GLADDING

"I have to say that [*Maximum Speed*] kind of led me to writing for *Sounds* and stuff like that. Which I enjoyed doing for a while until they asked me about bands I didn't like that much, and so I wrote what I thought about them and was a bit surprised when they weren't published. They paid for me to go to Paris to see a band. I remember the first line I wrote was 'Question: Why does a record company pay for somebody like me to go to Paris to see a band? Answer: Because they hope the person will write something really favourable about them and it would be a great review. Question: Does it always work? Answer: No...' Then I proceeded to write this really slag-off review. Of course, the first big chunk got deleted completely and it turned into just an average review of the band. At that point I thought to myself, am I really interested in doing this? I loved the music but I wanted to tell the truth."

By 1980, and with *Maximum Speed* now gone, other fanzines grabbed the baton. One of the earliest hailed from Stoke Newington. Ray Margeston's *Patriotic* certainly helped fill the gap left by Maximum.

Margeston remembers: *Maximum Speed* was a big influence on my own fanzine, however, it was really the punk ethos and 'get up and do something' attitude that made it. I used to help the guys at *Maximum Speed* put together their fanzine, in as much as collating and stapling. When they finished their fanzine, I decided to do mine as a continuation of what was going on in the Mod scene."

Margeston wasn't about to let something as trivial as not owning a typewriter stop him in his quest, so he found himself hand-writing, in capital letters, all 25 single-sided pages of Issue 1. Then he managed to print off 100 copies using the office printer at his job in the City. When Margeston accepted that he couldn't risk commandeering the work printers again, Issue 2 was delayed, although when it finally did arrive, one bonus of upping production values was that the issue now had double-sided pages. By Issue 3, Margeston had ditched the pen for his mother's old typewriter. Each issue took around two months to complete, but as the quality improved, the process lengthened.

Margeston: "I used to literally go out every night to gigs and clubs, then would come home and put together an article gone midnight. It was very helpful around '82, as I used speed to keep going in the clubs till the early hours, then came home and wrote the article."

As the fanzine gained popularity the output eventually topped 1,000 copies per issue, and was sent out all over.

"I think fanzines were very important during this period as they helped, for example, with people learning about what was going on in the capital, and helped them to create their own scene wherever they were in the UK, or even around the world. I literally had fanzines being sent out to Holland, Belgium, Italy and Australia, so it was turning into a really global thing, especially considering we didn't have the internet or mobile phones.

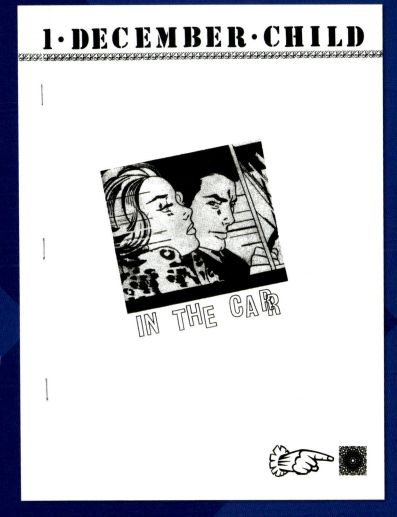

"What I'm really pleased about, in writing my fanzine, was that it influenced a lot of other Mods: what they listened to, what they wore, where they went to gigs, what bands to see... It also helped promote bands such as 007 and The Variations, bands respectively from East and North London. It also promoted clubs nights that I was involved with and also set up: Mildmay Tavern, Sebright Arms, Ilford Palais all-dayers, Barons, Regency Suite, Lords, Middleton Arms, Burlington's in Piccadilly."

If Paul Weller wasn't an advocate of the Mod fanzine, he certainly believed in the concept. In 1980, he released his own contribution, *December Child*. Over three issues it proved to be a showcase not only for his poetry but for pop art and his favourite bands, including The Creation, John's Children and The Action.

Weller explains: "At that time, around '79/'80, I was doing lots of writing. Not just songs but just lots of writing for myself – prose, poems or whatever it was. I suppose in a self-indulgent way I wanted to be able to put it out but then broadened it out to include other people's work as well. I was into a lot of literature and art at the time, plus I was going to a lot of art galleries. I think I was probably making up for all the time I was never interested in it at school. You know, when it's fuckin' rammed down your throat. When it isn't, and you come to it yourself, you see it differently. I think there was a kind of evangelistic thing in it to some extent, because of that thing of when you're young and get turned on to something, whether it's a record or a band or whatever it may be, and you just want to put everyone on to it. So I guess there was an element of that as well. Also, the way that generally working-class people were excluded from anything 'arty.'

"I did a few books as well, anthologies I suppose, that fans had sent in. It was kind of like these people can write fucking good poetry or something interesting. You haven't got to go to fuckin' Oxford or Cambridge to do that. It's about imagination and putting words together. There was a kind of message there, a sort of 'Why should this kind of stuff be excluded to us because you don't go to the right schools?'"

In 1981, a poem called 'Pop Art Poem', a musical interpretation of which was recorded by The Jam, featured in the first issue of *December Child* and made it onto a disc as a free giveaway in *Flexipop* magazine, which was run by ex-*Record Mirror* writer Barry Cain.

After The Jam split in 1982, a whole host of Mod groups disbanded too. The music press pretty much gave up on reporting on the remaining bands, so fanzines were more important than ever. In September 1983, *Jamming!* managed to go bi-monthly, and later monthly. But by January 1986, after 36 issues, the fanzine shut down.

But the mid-eighties saw a whole new raft of Mod fanzines, including *Shadows And Reflections* from Cambridgeshire, *That's Entertainment* from Woolwich, *What'cha Gonna Do About It* from Pitsea, Essex, *Fabulous* from Cardiff and *Right Track* from Ilford, Essex. Special mentions go to *The Hipster* from Coventry, which was properly typeset and looked great, and Derek Shepherd's *In The Crowd* from Guernsey, which ran from 1983–90, totalled 30 issues and grew from a first-issue print run of 100 to an average of 2,000.

SHADOWS AND **REFLECTIONS**

A NEW OPTIMISM FROM THE '60'S!!

NO. 3

SQUIRE
THE TIMES
THE SCENE
THE WAYOUT
SMALL WORLD
JETSET FLEXI DISC

RIGHT TRACK No.9

"...there was a kind of evangelistic thing in it..."

PAUL WELLER

POP-ART POEM.

kidwalksdownstreetbumpsintoemptiness   - POW!

kidlooksattheskylooksatwatchdecidestogohome - ZAP!.

KIDSPYSaPRettygiRlwalksuptOHerkisseshEronthemouth(whereelse?-).

anda ll d   a y longhesthinking

hesthinkingthisthatandth e o   ther

and WHAMM! so ami

(FOOT NOTE)
           i madethisu   p asiwentalong.
                  itsgoodinnit.

1 The lyrics to 'Pop Art Poem' appeared in Issue 1 of Paul Weller's fanzine *December Child*. They were recorded as a spoken poem with music alongside 'Boy About Town' on a flexi disc in issue two of *Flexipop* magazine in January 1981.

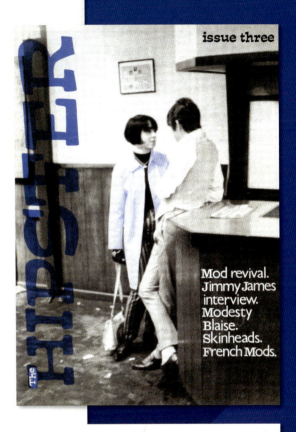

issue three

Mod revival. Jimmy James interview. Modesty Blaise. Skinheads. French Mods.

IN THE CROWD

ISSUE 29   80p   MODZINE

Long-time Mod from Loughton, Eddie Piller, started the fanzine *Extraordinary Sensations* in the mid-eighties: "Fanzines were the most important thing. Every town had a fanzine. You'd go to Derby, Stockport or Belfast and there'd be a fanzine. They might only sell a hundred copies, but it mattered. You go to Chesterfield, just up the road from Derby, and there would be somebody selling 150 copies of their fanzine, you go to Derry, you go to Oldham and there were fanzines.

"*Extraordinary Sensations* was the local fanzine on a national scale. So we used to sell 10–12,000 copies. But there was *Patriotic*, *Roadrunner* and *In The Crowd* all selling well, but mine sold the most. Why did I do it? Because *Maximum Speed*, *Get Up And Go*, *Direction*, *Reaction*, *Creation* and *Shake* stopped. In late '79 I realised the Mod backlash hadn't really started in the music press and [Mod] was still quite big at that point. I realised that these guys that I'd give my 20p to at football or a gig were bored of it because most of them were four years older than me. I thought that this is going to die unless I do my own fanzine. So I did, and the first one sold 10 copies, the second sold 30, the third 150, the fourth sold 500, the fifth 2,000, and this carried on until it was so big I needed a full-time office and an assistant, and Terry Rawlings to deal with the post bag alone. I was getting 60 letters a week. I would send 20 fanzines to one bloke in Northern Ireland, 20 to another, and so on, until I'm selling 12,000 copies of some fuckin' pieces of paper written for Mods by me and with a bit of help from Terry Rawlings. Suddenly this is the most important thing on the Mod scene."

The nearest thing to a 'professional' Mod fanzine was *The Face*, which started life in May 1980. Its editor, Tim Logan, had previously been editor of *NME*, as well as being creator of *Smash Hits* pop magazine. *The Face* was a monthly magazine that covered music, fashion and youth culture, with a fantastic range of contributors including Garry Crowley, Tony Parsons, Pennie Smith, Vaughn Toulouse, Julie Burchill, Derek Ridgers, Jon Savage, Virginia Turbett and Tony Fletcher. It started out very Mod friendly, with features covering Two Tone, Paul Weller, The Chords and Pete Townshend. As time went on, though, Mod fell out of favour, but the magazine ran successfully until May 2004.

❝...the most important thing on the Mod scene.❞

EDDIE PILLER

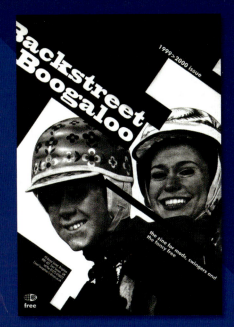

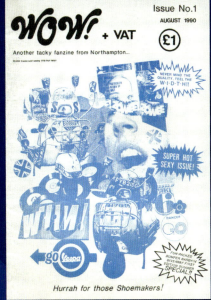

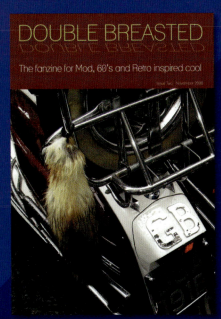

Mod fanzines from across the years, from the basic cut, paste and photocopy of *Roadrunner* and *Empty Dreams* through to the advancement in home computers and printing techniques of *Double Breasted* (2009).

The ultimate was *The Face*, which, whilst not a Mod fanzine, catered for Mod tastes in most of the early issues.

1

TERRY TONIK

"...I wanted to go in to graphic design. ...should have gone to art school..."

IAN HARRIS

1 Just a little Mod. In the back garden of the family home, Kingsbury, NW London, summer, 1965.

2 Promo photo shoot by Norman Brand. Suit by Johnson's.

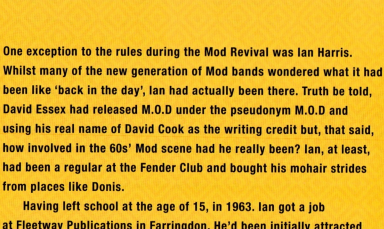

One exception to the rules during the Mod Revival was Ian Harris. Whilst many of the new generation of Mod bands wondered what it had been like 'back in the day', Ian had actually been there. Truth be told, David Essex had released M.O.D under the pseudonym M.O.D and using his real name of David Cook as the writing credit but, that said, how involved in the 60s' Mod scene had he really been? Ian, at least, had been a regular at the Fender Club and bought his mohair strides from places like Donis.

Having left school at the age of 15, in 1963. Ian got a job at Fleetway Publications in Farringdon. He'd been initially attracted by them because Fleetway were responsible for producing the War Picture Library comics and Ian thought he had landed his dream job of becoming an illustrator and would be drawing soldiers all day long. Alas, his hopes were shattered when he discovered that all the illustrations for his beloved comics were drawn in Spain. It seemed he would have to accept a role as a post-room messenger boy.

"I knew I wanted to go in to graphic design. It was called commercial art in those days. I was at Fleetway for a year until they wanted me to take an exam and become a clerk. A guy in the merchandising office where I was working recognised I'd been drawing all my spare time and told me he had a friend who had an art studio in Oxford Circus and perhaps I should contact him. So I got a job as a junior artist doing advertising promotion. I learned hand-lettering and graphic design. I didn't do any GCEs and I should have gone to art school but I learned my trade as a commercial artist in the studio."

Throughout this time, Ian had spent his nights at venues like the Flamingo Club, checking out Georgie Fame, and every other R&B filled club of that time. He had even formed an early Mod band with some like-minded mates: they had called themselves The Third Party before changing their name to Conviction, and belted out 'In the Midnight Hour' whilst sporting dyed waiters jackets with arrows stencilled on them.

Terry Tonik

❝...no idea why I wrote it as there was no Mod stuff going on... ❞

IAN HARRIS

Come 1971, Ian had been in various bands with little or no success. He found himself in Gooseberry Studios in Soho recording a song he'd written – titled 'Happy' – whilst playing his banjo. He touted the song everywhere and nearly got a deal at EMI. When that fell through, he left London in search of sea air and found himself in Brighton.

"At the time I was playing a four string tenor banjo, actually I did buy a tenor guitar, which is a four string guitar. I'd write all my music on that tenor guitar using tenor banjo chords, which are nothing like any other chord on any other instrument. I'd moved to Brighton in 1972 and was still constantly writing. I wrote the lyrics to 'Just A Little Mod.' I have no idea why I wrote it as there was no Mod stuff going on at the time but it was still in me."

It wasn't until 1978, however, that Ian saw the emergence of a new breed of Mods brought to his attention by The Jam. Having already made a demo of 'Just A Little Mod' he played it to his long-time friend Andy Powell, who had made a name for himself as the guitarist in rock band Wishbone Ash. Eventually Powell's manager, John Sherry, heard Ian's song and suggested it should be put out as a single. Just one drunken, pub meeting later and Ian had created for himself a new persona: "Me and Andy [Powell] sat there trying to think of a name for me. At first I thought about going under the pseudonym 'Fred Perry.' We were slowly getting pissed. My brother's name is Terry, and I thought about how I used to wear Tonik mohair back in the day so I became Terry Tonik. TT is good!"

Ian then purchased a Tonik suit from Johnson's in the King's Road and, in 1979, eight years after he'd recorded 'Happy,' he found himself back in that self-same studio on Gerrard Street to lay down a track for the B-side. Called 'Smashed And Blocked,' this song visited the drug scene of Mod culture.

"We recorded and mixed both sides in one day. Andy Powell was on guitar and we got two session guys on drums and bass. The drumming was supposed to sound like The Who. I did all the artwork for the sleeve and came up with the Posh logo for the label. I wanted the lyrics on the back of the sleeve because I had a story to tell. I was an old Mod and nobody else was doing that. At that time, I had my own business painting blinds in a little studio in Kingley Street. There was a photographer called Norman Brand on the top floor and he took the promo photos of me in his studio upstairs."

Unfortunately, the single never actually got released until early 1980 and by then the so-called revival was already on the wane. Ian even designed a fanzine called *Talkin' 'Bout My Generation* to accompany the single, telling potted histories of his heroes such as Georgie Fame, Graham Bond and John Mayall, but to no avail and the record sank without a trace. It didn't help that Ian never performed a single gig as his alter ego.

"I managed to get it on a playlist on Radio Pennine and it got one play!" laughs Ian. "I'd had 2,000 pressed. I'd sold a box of 50 to Virgin Records but it was hard and we were stuck with over 1,500 so I ripped off all the picture bags, stuck it in a plain white sleeve and re-released it with 'Smashed And Blocked' as the A-side... It got a review in *Melody Maker* and it said something like, 'a bit of a tubthumper. Says nothing, goes nowhere.' We eventually just threw the rest away. You have to bear in mind I'd written it eight years earlier. I know people think it, and it is a novelty single, but for me it was sincere. I really meant it."

Nowadays, Ian is usually to be found in his studio, working on paintings. He still loves his war stuff and pop art; he's still sports smart clothes and carries the Mod look to a tee. 'Just A Little Mod' usually changes hands for approximately £70 a copy.

1 Ian's modern-day artwork includes this piece *Branches Everywhere*, 2010.

2 Ian's frustration with not being able to illustrate the War Picture Library still manifests in his art today, regularly painting Spitfires, Hurricanes, Stukas and Messerschmitts.

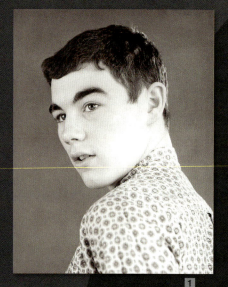

One evening in 1979, Mickey Modern was walking along the Old Kent Road with his daughter. As he passed the Thomas A Becket pub he was astounded to see a group of scooters parked up outside. Wailing R&B drifted out of the door, filling the night air with the long-lost tones of Little Walter. Having been an original sixties Mod, for a brief moment Mickey thought he had stumbled into a time warp. He dropped his daughter back home then went back the pub to investigate. Inside, he found a band that seemed to have been perfectly preserved from those bygone days. The short hair, the sharp suits... and that music! They had already been playing for two years and had built up a loyal following. When the band finished playing, Mickey sat down with the lead singer and guitarist Dennis Greaves and harmonica player Mark Feltham, and listened with fascination to their story of how Nine Below Zero had come together.

Mark Feltham: "Back in '77, Dennis convinced me to come down and have a jam in his living room. All the blues covers like 'Boom Boom, Out Go The Lights' and 'You'd Better Watch Yourself' by Little Walter, I took to Dennis. They'd been doing bits by Stan Webb, Chicken Shack, old Fleetwood Mac, you know, the British R&B rather than the American side where I came from, as it were. The band was actually called Stan's Blues Band after Stan Webb [Chicken Shack frontman]. Dennis was also a big Free fan so he had that rock side to him. At the time, punk was massive and we'd just missed the pub-rock boom so we were completely un-hip. Dennis had that Moddy side to him. He was very much a Mod, where I wasn't."

Dennis Greaves: "I'd got into the blues through my uncle. He and his mates went to the Marquee to see Clapton, John Mayall, The Action and all that early stuff. My mates at school were listening to Gary Glitter, Marc Bolan and David Bowie. I went through all of my uncle's records and found The Graham Bond Organisation and stuff like that – just amazing, I don't know why.

"When we supported The Who, Pete Townshend said we reminded him of them when they first started out with old R&B songs. Everybody else was playing punk. I didn't like punk fashion so what I did was find my dad's wardrobe with all his suits and his sixties stuff. There was also a place called Crampton Clothing on the Old Kent Road, where we could pick up a suit for about a quid. There were also the Salvation Army Stores where you could pick up a shirt for about 5p. We were retro back then, but we were always influenced by the old black guys. You know, the old black guys that dressed up to be accepted in Chicago by the white race. I suppose we copied that. It was all quite natural."

NINE BELOW ZERO: A SHOT OF R&B

❝ ...Townshend said we reminded him of them when they first started out... ❞

DENNIS GREAVES

Mickey Modern: "I thought why call yourself Stan's Blues Band because you sound like Chicken Shack and you're too young? I said to them, get yourself a name that you love and is something to do with the blues. So they came up with Rocket 88 for about a week, The Mannish Boys for about another week. I didn't think it sounded right and the publishers were getting to me. I put pressure on Dennis and he came up with the Sonny Boy Williamson song 'Nine Below Zero'."

Feltham: "I think Mickey Modern was a very talented bloke and was a great talent spotter. He just told us he'd sort us, and that he'd got the contacts. He took us out of the pubs. We wouldn't be here without him. He negotiated with A&M and got us the record deal."

At the time, Mickey was a musician contracted to A&M Records, but he became the band's manager and under Modern's creative direction and production, Nine Below Zero went full time, releasing their debut album *Live At The Marquee*, which was recorded on July 16, 1980. Michael Ross and Simon Ryan provided design and art direction.

By the end of that year they were one of the most popular club attractions in London.

Feltham: "We kept our credibility throughout the Mod Revival only because we had that blues image and a lot of the Mod bands at that time didn't have a harmonica. Now, if Dennis had been playing Mod music I wouldn't have been with him, so the harmonica gave us that edge."

Greaves: "We never had a hit and we were never on *Top Of The Pops* so I think that kind of saved our bacon."

The band's second album, *Don't Point Your Finger*, released in 1981, was recorded over 12 days at Olympic Sound Studios and produced by the legendary Glyn Johns. It came with a cover cartoon image of the band by Marco Ropes. Their 1982 album *Third Degree* spent six weeks in the album charts, reaching number 38. It featured a cover photograph by none other than David Bailey.

Despite their success, the band split up and Dennis Greaves fronted Mod pop/soul band The Truth for the remainder of the 1980s. Nine Below Zero reformed in 1990 and have played together with various line-ups ever since.

Feltham: "I think *Live At The Marquee* captures us, and it's one of the best live albums recorded. The atmosphere on the record is fantastic and I love 'Tore Down' on that. My favourite sleeve is the *Third Degree* cover, purely because it was David Bailey. I remember him being extremely difficult to please. He called me 'The Lawyer' because I guess I must have looked like a lawyer to him at the time. I didn't actually like the cover shot because of the furrow in my forehead but everyone said that's how you are! I would say we were with him around two hours. He was a taskmaster but he got the performance. It was A&M that picked what they wanted for the cover. We never saw anything else that came from that session."

1 Manager Micky Modern in his days as an original Face.

2 Early advert for Stan's Blues Band, before eventually settling on a cooler sounding name.

3 Dennis Greaves appreciated being shot by the same camera used to shoot the Krays far more than being shot by the Krays.

Greaves: "My favourite album is *Don't Point Your Finger* because it was the first album where I tried to write songs and we were in Barnes Studios with Glyn Johns. The *Third Degree* album has my favourite cover. What Bailey did was take one look at us and he said to his assistant, 'Get me the camera I shot The Krays with.' He hadn't used it since he'd taken those shots. The camera was a Hasselblad, I remember."

"We never had a hit... ...kind of saved our bacon..."

DENNIS GREAVES

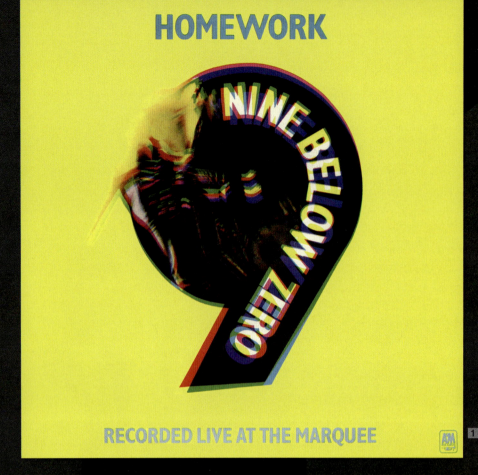

1 Three track EP promoting the band's great live sound.

2 Just as *Five Live Yardbirds* did for the Yardbirds, this album captured the band at their blueswailin' best on a hot summer's evening at the Marquee, London on July 16, 1980. Art direction by Michael Ross and design by Simon Ryan. Photography by Iain McKell (front cover) and Janette Beckman (rear cover).

3 Recorded over 12 days at Olympic Studios in Barnes, London, 1981. The album proved that the band was capable of writing storming R&B as well as covering it. Cover drawing by Marco Ropes and art direction by Michael Ross.

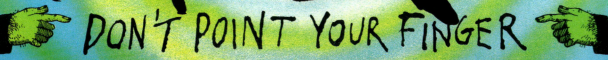

9 BELOW ZERO

DON'T POINT YOUR FINGER

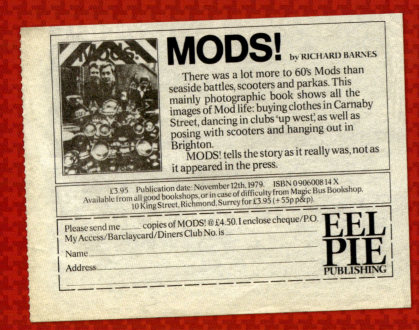

THE 1980s: LOOKING BACK TO THE ORIGINALS

> **"...I'd hate us to end up old and embarrassing..."**
>
> PAUL WELLER

By 1982, more and more Mods seemed to be swapping their parkas and suits for flight jackets and army greens as their priorities became more centred around their scooters and less their clothes. But while many embraced the 'Scooter Boy' culture, purists were still finding ways to discover more about their Mod forefathers.

For many, Richard Barnes' book *Mods!*, first published in 1979, had become a bible, a portal to a time of Scene Club dancers, suede jackets and Sue Records. Fans were craving a purer sixties look, and suddenly tailors and second-hand record shops were inundated with new Mods again.

Midway through 1982, Secret Affair split up and on October 30, The Jam announced that they, too, were going to split before the end of the year. These two bands were easily the biggest and most successful of the revival. The Jam had toured their UK number one album, *The Gift*, earlier that year, following British dates with tours of Europe, North America and Japan. When Paul Weller returned from Italy he revealed the news that fans dreaded: "At the end of this year, The Jam will be officially splitting up, as I feel we have achieved all we can together as a group. I mean this both musically and commercially. I want all we have achieved to count for something and most of all, I'd hate us to end up old and embarrassing like so many other groups do."

As the revival had mainly been built up around the bands, it seemed only logical that as more bands gave up, so did the fans. Many Mods drifted away, but while concert halls may have suffered, club and pub venues thrived as suddenly the scene became more focused on vinyl. Hundreds of old and rare sixties soul, R&B, ska, blues and jazz 45s were now the main attraction.

Birmingham was a focal point, and could boast a great DJ in Tony Reynolds, and great clubs such as the Barrel Organ, the Outrigger and Sinatra's. London, of course, had its fair share of clubs and by 1983, northern soul had to make way for the return of original R&B records. Bob Morris and Eddie Piller started up a 'Crawdaddy R&B' night in Whitechapel. Eddie also got involved with Ray 'Patriotic' Margeston at the Regency Suite in Chadwell Heath. 'Bang In The West End' was held at the Phoenix Club in Cavendish Square, with Toski and Ian Jackson DJ'ing. All these club nights were full of young kids wearing tailor-made or vintage clothes, dancing to some of the rarest and most obscure R&B, ska, beat, soul and jazz ever recorded.

Before the vinyl revolution, legendary Mod DJ Tony Class had dominated London's Mod scene. Scooter Boys clashed with purists, but Tony was happy to let anybody into his nights, one of which – Saturday night at the Bush in Shepherd's Bush – was open to everyone. But soon the 'elite' Mods wanted their own night, and they got it in the form of Sneakers, at the same venue on a Sunday, with Paul Hallam and Richard Early at the helm. It became the first club to put up a sign demanding: "Smart Dress Only. No Jeans. No Greens. No Casuals."

'Casuals' was the name given to the latest street tribe. As football fans followed their team around Europe, they developed a penchant for European designer sportswear, such as Lacoste, Sergio Tacchini and Robe di Kappa. While Casuals were seen as Mods' arch-enemy, the two rival groups were connected through their love of clothes. Some Mods even began mixing and matching both Mod and Casual clothing, and in so doing loosely gaining the nickname 'Modules.'

Paul Weller's new band The Style Council (in which he was joined by Mick Talbot, who had been organ player in the Mod Revival band Merton Parkas) was quick to pick up on and embrace this European-style influence.

Weller: "In the early days of The Style Council, around '83 and '84, we spent quite a lot of time in Paris doing promos and we recorded there too. We were quite big in Italy, too, and did lots of promos there as well. We were just taking in things generally in these places, such as clothes. Even though it was the early eighties it was still hard to find different colours. It was pretty fuckin' dull over [in the UK] to be honest, but when you went to places like Paris or Rome, you'd see jumpers in every colour, great shoes and things that you couldn't see in this country. Now it's generic and it's the fuckin' same everywhere you go. Back then it was quite different, so we would just go fuckin' mad and buy shitloads of clothes you could never see over here. England was really closed minded at the time, stuffy and old fashioned. It's different now; people are more travelled and generally enlightened."

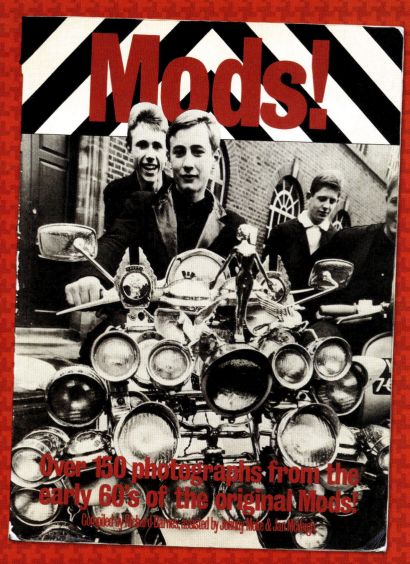

Mods!

Over 150 photographs from the early 60's of the original Mods!

Compiled by Richard Barnes, assisted by Johnny Moke & Jan McVeigh

"...was f***in' dull over [in the UK]... England was really closed minded at the time, stuffy and old fashioned. "

PAUL WELLER

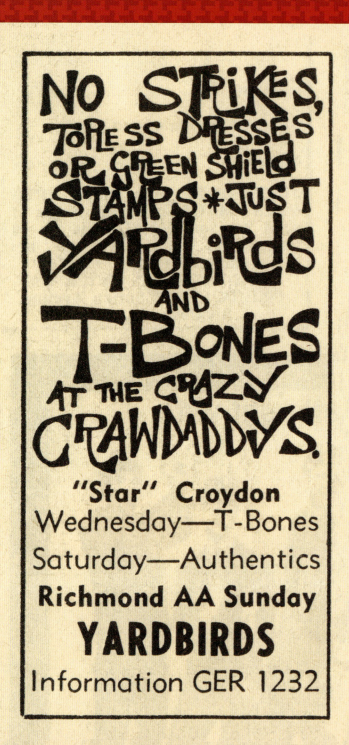

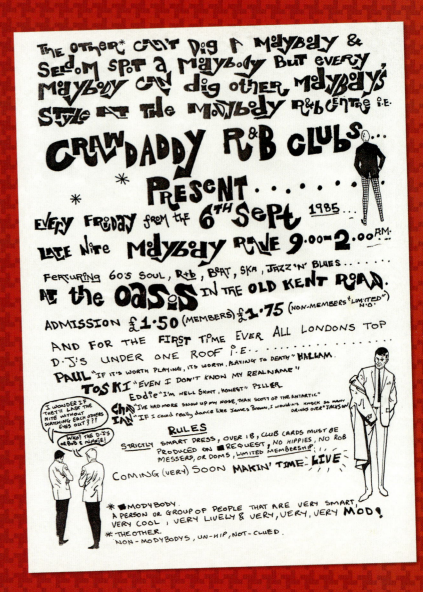

1 Original Crawdaddy flyer advertising Yardbirds and T-Bones, 1964.
By late 1984, a group of London Mods (Bob Morris, Paul Hallam, Andy Orr,
Mick Wheeler and Eddie Piller) resurrected the name 'Crawdaddy' for events.
Seen here and opposite, flyers from 1985.

Casual attire, though, certainly wasn't visible at most of the
Mod clubs in the London area. Bob Morris, Eddie Piller, Andy Orr,
Paul Hallam and Mick Wheeler organised the Crawdaddy network
of clubs. Their flyers gave a nostalgic nod to the original sixties
Crawdaddy Club, which was held in Richmond Athletic Ground.
Back then, in 1964, Giorgio Gomelski, was running the Crawdaddy.
His right-hand man, Hamish Grimes, a designer and graphics man by
trade, created the club's promotional material. His unique take
included creating a new 'language,' in which he called club regulars
'Modybodys.' The Crawdaddy was the club where "Modybodys meet,
mingle and nod in Modybody ways". Fast-forward to London 20 years
later and the Crawdaddy network of clubs was reviving the same
lettering style and 'Modybody' phrases. Authenticity was everything.

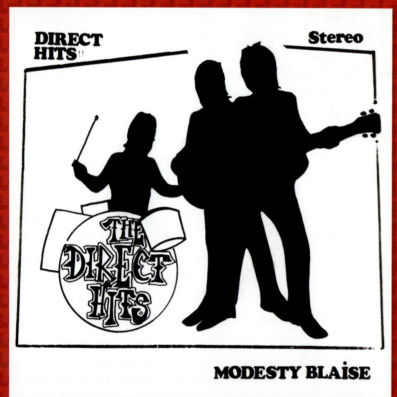

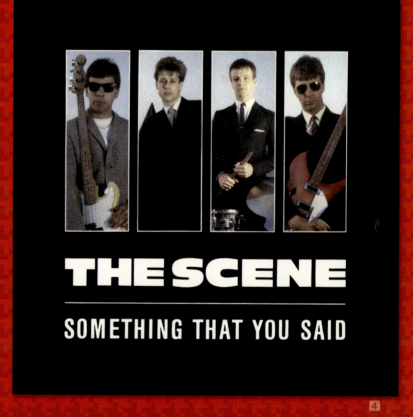

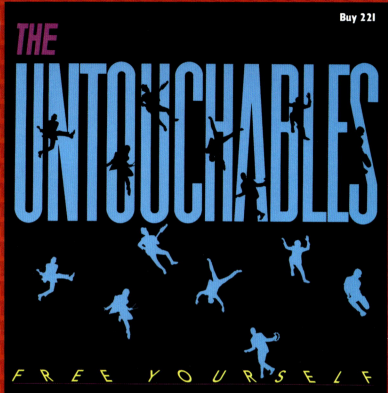

After the pounding Mod had taken during the revival, there were still plenty of interesting things going on. So much so that in a July issue, *Sounds* printed 'Mod 84,' a two-page article that profiled the current bands, such as The Direct Hits and Small World, the fanzines, and gave an overview of the scene. However, it made sure to end with "Don't panic! This is no 'next big thing' codswallop, no re-revival" and an explanation that something was going on, should you wish to investigate further. A November issue of that year would also see Garry Bushell cover the First National Mod Meeting, held at the Boston Arms in Tufnell Park.

Both 1984 and 1985 would see yet another resurgence of interest in Mod, although by and large it remained underground. Of the few bands that were accepted by Mods at the time, The Scene, Fast Eddie, The Rage, The Moment and The Prisoners all gained big followings but poor national publicity. The bands that did manage to break into the charts included The Truth (Dennis Greaves' new venture after Nine Below Zero split), and a band from Los Angeles called The Untouchables, who charted with 'Free Yourself.' The Style Council released their second studio album *Our Favourite Shop*, which divided Mod opinions, as some were still trying to come to terms with The Jam split and didn't get Weller's more contemporary take. Wolverhampton's Makin' Time would be the band most greatly accepted in 1985, as music papers, revivalists and retro Mod club-goers enthused over their debut album *Rhythm And Soul*.

1 Small World 7", Valid Records, 1984.
2 Fast Eddie 7", Well Suspect Records, 1982.
3 Direct Hits 7", Whaam! Records, 1982.
4 The Scene 7", Diamond Records, 1984.
5 'Free Yourself' 7", Stiff Records, 1984.
6 The Untouchables flyer, 1985.

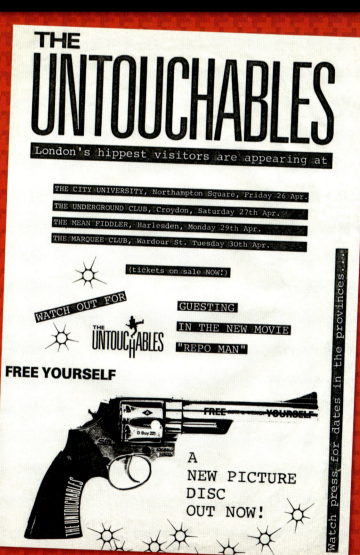

THE BEAT GENERATION AND THE ANGRY YOUNG MEN

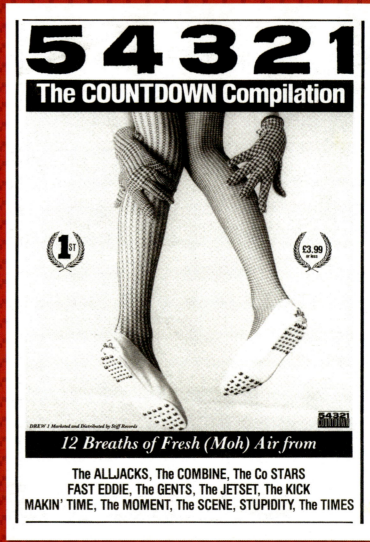

54321
The COUNTDOWN Compilation

1ST

£3.99 or less

DREW 1 Marketed and Distributed by Stiff Records

54321 COUNTDOWN

12 Breaths of Fresh (Moh) Air from

The ALLJACKS, The COMBINE, The Co STARS
FAST EDDIE, The GENTS, The JETSET, The KICK
MAKIN' TIME, The MOMENT, The SCENE, STUPIDITY, The TIMES

The Countdown Compilation *54321 Go!* exposed 1985's scene by presenting the current crop of talent and sporting an eye-catching sleeve. Terry Rawlings supplied the artwork, assisted by Bob Morris.

Morris: "We wanted to use a David Bailey shot on the cover but we couldn't afford to use it because of the copyright charge. So we actually remade the shot ourselves so that it looked strikingly similar. I'm quite proud of that." The last half of the decade would see the Mod scene go largely unnoticed, a counterculture that would lay dormant as rave music and dance culture began stealing headlines.

> **"...wanted to use a David Bailey shot on the cover but we couldn't afford to use it..."**
>
> BOB MORRIS

While promotional material for raves and rave music continued the earlier punk and Mod Revival traditions of hand-drawn, or Letraset rub-down transfer lettering with collages consisting of photocopied pictures, the early 1990s saw professional-looking, full-colour, high-gloss flyers conquer the scene. The Pritt Sticks, typewriters and Letraset sheets were destined for the bin. Sadly, a little bit of creative spirit went with them.

The
COUNTDOWN
Compilation

5
4
3
2
1

12 Breaths of Fresh Moh-air
for £3.99 or Less
Licensed through Stiff Records available through E.M.I. Distribution

Stiff Records

DREW I

//\ Pirate Mod Run \\\
TO
|||||| HAYLING ISLAND ||||||

On:- 15-16 JUNE (SUBSTITUTING SCARBOROUGH)

Strictly MODS ONLY!!!

R&b NITE TILL 2 a.m. (ON THE ISLAND)
D.J. "PAUL HALLAM" +GUESTS

SMART DRESS ONLY (AS ALWAYS!)

£3·00 ADDMISSION (ADVANCE TICKETS ONLY)
FROM PAUL HALLAM OR GARRY MOORE
AT SNEAKERS (SUN.) OR BEN TRUMAN (SAT.)

Holy Shit! It's here babies.

THE LEGENDARY CLACTON
bank holiday
BONANZA
23rd–25th August
WAVERLEY HOTEL BALLROOM, CLACTON

No Scooter Competions, No Escorted Rides Around Town, No Camp-Site, No Video Screen or Cameras and NO FUCKING PATCHES
Just..... PURE R+B for PURE MODS

Saturday night 'LIVE' (8 pm until 1:30 a.m.)

THE RHYTHM STEADIES   SUPPORT   Makin' Time

D.J's PAUL HALLAM, JIM WATSON
plus other masters gifted with prize sounds

Sunday night (8p.m. till 1a.m.)
r+b explosion

D.J's From Everywhere Playing An UNBELIEVEABLE Selection of RHYTHM & BLUES, EARLY SOUL, THAT JAZZY BEAT with maybee some SKA SENSATION

For Tickets and Abuse Confront either
GARRY MOORE, THE CAT WHO GAVE YOU THIS SHEET or ANY INTELLIGENT MOD OVER 5'2"

JOOLS
mod club ✳

Every Friday Night
200 Edgware Road. Paddington
Edgware Rd Tube
8 TIL 1
Soul, Rhythm & Blues, Ska & Jazz

ENTRANCE: A measley 2 Sous
YOU MUST BE A 100% MOD
TO GET IN SO PLEASE,
NO MUGS!?

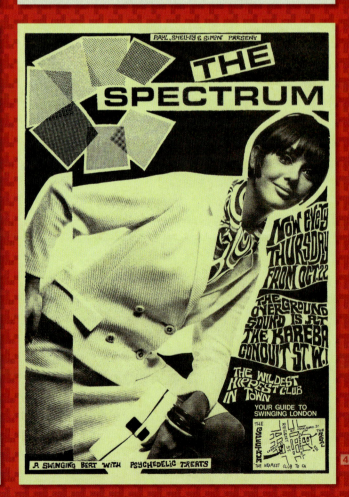

PAUL, SHELLEY & SIMON PRESENT:

THE SPECTRUM

NOW EVEY THURSDAY FROM OCT. 22

THE OVERGROUND SOUND IS AT THE KAREBA CONDUIT ST. W.

THE WILDEST HIPPEST CLUB IN TOWN

YOUR GUIDE TO SWINGING LONDON

A SWINGING BEAT WITH PSYCHEDELIC TREATS

1 Hayling Island, 1985. **2** Clacton flyer, 1985. **3** Jools Mod Club flyer, 1986. **4** The Spectrum, 1983.

MOD ART 208

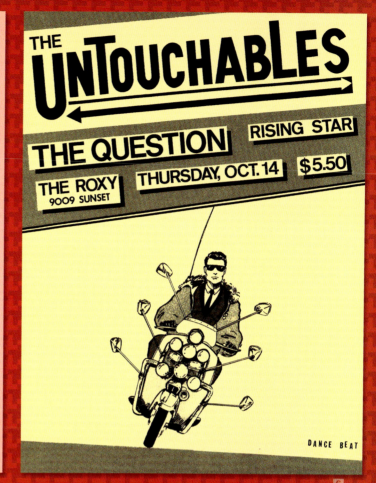

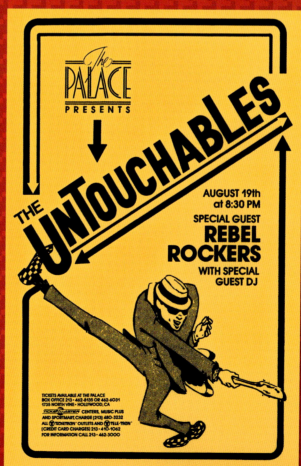

AMERICAN FLYERS: 5 Sidewalk Society pink flyer, 1983. 6 The Untouchables flyer, 1982/83. 7 Sidewalk Society blue flyer, 1983. 8 The Untouchables flyer, 1982/83.

WELL FRIDAY NIGHT HAS
FINALLY COME AROUND
AND ME AND MY BABY GONNA
HEAD FOR A SPOT WE FOUND
WE'RE GONNA FORGET OUR CARES
AND DANCE ON INTO THE NIGHT

CRUSH BAR, at the Continental Club, 1743 N. Cahuenga Blvd. Go-gostess Pamela Motown presents the only club in town that plays all '60s soul dance music, all night. Put on your hi-heel sneakers & dance to the Supremes, Temptations, James Brown, Chubby Checker & loads more. Free button giveaway. $1 drinks before 11 p.m. Fri., 10 p.m.-2 a.m. $5 cover, over 21. Call (213) 462-9858.

Sixties SOUL BEAT

EVERY FRIDAY

THAT MOTOWN SOUND

FREE BUTTON GIVEAWAY EVERY WEEK!

THE CRUSH BAR

THE CRUSH BAR, at the Continental Club, 1743 N. Cahuenga Blvd. Go-Gostess Pamela Motown presents "the only club in town that plays all '60s soul dance music all night, every Friday."

Two full bars, all drinks $1 before 11 p.m Dancing 10 p.m.-2 a.m. Cover $5. Over 21 Call 462-9858.

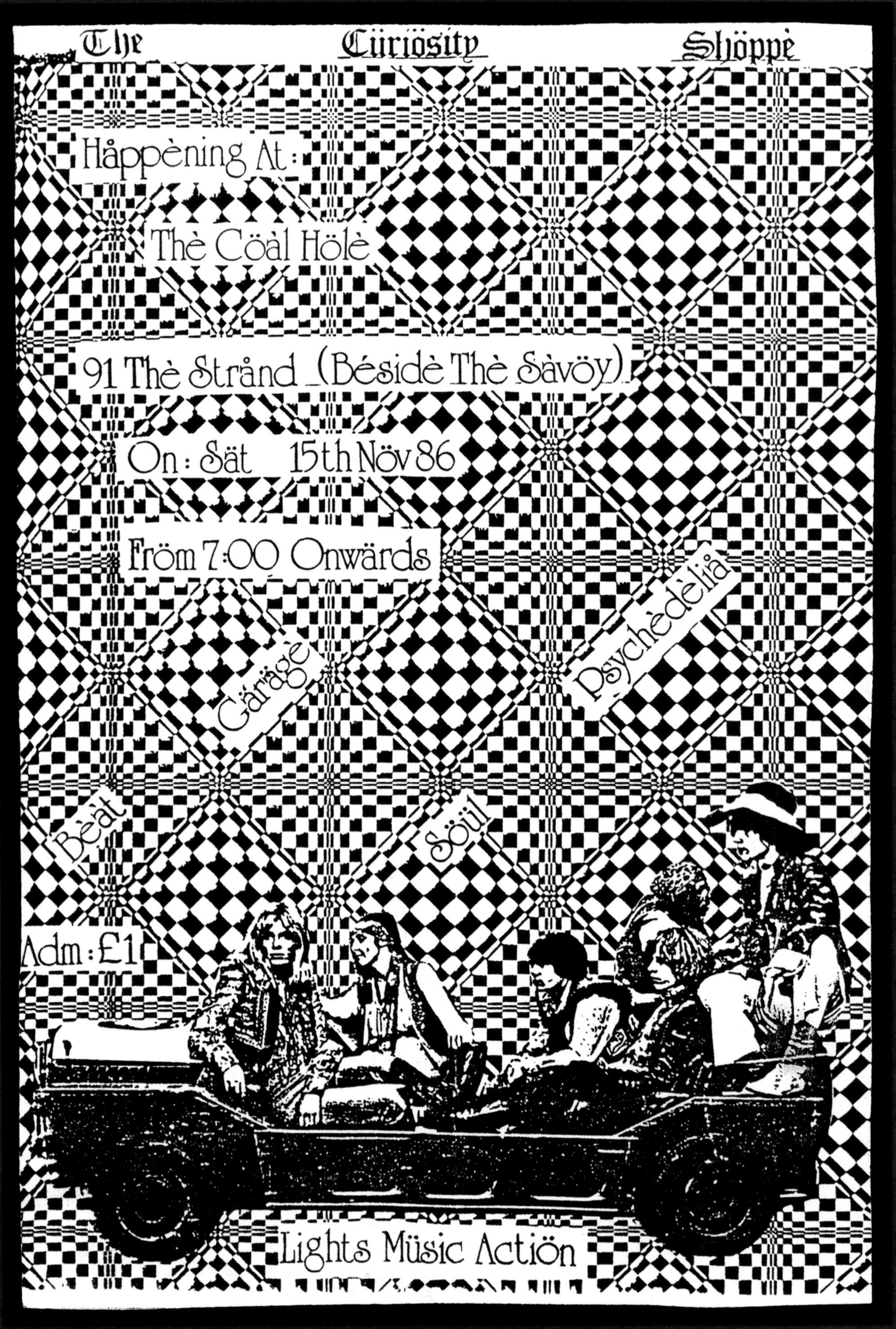
The Cüriösity Shöppè
Håppèning At:
Thè Cöål Hölè
91 Thè Strånd (Bésidè Thè Sàvöy)
On: Sät 15th Növ 86
Fröm 7:00 Onwärds
Bèåt
Gäräge
Söül
Psychèdèliä
Adm: £1
Lights Müsic Actiön
1

1 & 2 Bridget Riley revisited, 1986.

THE CURIOSITY SHOPPE happening

the black horse rathbone place w.1

(turning off of oxford street)

friday 18th sept

garage punk!

freak beat!

60's psychedelia!

from: 7.00pm

till late

adm:

£1.00 before 9.00p.m £1.50 after

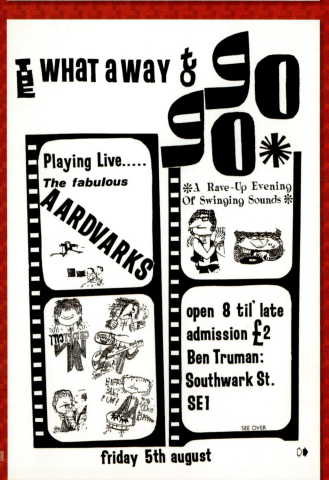

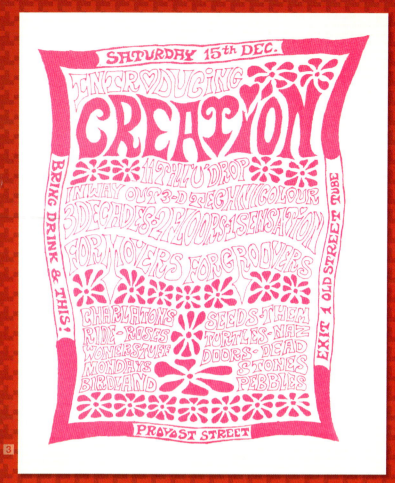

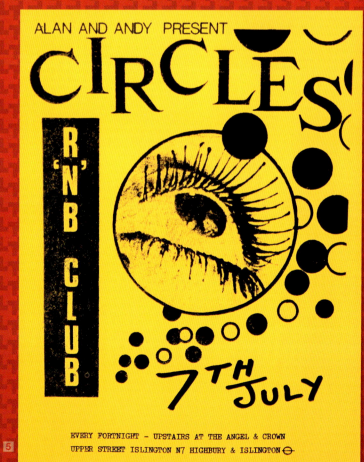

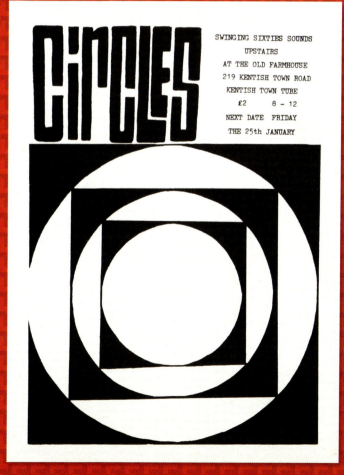

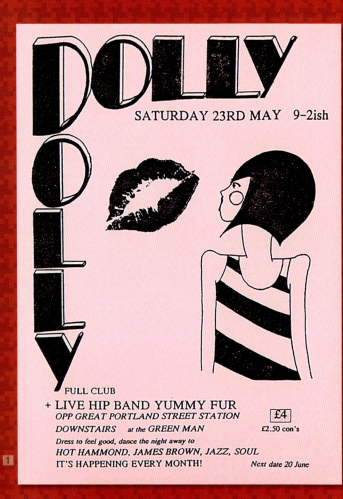

1 Dolly Dolly Flyer, 1992.

2 Hand-drawn Kings Tavern flyer by John McIllmurray, 1990.

3 Recipe For Dance flyer, 1989. This flyer was advanced for its time,
as it wasn't the usual cut and paste and was professionally printed in blue and black.
Most full-colour flyers didn't appear on the Mod scene until 1991.

4 Flyer designed by the author Paul Anderson, 1990.
It uses cut out photocopies of record labels and the same 'Crawdaddy' style as
used by Hamish Grimes in the sixties and the Crawdaddy Network in the mid-eighties.

CLACTON 91

SUN 26 AT THE LORD NELSON
SMART MOD/SIXTIES DRESS

7-1:30am   £4

BOURNEMOUTH 91
FRIDAY 2 AUGUST

SIXTIES DRESS ONLY

RUSSELL COURT HOTEL

8 - 1   £2

SMART MOD

BATH ROAD

LUNCHTIMES FREE
AT COURTLANDS

CLACTON 91

PRESENTING TOMMY CHASE
SAT 25   THE LORD NELSON

MOD/SIXTIES DRESS

7-1:30am £5

SATURDAY 3 AUGUST

7 - 1   £4

SMART MOD
SIXTIES DRESS ONLY

COURTLANDS HOTEL
16 BOSCOMBE SPA ROAD
EASTCLIFFE

BOURNEMOUTH 91

Above a selection of tickets for the original Untouchables rallies, 1991.

1 Two flyers for the original Untouchables events, 1991.

2 Tickets for original Untouchables event, 1991.

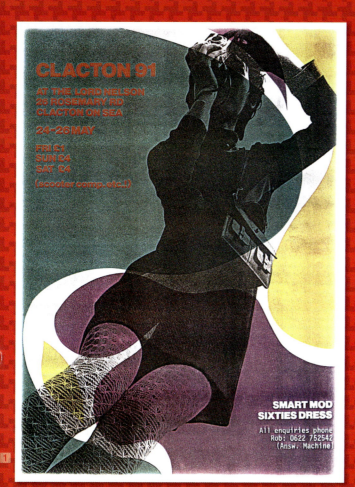

CLACTON 91

AT THE LORD NELSON
26 ROSEMARY RD
CLACTON ON SEA

24–26 MAY

FRI £1
SUN £4
SAT £4

(scooter comp. etc..!)

SMART MOD
SIXTIES DRESS

All enquiries phone
Rob: 0622 752542
(Answ. Machine)

UNTOUCHABLES

HASTINGS EASTER '91

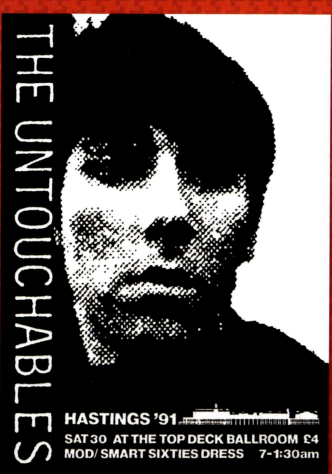

THE UNTOUCHABLES

HASTINGS '91
SAT 30 AT THE TOP DECK BALLROOM £4
MOD/ SMART SIXTIES DRESS   7–1:30am

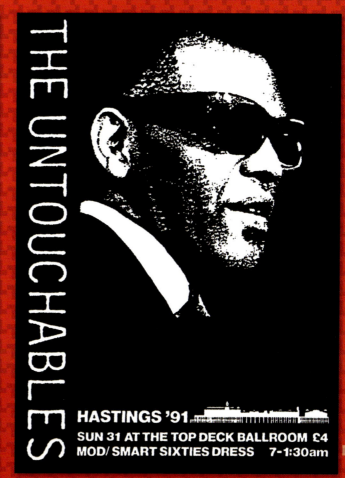

THE UNTOUCHABLES

HASTINGS '91
SUN 31 AT THE TOP DECK BALLROOM £4
MOD/ SMART SIXTIES DRESS   7–1:30am

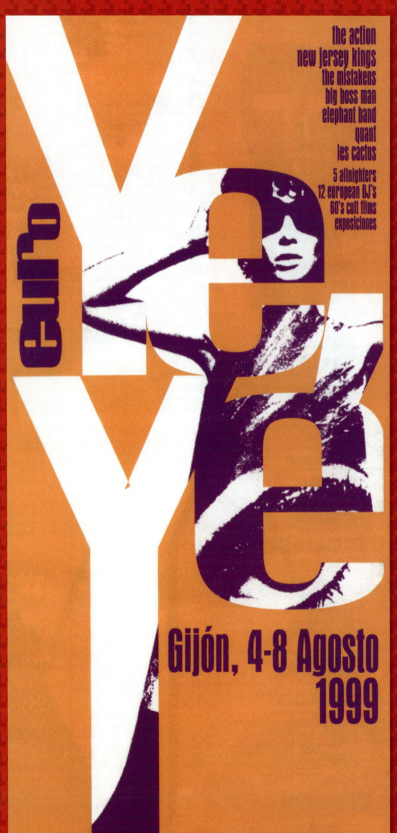

Throughout the eighties, Mod had become more intertwined with European events. By the time the nineties had arrived it had become truly global.

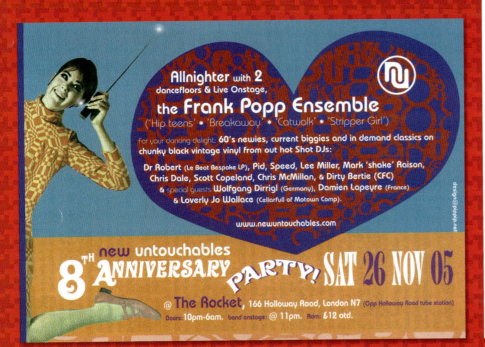

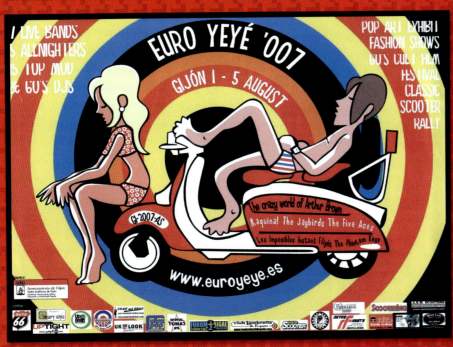

Throughout the nineties many events were co-organised and promoted by
Rob Bailey with The New Untouchables. Thanks to the internet, the world had become
a smaller place, flyers looked far more professional, and the advent of
computer technology made the eighties photocopy and paste flyers seem so basic.

Taunton Lions MOD Scooter Club

HERE COMES THE NICE

A NIGHT OF SIXTIES SOUNDS

AT

THE EAGLE

SOUTH STREET, TAUNTON

ON

23RD OCTOBER '99

8PM - 11PM

£3

Phone Ian (01823) 350326

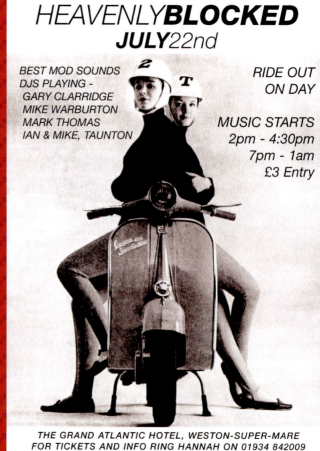

HEAVENLY BLOCKED
JULY 22nd

BEST MOD SOUNDS
DJS PLAYING -
GARY CLARRIDGE
MIKE WARBURTON
MARK THOMAS
IAN & MIKE, TAUNTON

RIDE OUT
ON DAY

MUSIC STARTS
2pm - 4:30pm
7pm - 1am
£3 Entry

THE GRAND ATLANTIC HOTEL, WESTON-SUPER-MARE
FOR TICKETS AND INFO RING HANNAH ON 01934 842009

HIPSTERS IMAGE

AT

THE PRINCESS ROYAL

FUNCTION ROOM

CANON STREET TAUNTON

SAT 15th MARCH

7pm til MIDNIGHT

R&B · NORTHERN SOUL
PSYCHE · TAMLA
MOD · FREAK BEAT

STRICT 60's MUSIC POLICY
FOR MORE INFO CONTACT :
JOHN (01823) 321056 or
MIKE (01823) 256118

£2 ON THE DOOR

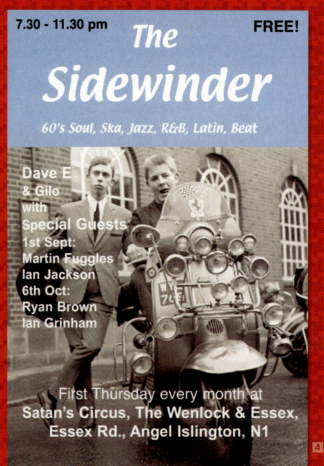

7.30 - 11.30 pm   FREE!

The Sidewinder

60's Soul, Ska, Jazz, R&B, Latin, Beat

Dave E
& Gilo
with
Special Guests
1st Sept:
Martin Fuggles
Ian Jackson
6th Oct:
Ryan Brown
Ian Grinham

First Thursday every month at
Satan's Circus, The Wenlock & Essex,
Essex Rd., Angel Islington, N1

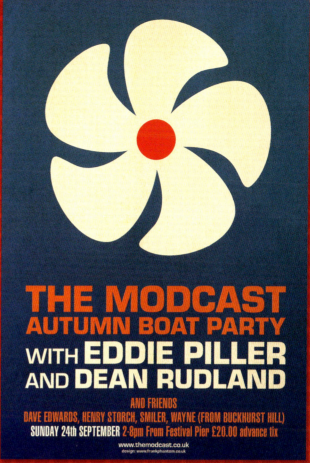

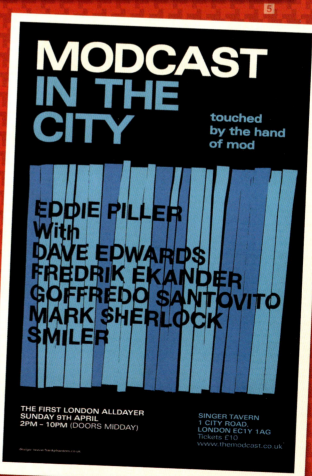

> **"...looking at the cover you can tell exactly what our influences are..."**
>
> PAUL WELLER

Released on May 9, 1985, *Our Favourite Shop* was The Style Council's second studio album. The album contains 13 original tracks on various themes, such as racism ('The Stand Up Comic's Instructions'), a eulogy to Weller's school friend Dave Waller, who had died of a heroin overdose in 1982 ('A Man Of Great Promise') and the miners' strike ('A Stone's Throw Away'). The album as a whole is politically based and full of biting lyrics that create a full-on assault on Thatcher's Britain and the Tories' selfish principles. That said, the lyrics do convey a sense of hope that things could change.

Our Favourite Shop would become The Style Council's most commercially successful album and would be their only number one album in the UK, largely helped by the album cover itself.

Weller: "Yet again, like the inside of the *All Mod Cons* LP, it's a collage. We did two photo sessions for that. The first session we did in Woking. I had this idea fixed in my head because there was this old gentlemen's outfitters shop by the station in Woking, not a trendy one, a real old school one. I said we should try some pictures of us just looking through the window of this old shop. We did this but they never turned out how we wanted. Anyway, the photographer, or maybe the designer, Simon Halfon, suggested creating our own shop in the studio, which is what we ended up doing. From looking at the cover you can tell exactly what our influences are, which encourages people to check things out, as we all do and it all gets passed on."

Band mate Mick Talbot has fond memories of putting the album sleeve together: "When Paul and I first met up, we both had various things in common outside of music, such as books. We both owned a copy of *Generation X*, both of us had Nell Dunn books such as *Up The Junction* and *Poor Cow*, and we had the trilogy of Colin MacInnes' novels *Absolute Beginners*, *City Of Spades* and *Mr Love And Justice*. So when we came to do the concept for *Our Favourite Shop* it was interesting that we could bring in objects that had influenced us.

CLASSIC ALBUM:
OUR FAVOURITE SHOP
THE STYLE COUNCIL

> **"...like the inside of the *All Mod Cons* LP, it's a collage."**
>
> PAUL WELLER

"The cycling shirt hanging on the wall is the one I wore in the 'My Ever Changing Moods' video and the trilby on the coat stand is what I wore in the 'Solid Bond In Your Heart' video. On the bookrack is *Arms And The Man* by George Bernard Shaw, which is a satirical look at war, so I guess there was a kind of subliminal message there. There's the Chelsea programmes, as well as my signed photo of Peter Bonetti on the wall that represents both mine and Paul's football team. There's a copy of Kenneth Williams' book of recollections, *Back Drops*, because both Paul and I had read [Williams' previous book] *Acid Drops*. Then there's Paul's copy of *Prick Up Your Ears* about Joe Orton, who we both loved, and maybe represented a darker side. On the shelf there's my book of Tony Hancock's scripts and a book on Humphrey Bogart, which is one of my favourites. There's an Otis Redding T-shirt that I think we bought in Amsterdam. That is hung up on my original Twiggy coat hanger. Paul had his George Best and John Lennon clothes hangers. The photos on the wall include Terry Thomas, Brigitte Bardot and the actor Alain Delon. We were both fans of those French new wave films, especially because of the clothes featured in them."

Weller cringes as he explains: "There's the 'Homo' Birthday card on the shelf, which was made by the designer Pete Barratt. It contained an explicit drawing of me and Mick. I think I was at my mum's when I opened it and she was a bit 'ooh-er.' There's stuff like Otis, Georgie Best stuff, my soul belt and there's the Hancock book, which is Mick's. Like a lot of English people we like a lot of camp humour as well, whether it's Kenneth Williams or *Carry On* stuff."

Talbot, in a reflective mood: "On the inner sleeve there are a few apt quotes. One is from the American comedian Lenny Bruce who challenged people's perceptions on subjects like race and religion. In a way he was the forerunner to the alternative comedians who were very big at that time. As for the record itself, I think it's a good diary of the state of the nation at the time. Sadly over 30 years on, most of these things are still going on."

"...it's a good diary of the state of the nation at the time."

MICK TALBOT

1 Paul Weller **2** Mick Talbot.

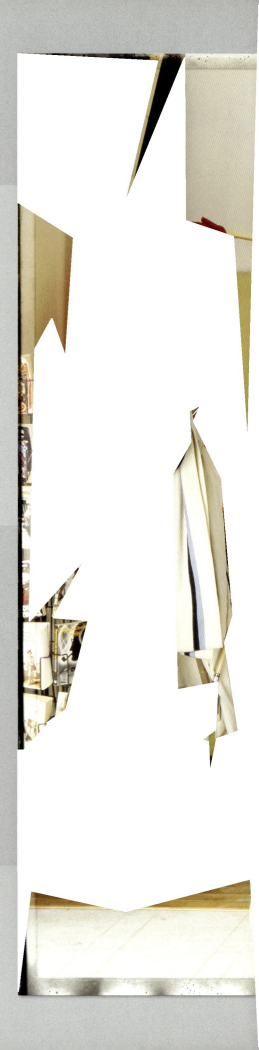

> **"...it was interesting that we could bring in objects that had influenced us. "**

MICK TALBOT

MAKIN' TIME

NEW L.P. *Rhythm And Soul* NEW 45 *Here Is My Number*

RHYTHM and SOUL

NEW L.P. *Rhythm And Soul* NEW 45 *Here Is My Number*
L.P. Down 1-Cassette C Down 1-7" Vain 1-12" Vain 112   1st from Countdown Manufactured and Distributed by STIFF Records

OUT   NOW

RHYTHM AND SOUL: MAKIN' TIME

"Makin' Time may look innocent on the sleeve..."

JONATHAN ROMNEY: *NME*

There aren't many bands that managed to come through the Mod Revival with credibility intact and untainted by music press vilification. One of the few bands that could boast such an accomplishment was Makin' Time, from Wolverhampton. Consisting of Mark 'Syd' McGounden (guitar/vocals), Martin Blunt (bass), Neil Clitheroe (drums) and 18-year-old Fay Hallam (Vox Continental organ/vocals), Makin' Time managed to swim against the tide of oppression of 'yet another bloody Mod Revival.'

When Garry Bushell of *Sounds* pressed the band regarding any Mod affiliation, Syd came up with "We're a band with Mods in it, but does that make us a Mod band? George Michael putting on a suit wouldn't make him a Mod singer. Nowadays I understand Mod as meaning the '79 generation of bands, and we don't sound anything like them."

> **"...you don't need to be a member of MENSA to pigeonhole Makin' Time as Mod revivalists. "**
>
> ZIYAD GEORGIS: *MELODY MAKER*

Sounds' July review of the band's 1985 LP *Rhythm And Soul* managed to attract the national music papers. *NME*'s Jonathan Romney started his own review of the album by slating the previous Mod Revival, but then he heaped praise on Makin' Time themselves, ending the review with "Makin' Time may look innocent on the sleeve, but they know what they're about, the crafty devils. No wonder they're glowing – they got it right." *Melody Maker* went even further: "One glance at the cover and you don't need to be a member of MENSA to pigeonhole Makin' Time as Mod revivalists. My first reaction was to shelve them under 'to be ignored.' Don't make that mistake because you'd only miss out." Journalist Ziyad Georgis continues: "*Rhythm And Soul* is easily the best debut album of 1985. Makin' Time remind me of a younger, sixties influenced version of the criminally neglected Distractions. The vocals are shared by Mark McGounden, who sounds like the magnificent Mike Finney's younger brother, and Fay Hallam. There's not much to say about Fay other than there's no female voice to touch hers. Like Sandie Shaw and Dusty Springfield before her, Fay Hallam sounds and looks perfect for the role of pop icon."

In 1980, Fay Hallam's parents owned the Castle pub in Wednesfield, Wolverhampton. She found herself drawn into the sixties revival scene when she was just 14 years old. Apart from being influenced by a gang of people hanging around, who were into The Jam, Fay also had a boyfriend who was really into The Who, the Small Faces and lots of other sixties bands.

But the biggest influence lay closer to home. Her father, who had played the piano, before moving to the organ, around various local clubs in the sixties and seventies, took it upon himself to share this gift with his daughter.

"He was out the whole time playing, and he taught me to play when I was eight. He made me stay up all night until I could play 'Amazing Grace' with both hands and bass pedals and not make a mistake. I remember sitting there crying. He wasn't a very PC teacher," says Hallam.

When she was 14, Hallam got hold of a record by David Bowie with 'She's Got Medals' on it (she doesn't remember exactly which record she had, although the song appears on Bowie's eponymously named debut album) and it inspired her to want to write her own songs. Interestingly, in later years, Hallam may have owned albums by Brian Auger & Julie Driscoll, Traffic and The Stranglers from which she took inspiration in terms of keyboard playing, but there certainly weren't any Small Faces albums or female soul albums.

Hallam: "Vocally I was influenced by my Mum... [she] has a very similar voice to mine. She used to sing with my dad. I remember her singing 'Bye Bye Blackbird,' Gladys Knight's 'Help Me Make It Through The Night.' I didn't try to emulate anybody else outside of that. The first white voice that I thought was really bloody good was Mama Cass. I've never really analysed it, I was just brought up with my parents singing."

Hallam had been in a little band called Minus One when she came across another local R&B band, which had Martin Blunt on bass and Mark 'Syd' McGounden on guitar. Fay was asked to join... but initially she wasn't impressed. Soon, the original singer and drummer were dumped and in came Neil Clitheroe on drums, and Makin' Time were born. From 1984, the band went on the road with a set list of driving, soul-tinged, sixties-style pop. It was obvious the band would attract a Mod following, and among the debris of old revival bands and a majority of new clueless pretenders, Makin' Time shone like a diamond under the spotlights.

> **"Vocally I was influenced by my Mum... "**
>
> FAY HALLAM

Hallam: "I was painting a lot at the time. My uncle had got some canvas from Goodyear, some big green tarpaulin. I was into pop art, and I think I was painting some food on it, you know cans and bread. It was a take on Andy Warhol's *Campbell's Soup Cans*. The thing in those days was to have a stage backdrop with your band's name on it. Somebody mentioned it and I thought, well, I've got this tarpaulin, the paints and a space to do it. So I had to do a design and that's where I came up with the man incorporated with the name. I'd made a rough sketch in felt tip pen and thought it could be used on posters for us. So then I painted that image onto our backdrop. Later on, when we got the record deal with Stiff, Will Birch, our manager, said he'd send it to an art guy to make it look more professional. They changed the design slightly; it was slightly refined. I really liked the white lettering on a black background. I actually hand-drew all our posters because we had no access to anything else."

After a gig at the Ilford Palais all-dayer, Eddie Piller liked the band enough to get the band more gigs down south, including at the 100 Club. As Piller was running Stiff's subsidiary label 54321 Countdown, he signed the band and Makin's Time's recording career began.

Hallam: "I never really thought we'd ever get big. I was only interested in the songs and the songs sounding as good as they could be. I thought it was amazing that the first song I ever wrote, 'I Know What You're Thinking' – which was a rip-off of 'She's Got Medals' that I wrote on the school gym piano when I was 14 – was on our debut album. I thought that was brilliant that that had happened, but it was just the sound that should have been different.

"I remember being in the studio a month recording the *Rhythm And Soul* album and by about week three all of us saying that it sounded a bit weak. The production on it was too nice and I think Martin [Blunt] said to Pat Collier, who was the engineer and co-producer, that he didn't want it to sound like the kind of album that your mum would like to listen to. They said it wouldn't, but I think it did. It sounded nothing like when we played live. I wanted us to sound powerful, like we were live. I think the demos sounded better even though they were a bit scrappy and a bit rubbish; they had a spirit that was somehow lost on the actual album."

RHYTHM and SOUL
NEW L.P. *Rhythm And Soul* NEW 45 *Here Is My Number*

Rhythm And Soul was released on July 5, 1985. Engineered at Greenhouse/Alaska/Workhouse Studios, it contains 12 songs of which 11 are originals, plus a cover of The Kinks' 'I Gotta Move.'

Hallam: "For the album photo shoot we had to come down from the Midlands and go to an old warehouse building somewhere in London with the photographer Miriam Reik in her studio. There was a table with a wooden board splitting it down the middle. So we had lots of different shots wearing different clothing options. The picture that finally made the cover is half of one photograph put with a half of another. My top may look perfectly ironed in that but there's a photo on the front cover of 'Here Is My Number' where we are all wearing stripy shirts, striking a pose. We all somehow had these stripy shirts and she said let's go with that theme. Well, because they'd all been crumpled in our bags, if you look closely at that picture they are just an absolute mess. I just bought everything I had in second-hand shops and if I couldn't find what I wanted, I just made it."

The album received good reviews including one that appeared in *City Limits* magazine, which started "Unbelievable as it may seem, Makin' Time are a Mod group from the Midlands and, being thus, have still managed with some ease to make the best debut LP I have heard in a long time." This review would cause immense embarrassment for Hallam as the reviewer, Dave McCullough, would sum it up with: "The star of the affair is joint-singer Fay Hallam. Fay Hallam is God."

Hallam: "In the end, Stiff did have problems so we decided we'd do the second album, *No Lumps Of Fat Or Gristle Guaranteed*, on our own. Pat Collier produced it but we recorded it really quickly. It was more like a week than the month we'd spent on the first one. It was also mixed and mastered really quickly as well, but I actually like the sound better as it's a lot rougher. We basically thought we'd release that then just stop playing any more.

"By that time I was going out with Graham Day of The Prisoners and they were just about to break up. Martin Blunt and I really weren't that happy in our band. We wanted to do something better and that's why we all stopped what we were doing and formed The Gift Horses, which didn't last very long at all."

Makin' Time split up in 1986. Hallam would eventually play in bands The Gift Horses (which included Martin Blunt, just before he joined The Charlatans), The Prime Movers and Phaze, and she can be found these days in The Fay Hallam Trinity. Hallam has designed most of the covers for these bands' releases.

Hallam: "Art was my favourite subject in school. I liked drawing a lot. When I was 16, I was told at school I might be able to make a career in art. So I thought I'd like to be a designer, and I applied to go to the Wolverhampton Poly. I applied a year early, at the time I was in a little kiddie band called Minus One, so I stayed on at school an extra year to get my art A-level and I did get into the foundation a year early. On the day I was supposed to go to enrol, I was in Makin' Time by that time, and I thought I'm going to do [Makin' Time] instead, so I never went. I finally did an art degree when I was 27 at Christchurch at Canterbury. A joint honours with art and education. First year we did screen printing, sculpture, painting, but for the main part of my degree I did oil painting and managed to get a first-class honours."

"Art was my favourite subject in school."

FAY HALLAM

Makin' Time

Rhythm
and
Soul

1 The band's critically acclaimed debut album.
Photography by Miriam Reik and artwork by
long-time Mod, Terry Rawlings. Countdown Records, 1985.

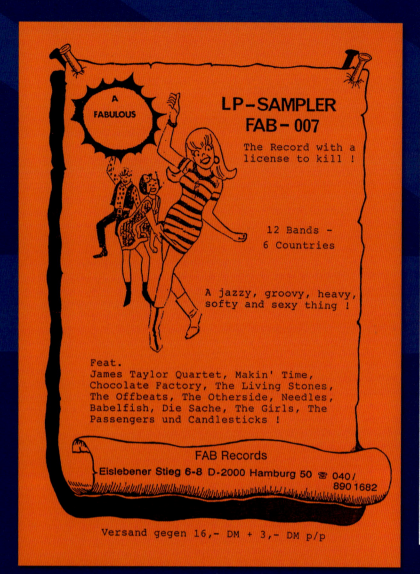

MAKIN TIME
OUT AND ABOUT

Jan 16th COLCHESTER Works
Jan 17th GREENWICH Tunnel Club
Jan 18th BATH Moles Club
Jan 20th SOUTHAMPTON Riverside
Jan 21st STOKE-ON-TRENT Shelleys
Jan 23rd LEICESTER Princess Charlotte
Jan 24th KIRK LEVINGTON Country Club
OUT NOW L.P. "Rhythm & Soul"
(Down 1) on Countdown Records

54321
COUNTDOWN

STIFF
RECORDS

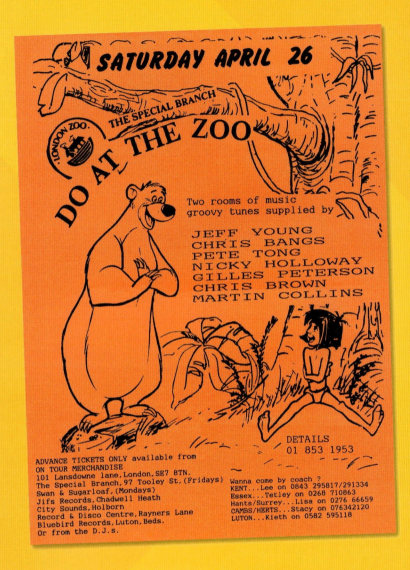

ACID JAZZ
AND NEO-MODS

❝...don't need f*in' Mod clubs any more... ❞**

EDDIE PILLER

The late 1980s were strange, fast times indeed for Mods. The world had certainly moved on. Club culture in the latter part of the decade seemed a million miles away from where Mod had started.

By June 1988, London's Astoria was holding club night 'Shoom,' and here DJ Nicky Holloway would champion a form of electronic music that had evolved in America, its epicentre in Chicago. The repetitive beats spilled from a Roland TB-303 synthesiser-sequencer and acid house, as it came to be known, soon had a major presence on dance floors across the UK, quickly followed by the emergence of a drug called ecstasy, or 'E,' street names for a psychoactive drug MDMA. The psychedelic-amphetamine qualities of the drug offered users a euphoric, inhibition-reducing sensation that, when combined with sound and colourful visuals, took them to their promised land.

Sadly for the participants of the new rave scene, the music (and euphoria) had to stop prematurely, as UK clubs were governed by a strict closing time policy. The media, especially *The Sun*, was also quick to take on the role of party pooper, looking beyond the image of happy kids in bright, smiley-face T-shirts and probing into the dangers of drug use. But this only had the adverse effect of forcing the culture underground, away from established nightclubs and into secret venues, disused warehouses and even the open countryside of rural Britain.

Football hooligans gurned away alongside bankers and businessmen, a cultural metamorphosis revolutionising people's perception of a night out clubbing. Of course, the scene also attracted ex-Mods looking for a new buzz. You may see it as a continuation of Mod heritage: staying out, dancing to rare and undiscovered music all night, consuming all manner of pharmaceuticals. Truth be told, most just got involved because it was bloody good fun.

By now the more traditional Mod clubs were on a bit of a downhill slide, usually restricted by the set list. The spectrum was wide in terms of genre, and included American R&B, soul, ska, Latin, beat and jazz, but there always seemed to be a mind-set of "don't play anything after '67." This policy wasn't always enforced because records such as Little Sonny's 'Wade In The Water' was released in 1970, but the general policy was to stay away from anything too heavy or funky.

Eddie Piller's take on the matter: "Around '84/'85 I was still DJ'ing on the Mod scene, but mainly in Essex. I'd hosted a night at the Wag with Dick Coombes and Ray Patriotic but that only really lasted six months. I think the last Mod rally I'd DJ'd on was Lowestoft '85, and I'll never forget that I played 'Tighten Up' by Archie Bell & the Drells and the dance floor cleared. After that I played 'Ain't No Big Thing' by Jimmy James, same year, different label, and the floor was full. I just thought I've had enough of this. I don't want to do this any more. They don't get what I get.

"A while later I went to a Tony Class do at the Royal Oak in Tooley Street on a Friday night and I was moaning to a bouncer how I'd had it with the scene and that I wasn't going to come any more. I was over it. The bouncer said to me 'You wanna try coming tomorrow because there's this geezer who does it called Nicky Holloway, and they play your type of music upstairs but I think it's better.' So I went the next day with two mates from Woodford to this Special Branch do with DJs Gilles Peterson, Chris Bangs and possibly Kevin Beadle. Downstairs was a little bit of B-Boy and a little bit of go-go. People forget that in the late eighties go-go was the thing before acid house, stuff like Little Benny & the Masters, and Chuck Brown & the Soul Searchers. That Washington sound was known as go-go. I just thought fuck me, this is it. I don't need fuckin' Mod clubs any more because I'm hearing boogaloo, Latin jazz, bossa nova and stuff like 'Spanish Maiden' by Tony Middleton. Plus stuff like Jimmy Smith & the Young Holt Trio doing 'Wack Wack', which were records that I was playing as a DJ but the big difference with this club is that there's girls. From that point, I didn't look back and became a regular at Special Branch."

Mods and the jazz scene was of course nothing new. Ever since the 1950s there had been a constant link between jazz music and modernism. While practically all aspects of jazz music were lost during the revival, as time progressed, it crept back in through DJs' playlists. The organ sounds of the 1960s that came from the likes of Jimmy Smith, Jack McDuff and Brian Auger soon had kids desperate to find out more.

Luckily, during this period in the mid-1980s, several compilation albums helped fans to navigate through a genre that could be a minefield if you weren't sure what you were doing. First, DJ Paul Murphy released several compilations, *Jazz Club Volumes 1* and *2*, as well as the *Jazz Juice* series of LPs compiled by DJ Gilles Peterson, all of which were highly influential. These came along at a time when many kids had also been turned on by the jazz element of The Style Council.

> **"...the big difference with this club is that there's girls."**
>
> EDDIE PILLER

Inquisitive minds switched on, some Mods moved away from the comfort zone of Mod clubs and ventured into the uncharted seas of the Wag, the Electric Ballroom and the Sol Y Sombra in Charlotte Street, where Paul Murphy reigned supreme behind the decks. Paul would put on the 10-minute version of 'Sidewinder' by Lee Morgan and head to the bar... effortlessly cool. Other nights followed, including Gilles Peterson at the Electric Ballroom and Dave Hucker playing Afro-Latin beats upstairs at Ronnie Scott's.

"...you could be a Mod but without slavishly having to be part of the Mod scene. "

EDDIE PILLER

The much anticipated release of the screen version of Colin MacInnes' novel *Absolute Beginners* also got people back-tracking 1950s and 1960s jazz, but when the film was actually released in June 1986, it was seen as a major disappointment. For live music you could check out The Tommy Chase Quartet and for home listening you could tune in to Gilles Peterson's *Mad On Jazz* show on Radio London.

By now Paul Murphy had started DJ'ing at a venue called the Purple Pussycat on the Finchley Road, in which you could shuffle to John Lee Hooker's 'Boom Boom' or Lou Rawl's version of 'The Girl From Ipanema.' Mods were discovering a new world away from their own clubs.

Meanwhile, The Prisoners, a Medway band who had been popular on the Mod scene, split acrimoniously in 1986. Ex-Prisoners Allan Crockford (bass) and James Taylor (Hammond organ) joined Simon Howard (drums) and Dave Taylor (guitar) to form a sixties and seventies organ jazz instrumental group known as The James Taylor Quartet.

Eddie Piller: "After a while I met Gilles Peterson because he's the main DJ. The Prisoners had split in '86 and I was managing their organist's band, The James Taylor Quartet. I played their debut single 'Blow Up' to Gilles because he was doing his *Mad On Jazz* show on Radio London and he was laughing, saying, 'I ain't gonna play this.' On his show he used to have a voting competition where he played four new releases from the jazz scene. Well, he never took me seriously but he played 'Blow Up' and everyone voted for it, and then he had to take me seriously. John Peel later made that his record of the year.

"After that I became Gilles' right-hand man. I answered the phone on Radio London and that kind of thing. Gilles always has a good warm-up DJ and after me there was Kevin Beadle, then James Lavelle and later Patrick Forge. Anyway, I became part of that world and I realised that you could be a Mod but without slavishly having to be part of the Mod scene. People like Chris Bangs, Peterson and a few other DJs were mixing it up in a way that the Mod scene would never let you do. Paul Murphy had built the jazz scene around London but was far more purist than Peterson. Murphy was Mr Jazz Dance and I used to go to his dos at the Electric Ballroom in Camden and I was a massive fan, but Peterson, along with Chris Bangs, was my introduction to a new world and I found that what they did was mix my past with what I saw as the future. So there's reference points such as Jimmy Smith, Joe Bataan and Young-Holt Unlimited. Murphy was proper jazz dance, which was Art Blakey, the Heath Brothers and other hardcore jazz, which was great but Peterson managed to take it slightly away from that and make it accessible to people."

> **"If that was acid house, then this is acid jazz!"**
>
> CHRIS BANGS

NITE FM AT WAG SHOCK. MON 2nd MARCH 10 30 - 3...4 QUID

Radio London's **GILLES PETERSON** and **CHRIS BANGS**

THE BAPTIST BROTHERS BIG BEAT BASH & SYLVESTERS LATIN LAUGH-IN

LIVE AND LIVELY

STEVE WILLIAMSON QUINTET

BATUCADA BOP BONGO BREAKBEATS?

HOT SKINS – CONGA KINGS

SNOWBOY PLUS VERY SPECIAL GUEST!

W.a.r. CLUB 35-37 WARDOUR STREET, LONDON W1 TELEPHONE: 01-437 5534

THE WAG CLUB 2ND FLOOR NOW OPEN

Suddenly, though, Paul Murphy was gone. He walked away from the scene and handed his crown to Gilles Peterson. Gilles was in a great position as he'd also played a part in the rare groove scene, so he was no stranger to the funkier side of things, too. The trouble was that even though the jazz sounds got ever more adventurous, the emerging acid house scene was affecting London's club scene.

One evening, Gilles found himself alongside fellow DJ Chris Bangs at an event at the Watermans Arts Centre in Brentford, hosted by Nicky Holloway. There were a thousand punters dancing and five DJs providing the sounds. At one point, Paul Oakenfold, fresh from a trip to Ibiza, dropped the futuristic electronic tune 'Acid Trax' by Phuture and the kids on the dance floor went mad for it. Gilles and Bangs were due next on the turntables and were already worried about how to follow it up. Bangs pulls out an old funky soul instrumental from 1969, 'Iron Leg' by Mickey & The Soul Generation and shouted down the microphone "If that was acid house, then this is acid jazz!"

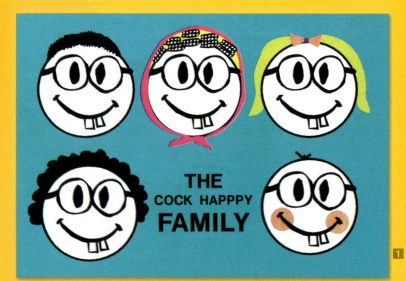

THE
COCK HAPPPY
FAMILY

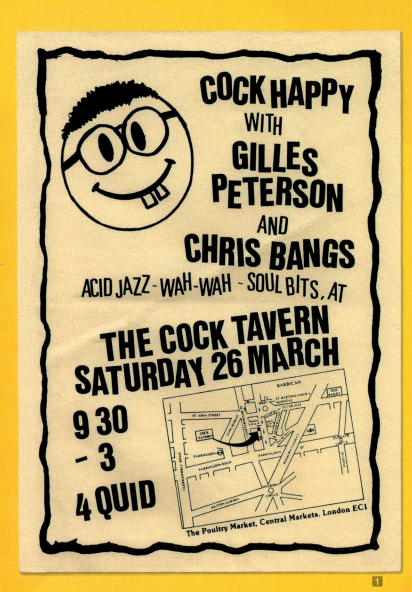

COCK HAPPY
WITH
GILLES
PETERSON
AND
CHRIS BANGS
ACID JAZZ - WAH-WAH - SOUL BITS, AT

THE COCK TAVERN
SATURDAY 26 MARCH
9 30
- 3
4 QUID

The Poultry Market, Central Markets, London EC1

ACID JAZZ
CHRIS 'ACID' BANGS
THE NEW EXPERIENCE IN SOUND
FRIDAY 12 30 - LATE, IN THE BLUENOTE

ACID JAZZ, BATUCADAS,
BE~BOP & BREAKBEATS
SPUN STUPID STYLEEE!

SIDE A

GALLIANO

JAZ ID1
ACID JAZZ

FREDERIC LIES STILL
(MAYFIELD/GALLIANO)

SIDE A. COPYRIGHT CONTROL
SIDE B. RE-ELECT THE PRESIDENT MUSIC

Piller: "I sold James Taylor to Polydor in 1987 but carried on managing him. Stiff had gone bankrupt by then so I had a small job working for John Curd [former manager of The Action and Mighty Baby; ID and ABC subsidiary (a mainly psychobilly label with a few Mod bands), and live promoter for places like the Klub Foot at the Clarendon, Hammersmith]. Curd was bringing over the very early hip hop bands like De La Soul and putting on people like Gil Scott-Heron. I found this whole world of influences opening up, which I felt on the Mod scene was closed to me.

"Anyway, while I'm hanging around with Gilles we started getting people coming up to us and giving us their demos. Meanwhile, Gilles' roadie, Rob Gallagher, who later became known as Galliano, used to get on the microphone at the Wag Club and rap over instrumentals. So me and Gilles said why don't we do a label. We then had to decide what to call it and because of Bangs' 'acid jazz' quote, we said we may as well call it that as we'll only bring out a couple of singles. We brought out 'Frederic Lies Still' by Galliano as our debut single. Then we had it cut like an American 7" with a big hole, which was my idea. We got people to send promo copies from America to DJs over here. James Hamilton, who wrote for *Record Mirror*, reviewed it as the latest thing from New York. He never forgave me or reviewed us again. I was just following a Stock, Aitken and Waterman angle, as they'd done it with 'Roadblock.'

"We'd always said it was for fun but having worked in independent labels before and Acid Jazz being my fourth label, I wasn't prepared for what happened next. Suddenly our first single sells 15,000 copies in three weeks. That would probably make you number one these days, or certainly in the Top 20. So after all these years of selling around 500 records, suddenly we're big. We then realised we had to continue and make it work. We signed a few other artists, such as A Man Called Adam, The Last Poets, Chris Bangs under his many guises and Snowboy, and ran Acid Jazz together for 18 months.

"Then, by 1989, Gilles got disillusioned. On reflection I think it was because he didn't like the retro feel that I'd embraced. I was what I regarded as a populist. I wanted to have hit records and have as many people as possible love what I loved. Gilles didn't; Gilles was an elitist, and there's nothing wrong in that. The thing we fell out about though was Jamiroquai. Gilles said, 'I don't want to sign another Brand New Heavies. I want to be creative and different.' I thought we were on to something. Anyway, he told me he'd just been offered a deal to sign for Phonogram to go and do Acid Jazz under a different name with them. I said great, I've worked for Stiff and I don't like major companies. So he left our set-up and we split the roster in half. He took Galliano and The Young Disciples, who had only done a demo at that stage and weren't even signed. I kept The Brand New Heavies and A Man Called Adam. We hadn't signed Jamiroquai at that time but [Gilles] didn't want to.

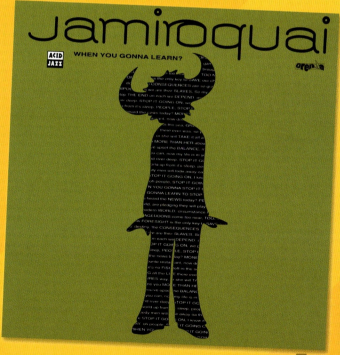

"So Jason Kay [better known as Jay Kay, Jamiroquai's lead singer] came to my office six months after Gilles had left. He put on a Brand New Heavies album track, from *Brand New Heavies*, the instrumental one, and he sings. He's doing the funny dancing around my office and I was so totally blown away that I immediately pulled out a blank contract and asked him to sign to Acid Jazz there and then. He performed 'When You Gonna Learn.' It was called something else at the time, it was 'How It Should Be,' but I asked him to change it. He didn't like it. Jay didn't like to be told what to do because he had this fuckin' vision and was really hard work, but he was worth it because he was a fuckin' genius.

"When Gilles set up Talkin' Loud he signed Incognito and Marksman. We ended up having more success than Talkin' Loud and they had a multi-million pound budget from a major and we were running out of a small bedroom in Hackney. Then we moved to Denmark Street and got the studio, and I'm proud of that."

When the magazine *i-D* featured the article 'Acid Jazz Mods' in their November 1989 issue it caused all sorts of reactions from both the Mod and jazz scenes. The two-page article, written by John Godfrey, seemed intent on causing something of a division in Mod ranks, even though it featured some of the scene's most respected figures.

> **"...they saw what we were doing at Acid Jazz as the new Mod."**

EDDIE PILLER

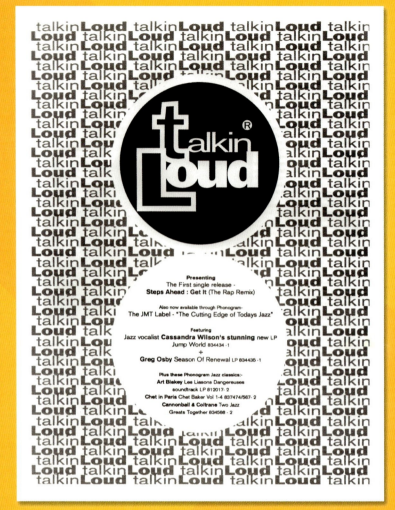

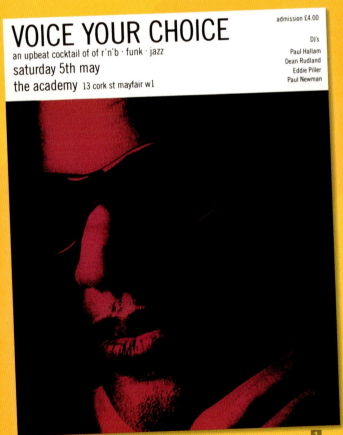

Ruby's **ASK YO' MOMMA** Carnaby Street

lickin' funk, fusion & psychedelic soul.

EVERY THURSDAY 10.30-3.30   BRING OWN ALCOHOL £5 OR £3 (concs)

2

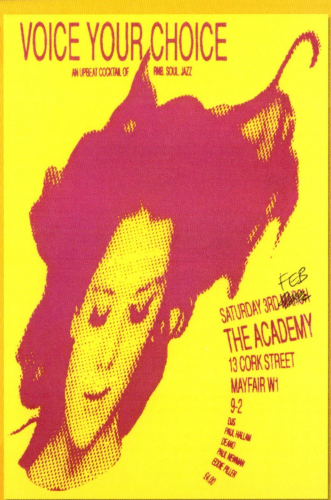

VOICE YOUR CHOICE
AN UPBEAT COCKTAIL OF RNB. SOUL. JAZZ

FEB

SATURDAY 3RD
THE ACADEMY
13 CORK STREET
MAYFAIR W1
9-2
DJS
PAUL HALLAM
DEAKO
PAUL NEWMAN
EDDIE PILLER
£4.00

1

Piller: "There was a magazine run by John Pidgeon called *Touch* which was the in-house magazine of Kiss FM, and they approached me to do a piece – they saw what we were doing at Acid Jazz as the new Mod. So they came to our gig called 'Voice Your Choice' at Cork Street, which I did with the former *Countdown* art director Jon Cooke, and they chose 10 people in the audience and asked if they'd be in a feature about new Mods. There was a couple of black girls, Jan Kincaid from the Brand New Heavies, Keiron Hurley from Acid Jazz. I was wearing a red leather jacket with 'Black Scots' written on the back, which was a Canadian junior baseball team. It was worth £350 and I thought I looked the absolute bollocks. Jon Cooke was much more Mod than me at the time.

"John Godfrey, who was the editor of *i-D* magazine, picked up on it and did the article 'Acid Jazz Mods,' then *The Face* magazine picked up on it, and suddenly it's the new Mod. *The Face* sent a journalist down to the Acid Jazz office and was amazed, because there were eight staff scooters parked outside the Acid Jazz office in Denmark Street. The journalist said 'Well, you're obviously Mods,' and we said 'Well, not really,' and they said 'But you are, aren't you?' So we said 'Well yeah... we probably are 'cos we're into Weller, jazz, funk and soul... but we're wearing trainers.'"

By the time the *i-D*'s 'Acid Jazz Mods' article appeared in November 1989 the jazz scene was buzzing again. Sadly, the retro Mod scene was on a downslide. Although it caused friction, the article was, in a way, completely tongue in cheek. It was even subtitled 'Modern Myths' and was in the 'Fantasy Issue.'

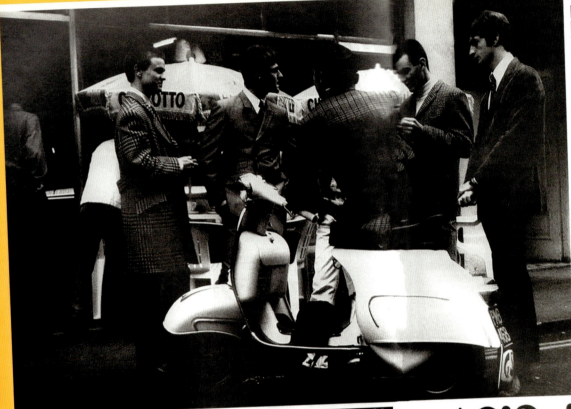

"I first saw them when I started DJing at The Wag four years ago, but it was when The James Taylor Quartet got into acid jazz that they started turning up en masse." Gilles Peterson, jazz DJ and progenitor of acid jazz, is talking about mods. Not the parka-clad 16 year olds who listen to 20 year old records and avoid the posses of b-boys who have taken over Carnaby St. Nor the armies of customised scooters that converge on seaside towns, bristling with fans of wing mirrors and combat green. These are true modernists who are keeping up with the times. "There's always been a jazz element in mod – what Gilles has done is open up a few kids' minds. It's affected quite a few mods in London, and it's only in London that it's happened, but before, if it wasn't a rare R&B record, mods wouldn't listen to it." John Cook, one of the faces on the London mod scene, is wearing a close-cut embroidered jerkin, black beret (not tilted), slim-line Levi's cords (don't forget the capital 'E' – extremely rare pre-'67 Levi's) and Bass Weejuns. He doesn't look like the archetypal mod. In fact, he looks more at home with 'Absolute Beginners' than 'Quadrophenia'.

"I wouldn't have worn this a few years ago, but it's all about being a 'sussed' mod. A lot of the mods wear '80s clothes, but the cut isn't right and some look so straight, so square; they look as though they've stepped straight out of a bank." The look is vital. You have to wear original '80s clothes, be prepared to go to Amsterdam to buy the original shoes ('they have warehouses full of them'), and never go anywhere near Carnaby St ("except for George's tailor-made suits"). And you have to want something more.

"I don't go to very many mod clubs now 'cos I find them a bit boring – it's the same faces every week. When I first started going to Dingwalls on Sundays and Cock Happy, I thought it was such a brilliant atmosphere. Personally, it's made me feel more like a mod – it's what a mod should be doing. Mod clubs only go on 'til midnight," says John. The drift to acid jazz within the mod scene shouldn't be that surprising. The organ sound of R&B jazz artists like Jimmy Smith and Jimmy McGriff has always been part of the scene, and Blue Note is an intrinsic part of the mod sense of 'cool' – all it took was a band to make it happen.

Ever since the mod revival of '79 when bands like Secret Affair and The Merton Parkas briefly provided a focal point for mods, there has never been a band who have stood up and nailed their mod colours to their Italian suits. The nearest was The Prisoners, a psychedelic garage band who commanded a large mod following almost by default. In the mid-'80s if you were a mod, you still hung onto the coat-tails of Paul Weller, waited for old '60s R&B starts to wait or shut your eyes and pretended The Prisoners were the Small Faces. James Taylor, leader of The James Taylor Quartet, was the organ-player in The Prisoners. "When The James Taylor Quartet moved away from '60s music, some of them followed us – the ones who weren't so narrow minded. It's definitely changed what music mods listen to."

This isn't a revival; it isn't even a new chapter in youth subculture. It is a small group of mods who want to break the clichés. "The actual mods involved with the mod scene are total knobheads," says Eddie Piller, one-time mod face, manager of The JTQ and co-owner of Acid Jazz Records.

MOD FASHION

Levi's (big 'E' – pre-'67).
Bass Weejun or Gucci loafers.
Long-collared button down shirts with sewn-in pleats.
Three-button suede jackets.
Tailor-made hipster trousers with kick-outs.
Check three-button sport jackets.
Clark's Desert Boots.
Roll-neck shirts.
Three-button double-breasted suits.
John Smedley turtle necks.
Silk socks.

MOD ACID JAZZ

James Brown: 'Funky Drummer
The JBs: 'Pass The Peas'
The Village Callers: 'Hector'
A Man Called Adam: 'Earthly Powers'
James Taylor Quartet: 'The Money Spyder'
The O'Jays: 'Shaft In Africa'
New Jersey Kings: new LP out on Acid Jazz
Julie Driscoll & Brian Auger Trinity: 'Save Me'
Billy Hawks: 'Ooh Baby'
Charles Wright & The 103rd Street Watts Band: Express Yourself'

MODERN MYTHS

Acid Jazz Mods in Soho

ACID JAZZ MODS

Story by JOHN GODFREY
Photography by SIMON FLEURY

"The mod scene was going downhill, the jazz scene was going up. Something had to happen. Apart from Cookie's crew – who are totally fucking mad – the mod scene is fucked." Whether or not any other mods will throw away their parkas with their prejudices and start dancing to acid jazz, is not yet clear. But to those who don't already know – Paul Weller doesn't go to Dingwalls on a Sunday afternoon for nothing.

70 I-D THE FANTASY ISSUE

I-D THE FANTASY ISSUE 71

> **"Some of the home-grown acid jazz stuff...
> ...was a bit too kitsch for me..."**
>
> PAUL WELLER

1 Swifty designed the cover for The Young Disciples debut 12" *Get Yourself Together*, as well as designing for artists like Galliano and Incognito.

Still, the acid jazz scene remained healthy and a whole lifestyle came with it. Gilles and Patrick Forge were DJ'ing Sunday afternoons in Dingwalls, Camden, at their 'Talkin' Loud And Saying Something' sessions to a packed dance floor. Jazz FM began, Kiss FM was legitimised after years as a pirate station, and both would offer jazz shows among their eclectic output. Paul Bradshaw's *Straight No Chaser* magazine provided the reading material for the scene by reviewing the music and clubs, while new music came in the form of Galliano, The Brand New Heavies, Mother Earth, Jamiroquai, The Young Disciples and others. This was usually mixed with American jazz rap provided by the likes of A Tribe Called Quest, Gang Starr and The Pharcyde. Add into the mix Brazilian music, seventies Hammond and wah-wah workouts and classic Blue Note releases, and you start to get an idea of the soundtrack.

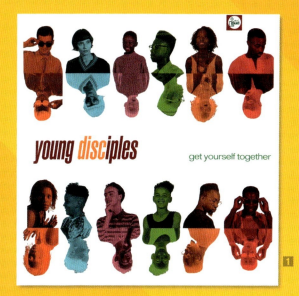

young disciples
get yourself together

1

One person who definitely saw the connection between these sounds and the whole Mod ideal was Paul Weller, who at that time was struggling to launch his solo career after the collapse of The Style Council: "The early nineties was a great time musically. It was happening on all musical fronts. I mean, I liked it as a punter, and the music that was around, but as for me doing my own music, I hated it for a couple of years. It was extremely hard work. It was a good two years before my debut solo album came out in '92, of me just trying to get it back together. It was fuckin' horrible man; it was like going back and starting again, and that's exactly what it was really. In hindsight it was a good lesson to learn, y'know: don't get too big for your boots because it doesn't always last.

"But there were some great things going and it was a very inspiring time musically otherwise, I thought. There were so many good things happening on so many different levels. I thought rap was good around that time, loads of good soul, R&B and pop records coming out as well. Lots of good tunes like 'Pushing Against The Flow' by Raw Stylus. Some great albums like Massive Attack, Young Disciples and Galliano. Some of the home-grown acid jazz stuff, though, was a bit too kitsch for me – you know, the wrong side of the sixties and seventies. Then there was all the rap stuff using samples by the likes of A Tribe Called Quest and Gang Starr. The funny thing was to hear those records at the time using great samples, they made me go out and find out about other tunes. So records such as 'Jazz Thing' by Gang Starr, which sampled 'Dujii' by really early Kool & the Gang amazed me. I didn't even know Kool & the Gang had made records before the pop shit. A Tribe Called Quest's 'Luck Of Lucien' sampled Billy Brooks 'Forty Days' from the *Windows Of The Mind* LP. I went out and tried to find these records, so the story keeps unfolding."

The clothing associated with the 'Neo Mod' look was a mixture of vintage, tailor-made and brand new threads. Footwear could be Adidas Gazelle trainers or Gucci loafers. One shop heavily associated with the look was Duffer of St George in D'Arblay Street, Soho, which did a great line in Italian-style knitwear.

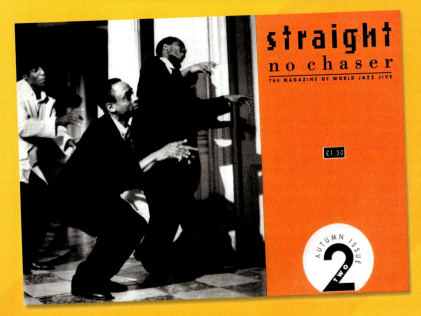

TALKING LOUD & SAYING SOMETHING

JAZZ WHA AFRO CUBAN

THE SESSION!

DJ

GILLES PETERSON

+

LIVE GUESTS

SUNDAY 12 - 5pm   Adm. 2.50

DINGWALLS

Camden Lock, Chalk Farm Rd. NW1

straight
no chaser
THE MAGAZINE OF WORLD JAZZ JIVE

£1.50

AUTUMN ISSUE
TWO
2

JWA = Jazz With Attitude. Swifty's designs for Talkin' Loud were iconic to the scene.

1 Eddie Piller: Acid Jazz Records boss.

2 Reading's Kings Tavern R&B Mod club switched to a new soundtrack.

Paul Weller remembers: "Clothes-wise, there was quite a Moddy thing going on at that time, with lots of good clothes around. Duffer of St George, Sign of The Times and Kensington Market were great. There were a few people I got to know through Marco Nelson and Femi of The Young Disciples. One of these guys was doing vintage stuff. I got some dogtooth hipster trousers, they were fuckin' amazing. I also got a load of old trousers from John Simons. He had two big piles of them, some were Sta-Prest, but they were all American."

There are some great graphics from that period, especially on some of the club flyers. One of the main exponents was Manchester's Ian Swift. 'Swifty,' as he was known, embraced emerging technology and, armed with twinned Apple Macintosh SEs, he revolutionised club flyers by ditching the cut-and-paste style for a sleeker, more luxurious look. When Talkin' Loud records was launched, Swifty was the obvious choice for art director, and he ended up designing the label's logo and record sleeves.

> **" Clothes-wise, there was quite a Moddy thing going on at that time... "**
>
> PAUL WELLER

The monthly music magazine *Straight No Chaser*, launched by Paul Bradshaw, went hand in hand with this new acid jazz world, and was packed with the latest club charts and featured articles on musicians both old and new. Of course, it would be Swifty who brought the whole magazine to life with his outstanding graphics.

One design, however, sums up that whole period: the Acid Jazz record label logo. Head honcho Eddie Piller remembers the frustration of its creation: "We were looking for a logo and the first single 'Frederick Lies Still' featured Galliano's face with a dinked hole, like an American issue. The first couple of records had that and Jon Cooke had found the font for the words 'Acid Jazz' in a book. After the first three records we realised we couldn't use Galliano's face for every record because it wasn't fair on him. We needed a logo, so I looked through my record collection... Blue Beat! What a fuckin' great logo that is. We tried to find a typeface for Blue Beat but there wasn't one so what me and Jon Cooke did was make our own letters from the Blue Beat typeface. So if you look at the Acid Jazz logo on any of the releases, the letters are all different. The two As and the two Zs are slightly different because they're hand cut by Jon Cooke and we stuck them down. Originally the design was curved in an arch like Blue Beat was."

" ...Blue Beat! What a f***in' great logo... "

EDDIE PILLER

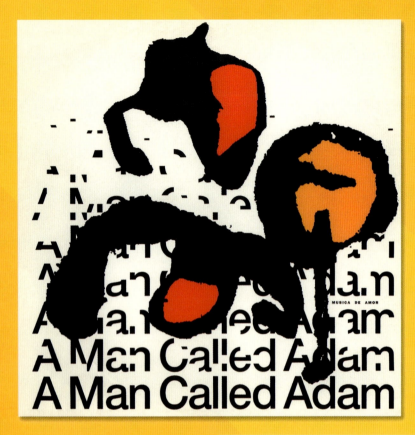

Jaffa's record cover creations.

HARD
BOPPIN'
ACID
DROPPIN'
FUNKY
BUTT
JAZZ
ACID

ACID JAZZ

❝...I love the typeface but it's not working... ...I've got an idea...❞

JAFFA

"Then we employed a proper designer, who was a bloke called Jaffa from a design company called The Unknown Partnership, who out of the 400-odd Acid Jazz sleeves he's done about 300 of them, while Paul McEvoy's done about 150. Jaffa said, 'I love the typeface but it's not working in the half moon design. I've got an idea,' and he put the words in a box, half black, half white. Fuckin' genius. It's the best logo and the most recognisable logo of the eighties.

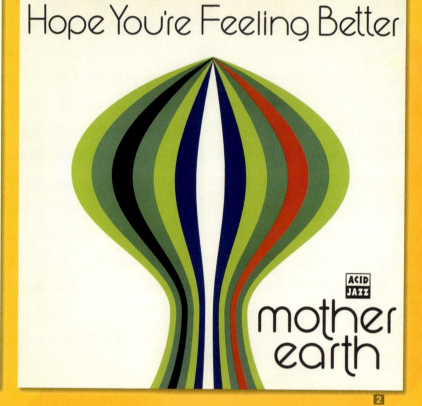

1

2

"I don't care what anybody says. I also came up with the tag line
'environmentally funky,' because people kept going on about recycling,
so what Acid Jazz did, being a kind of right on, funky, spliff smoking
label, we made all of our product out of recycled product. So all
our vinyl was recycled. All of our fabric for the T-shirts and clothes
was recycled."

1 & **2** Both record covers adding a splash of colour, designed by Jaffa.
3 The Brain Club in Wardour Street was used for the cover shoot in 1991.
Present on the day were many old 80s Mod club regulars, including Nick Aghadiuno
(seen at the forefront), Paul Newman, Dean Rudland and Jonathon Cooke,
as well as Simon Bartholomew of The Brand New Heavies band.

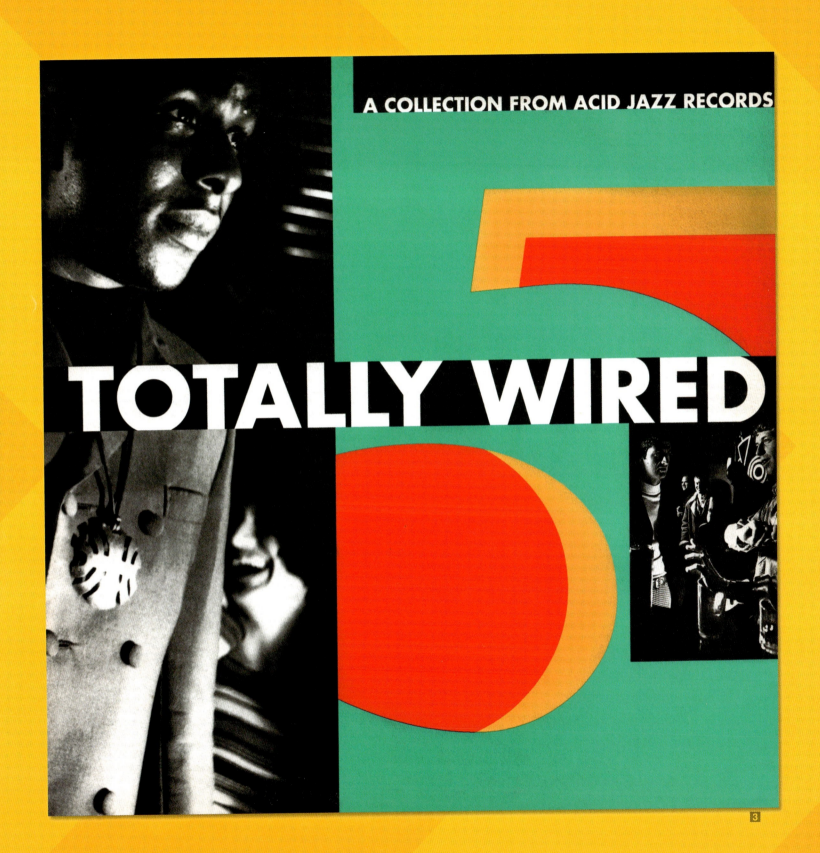

A COLLECTION FROM ACID JAZZ RECORDS

TOTALLY WIRED

5

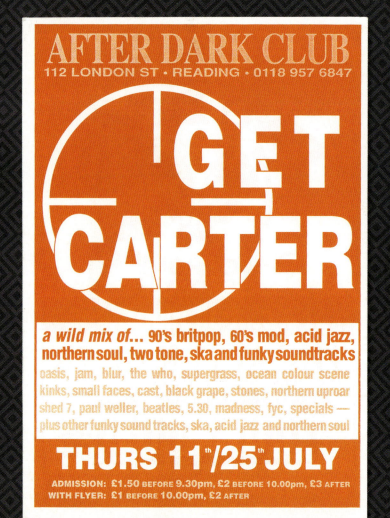

AFTER DARK CLUB
112 LONDON ST · READING · 0118 957 6847

GET CARTER

a wild mix of... 90's britpop, 60's mod, acid jazz, northern soul, two tone, ska and funky soundtracks

oasis, jam, blur, the who, supergrass, ocean colour scene kinks, small faces, cast, black grape, stones, northern uproar shed 7, paul weller, beatles, 5.30, madness, fyc, specials — plus other funky sound tracks, ska, acid jazz and northern soul

THURS 11ᵗʰ/25ᵗʰ JULY

ADMISSION: £1.50 BEFORE 9.30pm, £2 BEFORE 10.00pm, £3 AFTER
WITH FLYER: £1 BEFORE 10.00pm, £2 AFTER

BRITPOP: MOD OVERLOAD

" ...the Mod scene had disappeared up its own arse... "

ANDY LEWIS

1985's second Mod Revival had failed to take shape, and while at the beginning of the nineties magazines such as *i-D* and *The Face* had promoted 'Neo Mod' as *the* big look in club land, it certainly failed to materialise as any kind of high street fashion. That's why it was surreal to pick up a copy of *Melody Maker* in November 1994 and see the headline 'Touched By The Hand Of Mod' accompanied by an eight-page special feature stating 'MODS ARE BACK.'

Of course in truth the underground scene had never gone away. The trouble was that its ranks had been severely depleted in the mid-eighties as some Mods had discovered rave culture, acid house and ecstasy. The fact that the Mod scene was seen as inaccessible due to its puritan and elitist nature kept new blood away. The foundation of the '79 Mod revival was new young bands; by the late eighties, the Mod scene was largely lacking in them.

Back in the real world, the charts had flourished as bands such as The Stone Roses, Inspiral Carpets, Happy Mondays, The LAs and Charlatans flew the flag for British music. But it wasn't long before the home-grown assault on the charts was battling the new American sound: grunge. Long-haired, dishevelled-looking bands such as Nirvana, Soundgarden and the Stone Temple Pilots sang of apathy, social alienation and self-loathing. It comes as no surprise, then, that as grunge began to dominate music – both its look and sound – that there would be a British backlash.

Andy Lewis: "I started DJ'ing at St David's University College, Lampeter, which is part of the University of Wales, back in 1988, playing stuff like 'Bert's Apple Crumble' – The Quik, 'Nobody But Me' – The Human Beinz, 'Baby What You Want Me To Do' – Sons Of Fred, 'The Champ' – The Mohawks and 'Indian Rope Man' by Brian Auger & Julie Driscoll. So ordinary students were getting into the music that I thought was just the province of the hipper kids in London on the Mod scene. I also got into a lot of funky stuff, like 'Sex Machine' by James Brown. The James Taylor Quartet opened my ears to the rare groove and acid jazz scenes. One of the other DJs [at university] was a hip hop DJ who turned me on to 'I Believe In Miracles' by The Jackson Sisters and I started to hear all the samples from hip hop. By then I had a copy of the *Blow Up* soundtrack with 'Bring Down The Birds' by Herbie Hancock. A couple of years later, 'Groove Is In The Heart' by Dee-Lite came out and people realised that was the tune I'd been playing in the students' union bar along with all these other records that people were now sampling. All of a sudden I accidentally found myself being seen as a trendsetter. When I came back from university in the early nineties, the Mod scene had disappeared up its own arse, partly because all these heavy people were moaning and saying 'you're not a real Mod'."

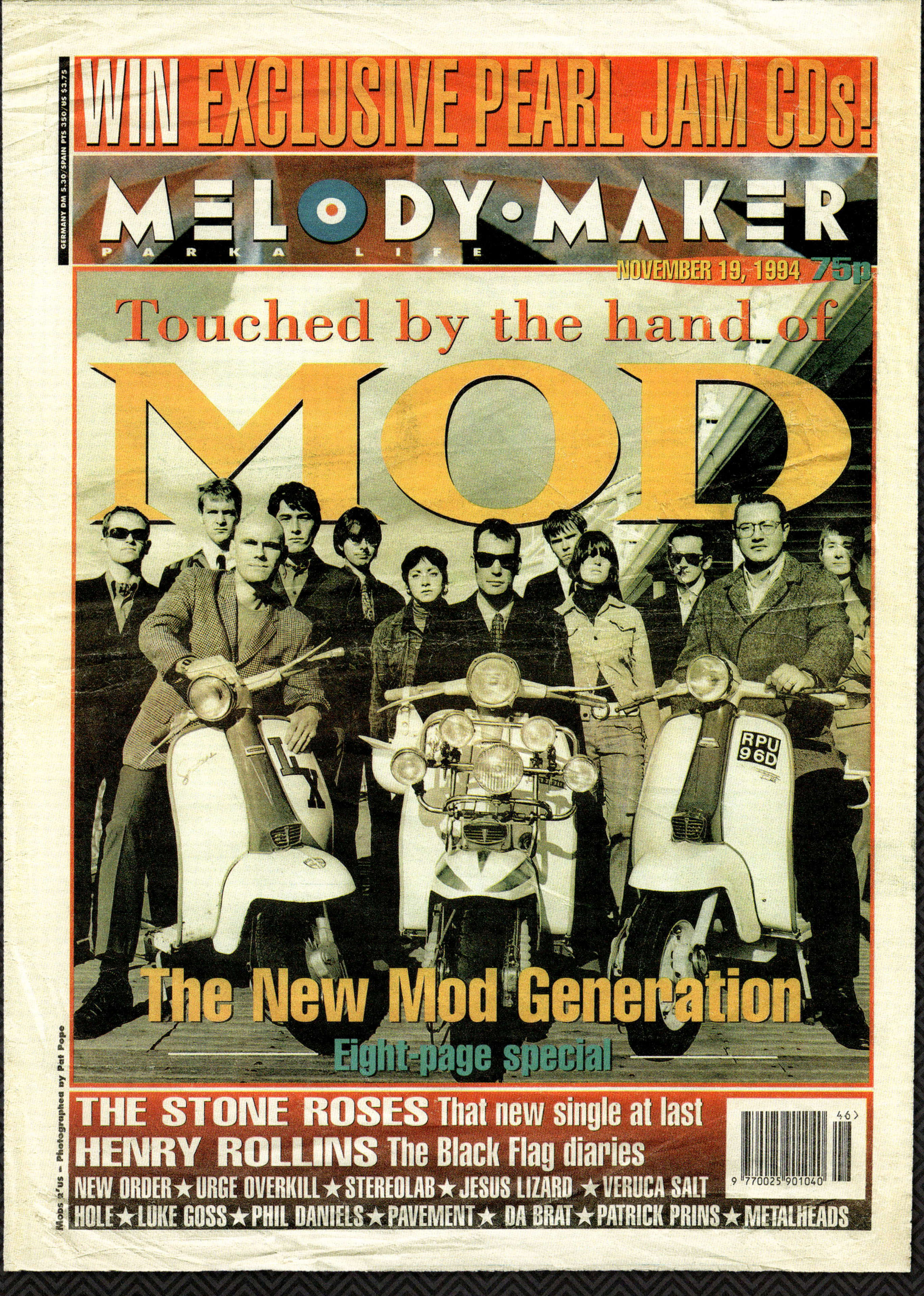

WIN EXCLUSIVE PEARL JAM CDs!
GERMANY DM 5.30/SPAIN PTS 350/US $3.75
MELODY·MAKER
PARKA LIFE
NOVEMBER 19, 1994 75p
Touched by the hand of
MOD
RPU 96D
The New Mod Generation
Eight-page special
THE STONE ROSES That new single at last
HENRY ROLLINS The Black Flag diaries
NEW ORDER★URGE OVERKILL★STEREOLAB★JESUS LIZARD ★VERUCA SALT
HOLE★LUKE GOSS★PHIL DANIELS★PAVEMENT★ DA BRAT★PATRICK PRINS★METALHEADS
Mods R'us – Photographed by Pat Pope

One of the places Andy started hanging out in was Wendy May's Locomotion Club at the Town and Country Club in Kentish Town. Here he discovered a melting pot of musical styles being absorbed by different youth cults. Andy passed Wendy a demo tape of his sounds and soon found himself being asked to DJ at the night. In August 1991, Andy Lewis was 21 years old and was a DJ in London earning good money playing a mix of sixties soul and R&B, seventies funk, hip hop and indie.

In March 1993, the Town and Country Club lost its lease, forcing Wendy's Locomotion night to move to the Underworld in Camden. By default, Andy began to spend more time in Camden and soon found himself in the downstairs rare 45s department of record shop Out On The Floor, where he got chatting to Paul Tunkin, who worked there.

"...I hated that grunge thing... "

PAUL WELLER

In October 1993, Tunkin decided to launch a night at the Laurel Tree pub "for nineties Swinging London." The names 'Londinium' and 'Swinging London' were both considered before he finally settled on 'Blow Up.' Andy Lewis was invited to DJ and he soon became a regular behind the decks. The club night proved to be popular with art school kids and indie fans alike.

Andy Lewis: "On any given night at Blow Up, especially in the early days, were young people in their twenties who were working for television production companies, advertising agencies and radio, or they were journalists. They were the people who really did us favours and were the people who bigged the club up. Once they started coming, it was only a matter of time before we had members of Pulp, Blur, St Etienne and other artists swing by. Graham Coxon of Blur came every fuckin' week so that's how we got to DJ for Blur on their 'Parklife' tour."

Camden became the centre of the universe for all up and coming bands, and the beginning of an entirely new scene: what would become known as Britpop. The Good Mixer pub in Inverness Street was the meeting place, the Monarch in Chalk Farm Road the place for live gigs and Blow Up in the Laurel Tree the main club night.

Then of course there were the bands. There had been great bands from 1991, such as 5.30 and The Revs, who had the same type of ideals as the emerging Britpop scene, but were just a bit too early to get properly noticed. So while Britpop will always be remembered for its huge bands, such as Pulp, Blur and Oasis, there were lots of smaller bands like Thurman, Mantaray, These Animal Men and S.M.A.S.H that should have got wider acceptance.

Lewis: "The music press decided to big up Menswear but in a parallel universe they could have bigged up all sorts of other people and maybe Oasis wouldn't have got anywhere. It could have been a band like My Life Story, which would have made life far more interesting in the nineties. Britpop [...] actually lowered the bar of pop culture that had been set pretty high, and then every generation moved it that little bit higher. Britpop kind of started bringing it down again."

Paul Weller: "Britpop was good in some ways. Once you give anything a name it limits it. It puts it into a bracket or a box of some kind, which is never a good thing to do. I did feel, though, that there was some kind of renaissance in British music and British culture and that it was recognised in a lot of other countries. With Oasis, it was good timing as well. There were a lot of 'lads' bands' that liked football, getting off their nut and playing music. I hated that grunge thing and all that bollocks, and if nothing else, Britpop sort of saw that off really. But the tag Britpop was daft, really, because suddenly groups like The Kinks and The Beatles were being called Britpop."

1 Poster for pre-Britpop band 5.30 that accompanied their '13th Disciple' 12", 1991.

2 The Revs EP cover, 1991.

3 These Animal Men 'Too Sussed' 12" EP, 1994.

4 S*M*A*S*H 'Real Surreal' 7", 1993.

The music papers covered the whole new Britpop-style Mod thing for quite some time after the *Melody Maker* feature in 1994. *GQ* ran a 'Mod Gets Modern' feature in February 1996 and *Vox* magazine ran a 10-page 'Mod For It' special in 1996. From a fan's viewpoint it also paved the way for a whole new raft of fanzines, such as *New Perspective*, *All Our Yesterdays* and *Sussed*, which would promote the new wave of guitar-based British bands. While Noel and Liam Gallagher were pictured almost daily in some form of fur-hooded parka, sat astride their Velocifero scooters, it became the norm to see some form of Mod iconography on anything from posters to tins of beans.

Lewis: "Looking back I think there were certain aspects of [Britpop] that were totally Mod and other aspects that were desperately un-Mod. I think there was a point where this faith in the future got lost, and the whole point about Mod is that it's all about having faith in the future, taking things forward and moving things on. Suddenly it was all about looking backwards, and it lost its desire to move things on a bit. I thought things were going to get interesting again but it kind of stagnated. I think by '97 the wheels had fallen off it."

The one thing that Britpop did achieve was to give Mod respectability. The music press seemed to adore it so much that it encouraged the public into seeing Mod as a Great British tradition. Mods and Rockers are now as much of a British seaside town icon as ice cream and deckchairs.

In August 2012, Bradley Wiggins became the most decorated British Olympian when he gained his seventh medal at the games (six golds, one silver) for his win in the 44km time trial. *The Times'* front cover the next day carried a photo of him on his bike, his helmet carrying a 'target' design. The headline accompanying the photo ready simply: 'Mod Rule.'

During the closing ceremony of the 2012 Olympics, The Who performed a short set culminating in 'My Generation' and The Kaiser Chiefs performed The Who's 'Pinball Wizard,' as Mods and scooterists rode their Vespas and Lambrettas around the arena. The light sequence projected images of Union Jacks and targets across the arena and audience. It was modern pop artist Damien Hirst who set the scene, which, in his words, celebrated the "anarchy and diversity of British pop art, and by extension the energy and multiplicity of contemporary British culture." Hirst had been approached in November 2011 and agreed to do the design, which he called *Beautiful Union Jack Celebratory Patriotic Olympic Explosion In An Electric Storm Painting*. Many Mod purists cringed with embarrassment, while others were happy to smile and utter the words "we were right all along."

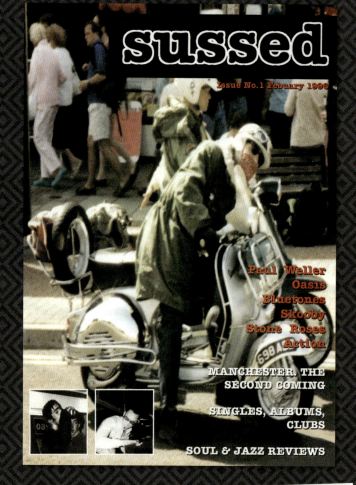

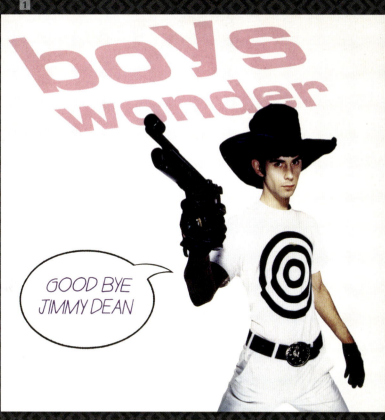

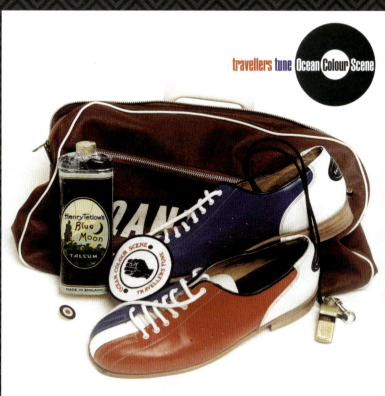

travellers tune Ocean Colour Scene

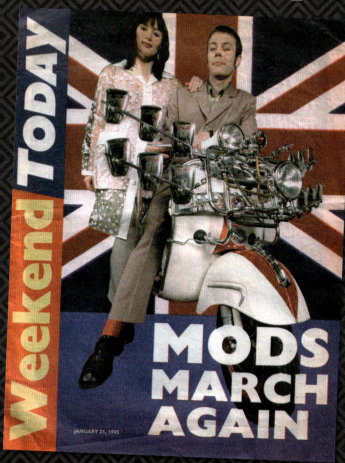

1 Too early for Britpop. Boys Wonder third single, 1998.

2 *Q* magazine feature, December 1996.

3 A retro nod to Northern soul on the OCS single, 1997.

4 *Weekend Today*, Sunday paper supplement, January 1995.

CLASSIC ALBUM: *STANLEY ROAD* PAUL WELLER

> **" Mod will never go out of fashion... "**
>
> PAUL WELLER

Stanley Road was Paul Weller's third solo album. Released on June 7, 1995, during the peak of the Britpop era, the album features 12 songs recorded at the Manor Studios in Oxford. It contains several notable contributors, including Noel Gallagher, Carleen Anderson, Mick Talbot and Steve Winwood. It was recorded over eight and a half weeks in 1994 and 1995 and became the UK's number one album between May 27 and June 2, 1995.

Paul Weller was 37 years old at the time, The Jam and Style Council but distant memories. But this period of Paul's life is when he seems keen to reconnect with his distant past. For the first time in over a decade, he reached out to his home town Woking, touched those lush green-belt fields, ran his fingers over the sign to Boundary Lane and opened up his ears again to the sounds of the Small Faces, Traffic and The Beatles, his original motivation for much of his own creativity.

The album shines among a sea of wannabe acts desperately clambering onto the bandwagon christened 'Britpop.'

In a May issue of *NME* promoting the album, Paul tells the writer Paul Moody: "Yeah, it is pretty much full circle in those terms. For me, Mod will never go out of fashion, and I think there will always be people who understand that and get what they want from it. I hate the way it's getting used at the moment. I mean, I don't want to talk about bands individually, but they aren't Mod bands are they? How can they be? It pisses me off a bit. It's like none of them are making Mod records, no matter how Mod they might look. If you want to hear a Mod record, stick on a good James Brown album. That's Mod."

Stanley Road came in a gatefold sleeve and featured a booklet of photographs entitled 'Excerpts,' with photographs from Lawrence Watson and words by Paolo Hewitt. These formed part of a book released later that year called *Days Lose Their Names And Time Slips Away*. But it was always the album cover that would stand out among covers released during that period, including The Verve's *A Northern Soul*, Alanis Morrissette's *Jagged Little Pill* and The Chemical Brothers' *Exit Planet Dust*. The bright, colourful, cartoon-like image leapt from the record racks. Once again, Weller had chosen a collage to share his influences, just as he had with The Jam (*All Mod Cons*) and The Style Council (*Our Favourite Shop*). *Stanley Road*'s cover included photos of Aretha Franklin, George Best, John Lennon, an old photo of Piccadilly Circus, George Doswell-designed figurines of Steve Marriott and Ronnie Lane, photos of his mum and dad on holiday, the Eiffel Tower and a painting of *The Lady Of Shallot* by John William Waterhouse.

Peter Blake: "That came about because Paul is a terrific Beatles fan. The way it came about was through a phone call with this very nervous, shy voice, asking would I be interested in doing a record cover, and it was Paul on the other end. He'd apparently always wanted me to do it but had always been too nervous to call, so when he eventually did call, we met up. He was incredibly polite, as he always is; he called my wife, Chrissy, 'Mrs Blake' and was very shy. That is when we first met and worked it all out. The form it took was that I'd had this idea of doing a kind of portrait of somebody through their likes. You know, all the things they like included in a picture. He gave me a list of favourite things and so it's made up from that. It was quite complicated because the LP would have been printed as it was but the EP would have sat in the LP in a shallow box. That element on its own as an EP was Paul as a little boy holding an image of himself as a man, which is a kind of surrealistic idea. I think the footballer he wanted didn't seem to fit in so we settled for Georgie Best, and then there was the local bus he used to catch. I was a bit surprised about his information on the art world. He really liked a painter called Waterhouse [John William] and he had a list of other people."

Paul Weller: "It wasn't my idea to get Peter Blake, it was the designer Simon Halfon's. When he suggested it, I wasn't sure to begin with. I thought it would cost us a fortune and that he really wouldn't be up for doing it. I really thought he was inaccessible to us, but he was really more than up for doing it. At the time he was curating the National Gallery, so we went to see him there. It was really quite amazing how he was really into it. The fact that he'd designed the *Pepper* album definitely factored into it. But it was only part of the reason, and certainly not the whole of it, as both me and Halfon liked his work.

"Again, it's a collage and we did the same sort of thing we did on *Our Favourite Shop*, with me bringing him some of my stuff, and so did Simon Halfon. I think the first cover he did originally we didn't like, and we were thinking how do we tell him we didn't really like it? But he was fine, and I think it was Halfon who said that we really wanted to see the targets, the heart and some of the famous iconic stuff that he was known for. Once he knew we wanted those he was OK with it and had the idea. You hadn't really seen those images for a long time so they were quite striking, but now they're everywhere, aren't they? Which is good in a way because it celebrates Peter and the whole pop art culture thing."

In my eyes, Britpop was the last significant phase of Mod. Today, it is a culture that is truly accepted as a major influence all over the world. In a way, many of the innovative processes formulated in the early days of the scene have been lost through technology.

Blogs, websites and online forums have mostly replaced fanzines, while social media, such as Facebook and Twitter, has mostly replaced the need to flyer events. This is not to say that there isn't a creative process involved in any of these mediums, just that the whole 'dirty hands and coping with basic materials' mentality has vanished.

The story of what has happened in the last 20 odd years could be another book in itself, so I have decided to end this book with what is happening now. The artists featured here all have very different styles. That whole individual ethos is part of the true Mod spirit, and we can truly see its legacy in these creative souls.

JOHN KIDD

London-born John Kidd is a self-taught photographer and artist. Having been a Mod since 1983, John's current specialist themes are pin-up art and psychedelic/Mod mono portraits.

He lists his main influences as Gustav Klimt, Alphonse Mucha, Jim Fitzpatrick, Stanley Mouse, Aubrey Beardsley, Kay Neilson, Gil Elvgren, George Petty, Alberto Vargas, Wes Wilson, Peter Max and Frank Frazetta.

Kidd's favourite forms of art are pin-up, art nouveau, pre-Raphaelite and sixties psychedelic posters. Having been born in 1967, it would seem that this reflects in his work.

John Kidd: "There are two distinct sides to my work – three, if you count the photography as well. On the one side is all the traditional mediums; I draw in either pencil or technical pen (I have a huge collection of Rotring technical pens, including original sixties ones that still work perfectly) and then add colour, usually watercolour or gouache for the more subtle images, or artists markers when I want bolder images. I also use metallics and embossing powders on marbled paper to create the images of Hendrix, Morrison and the like. The other side of my work is all created on the computer, the pin-ups are all airbrushed in Photoshop from a basic line drawing and the swirly mono portraits are drawn by hand then scanned in and the patterns dropped in afterwards; the modern equivalent of a craft knife and a Pritt stick, or 21st century smoke and mirrors."

MODERN ARTISTS

" There are two distinct sides to my work... "

JOHN KIDD

1 *Jo*, gouache on watercolour paper, 2011.

2 *Hendrix*, gold embossed on to hand-marbled paper, 2014.

3 *Mrs Peel*, artists markers and silver embossing on bamboo paper, 2017.

4 *Quant*, pen and ink, 1993.

BEN BOSTON

Ben Boston was born and raised in Bristol. Although Boston studied art at college, he is mostly self-taught. He has been tattooing since 1996 at the same studio in which he did his apprenticeship.

1 *The Calm Before The Storm*, acrylic on canvas, 2016. It is set before the beach fights, hence the gig poster, and the number plates give a nod to Lemmy and Bowie.

2 *Scooters*, acrylic on canvas, 2011.

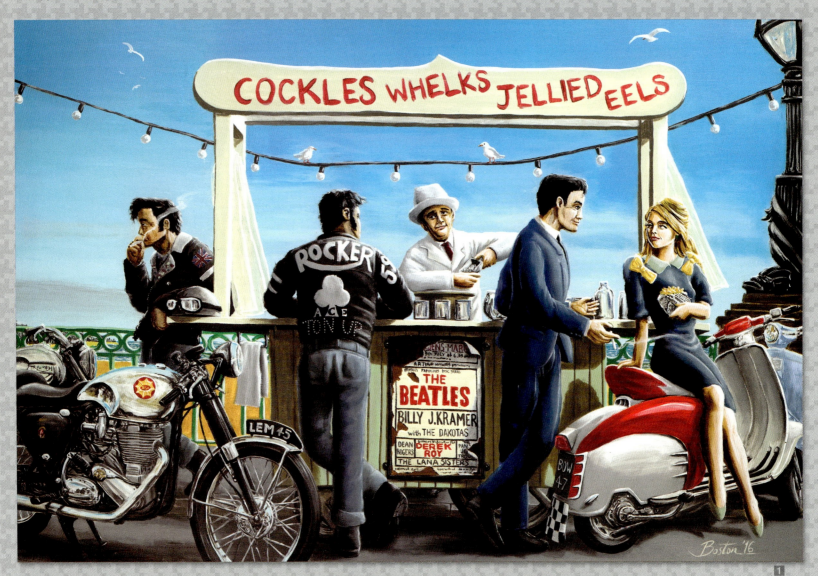

He lists his artistic influences as comics, science fiction movies, architecture, bridges, motorbikes, scooters, planes, trains and automobiles – in fact, all things engineering. Born in 1976, he loves music of most types and periods including country, rock, metal, blues and jazz, but says he would mainly identify as a Rocker.

"My mum and dad encouraged me to follow a creative path and supported me all the way," says Boston. "I like using acrylic paint, pencil, colour pencil, pen and ink. Any subject, any style, just like my tattooing."

Boston lists artists MC Escher, Frank Frazetta, Beksiński, HR Giger and James Jean among his influences.

❝...just like my tattooing.❞

BEN BOSTON

JUSTINA DEWHURST-RICHENS

Having been born at the end of the 1960s to two art students, Justina Dewhurst-Richens has always been surrounded by all art forms. As a small child she loved both the pop art and pre-Raphaelite movements, and that love has never faltered.

Dewhurst-Richens became a Mod in the mid-1980s having watched *Quadrophenia* when she was 13 or 14 years old. This led to her spending the following years obsessing over clothes and travelling up and down the country on the back of a scooter just to dance to fabulous music.

Having left school early before taking any O-levels, it was fortunate that she'd taken art a year earlier in evening classes at Brixton College. She went to work in various record and clothes shops until she fell pregnant at the age of 20. She returned to education when her daughter was two years old, and took a two-year part-time Foundation in Art and Design at Goldsmiths University. On completion, she then started a part-time BA Hons in Fine Art at Guildhall University.

In 1999, Justina held her first solo show of photography painting at the Workhouse Fine Art Gallery on the King's Road, Chelsea. Pete Townshend, the Target Apple and the Target Pear were all in this exhibition.

Dewhurst-Richens: "It was not intentional to begin with but as I worked on the pieces I realised they all had some connection to Mod. I love screen printing but as it's such a messy business, where you need a lot of space, I was unable to print at home, so I developed my painting to mimic screen prints. I paint free hand, no masking fluid or tape is used. Clean, sharp, hand-painted lines. A nod to Mod! After the exhibition I received many commissions, which kept me extremely busy for the next few years."

During the long dark winter of 2004 Bea's Beastlies was born, a business Dewhurst-Richens set up creating soft toys from recycled and vintage fabrics. For the last few years, alongside running Bea's Beastlies, she has picked up the brushes again and has been working on a new body of work exploring new mediums.

1 *Apple*, acrylic on canvas, 1999.
2 *Pear*, acrylic on canvas, 1999.
3 *Townshend*, acrylic on canvas, 1999.

❝ A nod to Mod! ❞
JUSTINA DEWHURST-RICHENS

MAGGIE MATTIONI

Since Maggie Mattioni was a small child she has always drawn little cartoons, such as comic-book characters from *The Broons* and *The Dandy*. Drawing was something Mattioni always did, and she was always found with a pencil and a pad in hand. Mattioni comes from a small mining village in County Durham, so industrial and working-class themes definitely influenced her style of drawing.

Maggie Mattioni: "My dad used to draw as a hobby so we both used to sit there when he finished working at the pit and draw for hours, until my mum came in from work and I could show her my drawings. It was something I was good at and filled me with happiness. I used to sketch everything that was going on around me, and growing up in a mining village in the eighties gave me lots of material to work on."

1

Watching old movies with her grandmother definitely got Mattioni interested in clothes and hairstyles, so along came her 'Peggy Jane' style of drawing, through which she realised a dream world that seemed so far away.

Mattioni: "I used to love looking at LS Lowry drawings and entering into his world through his art. The creative escapism, the dream-like world was definitely what influenced me as a child. I left school with not many GCSEs but managed to get into Newcastle Art College thanks to my graffiti style graphics [early Peggy Jane style]. For four years I studied fashion design and then went on to do my degree in fashion promotions at Preston University, so for years my Peggy Jane designs remained as doodles on scraps of paper, while I built up my career in fashion design."

Mattioni has been into the Mod/soul scene for many years, so that certainly inspires her ideas.

Mattioni: "Peggy Jane came into life in 2011, when I decided to do a website for cards. Greeting cards were something I struggled to find in the shops, there was nothing that I could buy for friends with similar interests, so an idea to do a website where I could sell something like that came about. I had the characters and the artwork but now the hard bit, I had to find a name... Peggy is short for Margaret, so it's my name (even though I'm a Maggie) and it was also my nanna's name – Margaret Jane – so the name Peggy Jane was created, and it obviously means a lot to me.

"The artwork used for the cards then came to life on shopping bags, canvas prints, passport covers and other merchandise. I have customers all over the world and it's amazing to see the photos that people send me of their Peggy Jane bag out and about around the world. I'm still a fashion designer but Peggy Jane has always and will always remain a part of who I am, as she's been in my life for so long and I could never give her up."

1 *Soul Time*, 2012.
2 *Time Goes By*, 2012.
3 *Morning After The Night Before*, 2013.
4 *London, Let's Go*, 2015.
All Maggie's pictures are sketched out on paper, then created on computer.

"...growing up in a mining village in the eighties gave me lots of material to work on."

MAGGIE MATTIONI

STEVEN MILLINGTON

Steven Millington is a graduate of the Bolton Institute of Fine and Applied Arts. Born in 1969, Steven has embraced whole-heartedly the concept of the 'jobbing' illustrator/designer, working across a wide range of media, to meet a similarly wide range of briefs. Born in the north west of England, Millington's career began as an apprentice glass engraver; an apprenticeship that helped to hone his skills in the technical aspects of hand lettering and left him with a lifelong obsession with the craft.

A desire to explore in greater depth his fascination with draughtsmanship led to Millington going freelance and working under the nom de plume (quite literally) of Lord Dunsby, a nod towards a tailor he and his friends frequented in his 'Mod' youth. His path has been set ever since.

Working in a style informed as much by the likes of Ronald Searle and Saul Steinberg, and harking back to a pre-Mac Book era of nib and Quink, his achievements are as long as they are broad, covering a range of projects including books such as *The Perfectly Dressed Gentleman* and *The Little Black Dress* etiquette and style guides, cocktail books and numerous other iconoclastic volumes. He's also designed skateboards and skate shoes for the highly successful cult skate team FLIP, and Vans apparel.

These days he goes under the name 'Dry British' and has a large, and growing, following on Instagram. You can find his illustrative work popping up in various magazines such as *Cycling Plus*, *The Cyclist*, *Pell Mell*, the in-house magazine for the Royal Automobile Club, and Italian design magazine *Studio*.

1 *Jazzers*, 2016.
2 *Cover Version*, 2010.
3 *First Impressions*, 2017.

1 *Code-Orange*, 2017.
2 *Molteni TDF*, 2016.
3 *Scootaur*, 2010.
4 *Moddy Boy*, 2016.

IMAGE CREDITS

© ADAGP, Paris and DACS, London 2018: p.25 (image 4)

Paul Anderson: p.60 (image 1)

Buddy Ascott: p128 (below, supplied promo),
p169 (images 1 & 2, supplied promos)

Olly Ball: p.226, p.227

© Peter Blake. All Rights Reserved, DACS 2017:
p.16, p.25 (image 3), p.125

Ben Boston: p.262, p.263

Norman Brand (supplied by Terry Tonik [Ian Harris]):
p.191, p.192, p.193 (left)

Pauline Boty Estate/Whitford Fine Art: p.13

© Boyle Family. All Rights Reserved, DACS 2018: p.17

Curbishley-Baird/Kobal/REX/Shutterstock: p.127

John Davis (owned by Paul Kelly): p.130, p.131

Sonia Delaunay (1885–1979). © Reserved.
Tate, London 2018, p.126

Justina Dewhurst-Richens: p.264 (images 1 & 2), p.265

David Dragon: p.135, p.136

Malcolm English (b.1946) Private Collection/
Bridgeman Images (from *Carnaby Street* by Tom Salter,
1970, colour lithograph): p.34 (image 2)

Nicholas Ferguson: p.55, p.59, p.61

Grant Fleming: p.152 (image 1), p.153

Tony Gale/Pictorial Press/Alamy Stock Photo: p.118 (image 1)

Richard Gardner/REX/Shutterstock: p.121

Goffa Gladding: p.174 (below right), p.179, p180, p.181,
p.182, p.183

The Grimstead family (owned by), supplied by Dave Dry:
p.66 (images 1 & 2), p.67 (images 3, 4 & 5), p.68

Fay Hallam: p.230 (image 1)

© R. Hamilton. All Rights Reserved, DACS 2017:
p.9, p.24 (image 2)

Jeff Hurst: p.119 (supplied promo), p.120

Annie Hutchison: p.85 (image 1), p.86, p.87,
p.89 (images 1 & 2)

© Jasper Johns/VAGA, New York/DACS, London 2017: p.123

Lloyd Johnson: p.169 (Polaroids)

Keystone/Hulton Archive/Getty Images: p.18 (image 1)

John Kidd: p.260, p.261 (images 2, 3 & 4)

Robert Lee: p.177

Phil Luderman: p.73 (image 2), p.94 (image 1)

Ray 'Patriotic' Margeston: p.184

Ben Martin/Getty Images: p.122

Maggie Mattioni: p.266, p.267 (images 2, 3 & 4)

Dave Manvell: p.115 (below left)

McDonald/Mirrorpix: p.114

R. McPhedran/Express/Getty Images: p.35 (below right)

John McHale poster for 'This Is Tomorrow' exhibition
catalogue, Whitechapel Gallery, 9 August–
9 September 1956, Whitechapel Gallery Archive: p.8

Steven Millington: p.268 (left, images 1 & 2), p.269,
p.270, p.271

© Mirrorpix: p.29 (images 3 & 5), p.62, p.63, p.64, p.65

Mickey Modern: p.196 (supplied promo)

© Estate of Kenneth Noland. DACS, London/VAGA,
New York 2018: p.14

Paul Norton: p.115 (images 2 & 3)

© Peter Phillips. All Rights Reserved, DACS/
Artimage 2018: p.10

Pictorial Press/Alamy Stock Photo: p.116, p118 (image 2)

Supplied by Eddie Piller: p.247 (image 1)

© Bridget Riley 2018. Arts Council Collection,
Southbank Centre, London. All Rights Reserved: p.15

Ray Roberts/Getty Images: p.35 (above right)

Rex Features: p29 (images 2 & 4)

Arnold Schwartzman: p.50 (image 1, supplied promo),
p.51 (images 3, 4 & 5), p.52, p.53, p.54,
p.57 (images 1 & 2)

Shawshots/Alamy Stock Photo: p.11 (image 3)

Smithsonian American Art Museum, Washington, DC/
Art Resource, NY: p.12

Time Out (photo by Roger Perrt): p168

Time Inc: p.26, p.27, p.88 (image 1), p.155, p.253, p.259

Terry Tonik [Ian Harris]: p.190, p.193 (image 1 & below,
supplied by Ian Harris), p194, p.195

Topfoto/PA Images: p.124 (image 1)

Nick Tweddell: p.110, p.111, p.113 (image 1)

Michael Ward/Getty Images: p.22

John White/BIPs/Getty Images: p.35 (left)

ACKNOWLEDGEMENTS

Thanks to Peter Blake, Paul Weller, Mick Talbot,
John Dunbar, Ian Page, Dave Cairns, Paul McEvoy, Paul Kelly,
Fay Hallam, Theresa Kerr, Denis Confrey, Jim Donovan,
Dave Edwards, Ian Hurford, Arnold Schwartzman,
Nicholas Ferguson, Annie Hutchison, Phil Luderman,
Dick Jordan, Bob McGrath, Colin Mansfield, Brian McCabe,
Nick Tweddell, Andy Ellison, Paul Norton, Jeff Hurst,
Buddy Ascott, Goffa Gladding, Andy Lewis, Barry Cain,
Grant Fleming, Bob Lewis, Eddie Piller, Bob Morris,
Del Shepherd, Mickey Modern, Dennis Greaves, Mark Feltham,
David John Dry, Dave Dragon, Willy Deasy, Lloyd Johnson,
Steve Millington, Ray Patriotic, Maggie Mattioni,
John Kidd, Ben Boston, Steuart Kingsley-Inness, Polly Love,
Justina Dewhurst-Richens, Michael J. Lotus, Tom McCourt,
Ian Jackson, Mikey Sherwill, Tim Fuller, Neil Lee,
Mike Collins, Wayne Northern, Lynsey Fox, Bob Manton
and my beautiful wife Lorraine and son Joe for putting
up with me!

Special thanks to Alex Briggs at www.usebriggs.com
and Damian Jones at www.pop-classics.com
for supplying the posters and general help and advice.